DOUGLAS GIFFORD holds the Chair of Scottish Literature at Glasgow University and is the Honorary Librarian of Sir Walter Scott's library at Abbotsford. He is the author and editor of numerous books and critical studies of James Hogg, Neil Gunn, Lewis Grassic Gibbon and modern Scottish literature.

ALAN RIACH is a poet and Head of the Department of Scottish Literature at Glasgow University. He is the author of four books of poetry and two critical works on Hugh MacDiarmid, editor of the Carcanet edition of the *Collected Works* of Hugh MacDiarmid and the author of *Representing Scotland in Literature, Popular Culture and Iconography* (2004).

Scottish poets from Carcanet
Iain Crichton Smith
W.S. Graham
David Kinloch
Frank Kuppner
Hugh MacDiarmid
Sorley MacLean
Edwin Morgan
Richard Price
Muriel Spark

SCOTLANDS
Poets and the Nation

Edited by
Douglas Gifford and Alan Riach

Editorial assistant
Susan Neil

CARCANET

SCOTTISH POETRY LIBRARY

First published in Great Britain in 2004 by
Carcanet Press Limited
Alliance House
Cross Street
Manchester M2 7AQ

and
The Scottish Poetry Library
5 Crichton's Close
Canongate
Edinburgh EH8 8DT

in association with The Department of Scottish Literature,
The University of Glasgow

Acknowledgements of permission to reprint in-copyright material can be found
on pp. 259–64 and constitute an extension of the copyright page.
Selection, Introduction and editorial matter © Douglas Gifford and Alan Riach
2004

A CIP catalogue record for this book is available from the British Library
ISBN 1 85754 740 3

The publisher acknowledges financial assistance from Arts Council England and
the Scottish Arts Council towards the publication of this volume

Typeset in Bembo by XL Publishing Services, Tiverton
Printed and bound in England by SRP Ltd, Exeter

CONTENTS

Introduction
MAKING POETRY OUT OF SCOTLAND

Scotland is a major theme in the poetry of Scotland. This might appear self-evident, yet it is the most obvious that is most easily overlooked, and this theme is a distinctive and differentiating feature of Scottish literature. The comparisons make this clear. In the literature of the United States, the frontier, 'lighting out for the territories' or the idea of the man alone, outcast individualism set against society's pressures to conform, are main themes; in West Indian literature, notions of hybridity and multi-faceted identity are prominent; in New Zealand and Australian literatures, different experiences of indigenous peoples and colonial encounters open into different social worlds; and nothing in English literature compares in consistency and continuity with the theme of the matter of national identity in the poetry of Scotland.

Comparison with Ireland may be particularly instructive. The feminised nation, Kathleen ni Houlihan or Mother Ireland, is an idea so potent that many songs were made, and motives forged, that would send men and women to martyrdom for it. Scotland too shares some of that, particularly in its Jacobite legacy, but the modernising trend towards imagining Scotland as a possible state (a 'Dream State' perhaps) is a recognition of the pluralism the country is capable of encompassing, not a call for constricting uniformity. And yet the idea of national identity remains sustaining. As Cairns Craig has said, no matter how Anglicised Scots become, they do not become English. On the evidence of the poems collected here, Scottish nationality nourishes many differences within itself – and after all, recognition, understanding, and celebration of difference is the principal work of culture and the arts.

This anthology is therefore unique, both in its aim and scope. It is not a comprehensive anthology of Scottish poetry, nor is it an annotated and academic survey. Rather than trying to select examples of outstanding poetry to illustrate aspects of Scottish culture and history, it recognises from the outset that such selection is an impossible task for a book of this size. Arguably, the vast bulk of poetry by Scots could be seen as exemplifying aspects of Scottish life and character, from Robert Henryson's 'The Uponlandis Mous and The Burges Mous' or William Dunbar's 'The Twa Mariit Wemen and the Wedo' to Liz Lochhead's 'Memo for Spring' or Tom Leonard's 'Intimate Voices'. Instead, this anthology focuses on how Scottish poets have used the overarching and imagined idea of Scotland as a nation, so that as far as possible the poems work with the notion of a kind of *meta*-Scotland. The selection enables readers to see for themselves how different periods have produced radically different perspectives, from lamentation for the perceived harm to the nation to celebration of its perceived virtues, in its landscape and people, and from positive assertion and triumphalism to bitterly satiric, and sometimes despairing, reproach directed at the collective entity the poets continue to regard as Scotland.

Many of the poems indicate their concern with the nation by having 'Scotland', 'Scottish' or the like in their titles. It very quickly becomes apparent, though, that poems like Kathleen Jamie's 'The Queen of Sheba' or Anne Frater's 'Divorce', for all that their titles are oblique in reference, are completely focused on a holistic vision of Scotland. The reasons for including poems addressed to, or lamenting, kings, queens and national leaders are perhaps less obvious; but on the assumption that so many of these figures transcend history to become legendary, or indeed mythical, and thus iconographic national symbols, we have regarded such poetry as important in illustrating this process.

Scotland Emergent

Where should a selection like this start? Given the confusions which surround the issue of the first appearance of concepts of Scottish nationhood, the volume opens with a collage of fragments relating to the emergence of the idea of Scotland as a nation. A problem immediately arises with this early material, in regard to the discrepancy between actual chronology of events and lives and the story-making about them.

There is no satisfactory solution to this. To present these early fragments in the order in which they were written would give the reader a confused sense of Scotland in the first millennium. Alternatively, ordering them according to the chronology of their historical subject-matter conceals the fact that most often these poems were written centuries later than the events they describe (as in the two poems about Columba or Walter Bower's fourteenth-century account of the Battle of Stirling Bridge in 1297 in his *Scotichronichon*). Even so, it was decided to follow this second course. And although the image of the dying Gaul (the doomed but defiant hero facing outnumbering odds) goes back from Wallace to Tacitus's Calgacus confronting the Roman forces at the battle of Mons Graupius, we chose to begin with the figure of Columba, both actual and mythic, initiating an ideal of kinship that may have helped to begin a conversation between different peoples that remains open-ended.

Perhaps this presentation, with all its distortions, can be read as mirroring the real difficulties and confusions attending the emergence of Scotland from its tribal territories and its earliest sense of identity as Alba, into what historians recognise as a nation. This also provides in succinct form a clear indication of how certain people or events, or ideas of what Scotland is and might be, acquire accretions of significance in writing emerging from different ideological imperatives. This is clear in the different ways in which later writers have chosen to view figures such as Macbeth or Malcolm Canmore. After this introductory collage, however, the poetry is presented as far as possible in order of the poets' birthdates.

We are indebted here to Thomas Clancy, editor of *The Triumph Tree* (1998), that groundbreaking and revelatory collection of early Scottish poetry, for many of these early poems. They show some of the first glimpses of poets, and people in general, acknowledging a unifying idea of the nation, whether it be called Alba or Caledonia or Scotland. Columba, Kenneth MacAlpin, Macbeth, Malcolm Canmore and Alexander III were figures who began to create a national awareness among people, but it was Wallace and Bruce who bound them securely into a nation. This volume in a sense really begins with that binding, in its many aspects; historians agree with Thomas Clancy and his collaborators that Scottish national identity in any sense we would now recognise really begins with the Wars of Independence and the time immediately following.

The anthology can be read as roughly falling into eight main periods. The first of these is represented by the collage of fragments concerned with the emergent nation and some of its outstanding leaders, up to and including Wallace and Bruce and the apparent end to the Wars of Independence. The second, to which we now turn, sees the late medieval world enter an early cultural renaissance in the Golden Age of James IV.

Renaissance and Reformation

Robert Carver, arguably Scotland's greatest composer, flourished at the court of James IV, and the degree of cultural sophistication in musical, literary, linguistic, artistic and architectural forms during the decade between James's marriage to Margaret Tudor in 1503 and the slaughter at Flodden in 1513, remains an astonishing example of national efflorescence. It is perhaps not too far-fetched to suggest that the critical musical development from plainchant to polyphony (for example, from Columban and Celtic plainchant represented in the *Inchcolm Antiphoner* and the *Sprouston Breviary* to the magnificent motets and masses in the *Carver Choirbook*, many of which have been recently recorded) somehow reflects the emergence of a polyphonic state, a nation whose independence seems characterised by the dialogic disposition of its inhabitants.

Poets like Henryson (who began writing in the reign of James III), Dunbar and Gavin Douglas were now less concerned with issues of national identity than John Barbour or Blind Harry had been in their epic narratives of Bruce and Wallace. Henryson's Scottishness comes out as an often grim under-commentary in moral fables like 'The Burgh Mous and The Uponlandis Mous' or in aspects of his 'continuation' of Chaucer's *Troilus and Cressida* in *The Testament of Creisseid*, where the Trojan priest Calchas has 'ain kirk'. The conclusion, as in many of his fables, is that quiet rural content is vastly preferable to the glamour of courts and wordly success. But is it an aspect of national identity or a sense of the tragedy in human life that makes the morality and compassion of *The Testament* timelessly relevant? Perhaps they are connected.

Likewise, Dunbar's national characteristics are unmistakeable in the *grotesquerie* of 'The Dance of the Seven Deadly Sins', the sidelong, wry physicality of 'The Twa Mariit Wemen and the Wedo' or the ironic reductiveness of his local satires. However, along with his poetry of court pageantry, 'The Thrissil and the Rois' shows the influence of Chaucer in its use of dream and aureate diction, as well as an overall desire to celebrate peace between Scotland and England. Margaret Tudor is depicted as the Rose, 'of cullour reid and quhyt' (thus symbolising the harmony of the houses of York and Lancaster), while James IV is depicted heraldically as Lion, Eagle and Thistle. The poem comes from a feudal society and celebrates hierarchy, degree and appropriateness, yet it commands a critical and cautionary attitude even to the authority of the Crown. It clearly instructs royal authority to rule for the benefit of all, and not to exploit the position of power it holds. As so often, justice is a major theme. Throughout its meticulous detail, the poem sustains a beautifully tender, prayer-like, tone. Its festive gathering evokes a hopeful sense of future harmony, balance and well-being, bringing earthly authority into accord with the pre-eminent law of 'Nature', the creator, ruler and teacher. This period ends, though, with the tragedy of Flodden in 1513. An anonymous Gaelic address to the Duke of Argyll on the eve of that battle urges and incites anti-English passions in defence of Scottish nationhood, spurring towards disaster. Later, David Lyndsay makes magnificent but ultimately unheeded pleas in poetry and drama to the young James V, and Scotland, to make reformation, or have reformation forced upon them. Lyndsay and the anonymous poet of 'Jok Upalland' both address the same issue: the corruption of authority.

Arguably, an embryonic ideal of democratic egalitarianism is at the heart of this address, and it is the egalitarianism of 'the democratic intellect' that is the quintessential myth of Scottish distinctiveness, in education and religion and before the law. The vernacular voice in Scottish poetry insists on an equal right to be heard: 'received pronunciation' is no guarantee of personal or social worth. This myth forms part of the work of poets from the earliest times, through Henryson to our contemporaries, and like all myths, may be grounded in fact. The Declaration of Arbroath of 1328 remains a lasting reminder of the responsibility of leaders to the people they must represent, and its resonance is still current.

The Union of the Crowns

Our third period follows the Reformation of 1560. Scottish identity and culture suffered a double blow, with the departure of James VI and his court poets to London. Scottish poets are preoccupied at this time with problems of monarchy and religion, and with the difficulties and possibilities of the relationship with England (especially after 1603). Alexander Montgomerie's complex allegorical poem of 1597, *The Cherrie and the Slae*, draws on the symbolism of the two fruits. Helena Shire reminds us in her book *Song, Dance and Poetry at the Court of Scotland under King James VI* (Cambridge, 1969), that these represent, respectively, the delicious, refreshing, but also high and inaccessible fruit of Heaven (the Christ-Eucharist symbol on its Tree) as against the bitter, black, harsh, low and accessible sloe on its bush (and the burning bush was a heraldic badge on the seal of the Reformed Church of France). This symbolism is part of the contemporary religious debate in the country: Montgomerie supported the Catholic, as opposed to the Reformed, church. However, the poem's allegory was politically pertinent to a king approaching the sovereignty of all Britain and, arguably, had less to say about the national identity of Scotland than the forms of religious faith to be endorsed in an expanding proto-empire. And in the seventeenth century's religious wars between Protestant Covenanters and Royalist Catholics, overarching national vision was obscured.

The Union of the Parliaments

Paradoxically, it is with the Union of Parliaments in 1707 that national vision returns, marking the beginning of the anthology's fourth period. A sense of loss, of the end of an old song, led to the rise of Jacobitism and the great rebellions of 1715 and 1745. Anger is pervasive, and not just that of the anonymous post-Union pasquils and Tobias Smollett, but also of Anglo-Irishman Jonathan Swift, who predicts rightly that 'tossing faction will o'er whelm / Our crazy double-bottomed realm'. David Malloch (who, on going to live in London, altered his name to Mallett to divest himself of unfortunate Scottish associations) joined with James (*The Seasons*) Thomson to rejoice in Greater Britain in their bullish 'Rule Brittania'. Anger predominates, however. Allan Ramsay's 'The Vision' is an outstanding example of this angry nationalism. Written in an archaic Scots, it was published in *The Evergreen* in 1724 as an old Scottish poem, supposedly by 'A.R. Scott' but in reality by Allan Ramsay, Scotsman. It exploits a characteristic of Scottish poetry which goes back to Henryson and Montgomerie and was to become a recurrent feature of the ambivalence of interpretation in Burns, James Hogg, and Scottish fiction.

Ramsay's trick is to pretend that he is writing about the Wars of Independence, when his real message, invoking the spirit of the past in Wallace, is an exhortation to present rebellion and the re-assertion of Scottish independence. And his successors Robert Fergusson and Burns continue his nationalist, visionary poetry.

One predominant theme, from the lament for Alexander III down to the period of the Scottish Renaissance of the twentieth century, is that of Scotland as a personified, often female, entity. From the earliest poetry, to the death of Wallace and Bruce, she weeps for the loss of her great ones. She sheds tears after 1603 and 1707; Allan Ramsay has his dreaming poet ask Wallace if she can ever be free, to be told by the Guardian that 'Thocht auld shois yet bauld shoiss / and teuch lyke barkit lether' and, pushed too far, will rise up to regain her freedom. In the eighteenth century she is 'hapless Caledonia', mourning her Culloden dead, or 'loved Albania, hardy nurse of men' – and Walter Scott, of course, will have her as 'stern and wild / Meet nurse for a poetic child'.

Fergusson's 'The Twa Ghaists', in which he raises the spirits of the Edinburgh merchants Heriot and Watson, and his 'Auld Reikie', have strong visionary elements, but due to their more restricted local focus did not quite qualify for inclusion. Burns's 'The Vision' similarly confines its presiding genius Coila to a local rather than a national vision, here of the west of Scotland. Perhaps 'Tam o' Shanter' could be read as 'The Presbyterian's Nightmare', allowing Tam to stand as the archetypal Scotsman, longing for the pleasures of wine, women and song to be prolonged, and thus inventing through hallucination, rather than actually experiencing, the forbidden pleasures he desires – but we felt that shorter poems like 'A Parcel of Rogues' and 'Scots Wha Ha'e' better expressed Burns's more complete view of Scotland. That said, it can be seen that as the century wears on, anger by and large gives way to gentler sentiments of loss regarding language and custom, as in Fergusson's 'Elegy on the Death of Scots Music' or to sentimental and less immediate sadness, as in Jean Elliot's 'The Flowers of the Forest', which remembers not Culloden, but Flodden. These are both verses of an age of sensibility, yet the hard and tragic sense of irreparable loss underlies them. They carry what Sorley Maclean was to call 'the heartbreak of the tale'.

Another mid-century development, foreshadowing later Scottish literature's tendency to take pride not in events of history, too often tainted by national failure, but in timeless aspects of the land and its people, is found in the anonymous celebration of Scotland, 'Albania'. This allegorical Scotland foreshadows the exotic and mysterious potential of the 'Dream State' we may still, at least partially, inhabit.

The Nineteenth Century

During the nineteenth century, the anthology's fifth period, the spirit of a mythical, allegorical Scotland or 'Albania' predominates, even if it is too often presented in terms of pious romanticisation, with aspects of the Kailyard. Walter Scott's famous passages of love of country avoid this, but they also avoid any questioning of political issues, as befits the man whose novels tried so hard to make the Union a partnership of equals. Perhaps a counterpoint begins to develop here, owing something to *The Seasons* and the pastoral tradition, in a celebration of the land, a national terrain idealised both by observers close-at-hand and viewers from all around the world.

As Scottish Romanticism developed an international provenance, patriotic unionism was conveyed emphatically in the nineteenth-century tradition of Scottish landscape painting. The declaration of national loyalty so uninhibitedly proclaimed by Scott was to take on a transcendental direction, too often departing from the mundane lives of earth-bound mortals. It is sobering and salutary to track how this became ground down, through irony to bitter self-abjection, from Scott's affirmative credo to the disillusioned modern fiction of Robin Jenkins and Irvine Welsh. Yet this later strand of ironic counterpoint does not disqualify Scott's idealising, assertive vision. Rather, it roots it in material problems and stands as a warning against complacency and banal nationalism.

The influence of Burns and Scott led to a host of nineteenth-century imitators unfortunately lacking their poetic talent. Nineteenth-century Scottish poetry about humble Scottish people, humble cottages, humble but sincere beliefs, in a stern but magnificent landscape, with its plenitude of ruins, rivers, flowers, birds, could fill endless volumes. We have chosen a representative few. Almost equal in quantity to this poetry of austere purity and simplicity, proud in its poverty, are the poems celebrating Scottish valour and strength, such as Allan Cunningham's 'The Thistle Grown Aboon the Rose', where dented Scottish pride is now bolstered by the thought that Scots are the muscle of military and imperial Britain. Robert Southey's poem on Wallace implicitly reconfigures the Guardian of Scotland as an essentially British hero, and Edward as an unconscionable villain. This kind of poetry begins to recover Wallace and Bruce, or the Covenanters, as subsidiary motifs, so that their spirit somehow infuses itself into a more peaceable Scotland which channels its valour into the service of Britain. Rather than regret for the loss of national independence or ideas of political unrest, it is nostalgia for old ways that predominates, together with quiet pride in local characteristics of language and tradition.

In the later nineteenth century, Scottish emblems soften. A single female persona diversifies to represent home and begetter of a hardy people, or Scotland's songs, the mother tongue, ghosts of the past such as martyrs for covenant, or aspects of landscape, from the lone shieling to bluebells, the fir tree, the white rose which breaks the heart. These are now among the bric-à-brac of familiar Victoriana.

Moreoever, in an age of increasing emigration and exile, 'home' becomes a potent term, with poets from Cunningham to Robert Louis Stevenson expressing a poignant sense of loss. At its worst, the 'Home Thoughts from Abroad' tradition is cloying, sentimental and false. It also reveals curious international perspectives, though, from New Zealand's 'The Thistle and the Fern' to the 'Canadian Boat Song' and the numerous nineteenth-century farewells to Scotland that are linked to famous contemporary paintings such as Thomas Faed's 'The Last of the Clan' (1865) or William McTaggart's 'The Sailing of the Emigrant Ship' (1895). Yet the poems of exile may also be traced all the way back to Deirdre's farewell to Alba, the ancient Celtic song of lament and leavetaking which makes its poignant effect simply by naming all the places – thus evoking the hills, valleys and rivers – that the singer will never see again. (The song has been reconstructed by John Purser in his radio series, book and CDs, *Scotland's Music*, of 1992). Exile is a recurrent theme, and the refrain continues most hauntingly in Iain Crichton Smith's poetry in *The Exiles* (1984).

Three different strands of the theme may be identified. The first is that of the traveller whose Scottish identity and eventual return home is hopefully, and riskily, assured. William Lithgow stands at the head of this tradition, perhaps the first Scottish writer who was a world-traveller. He journeyed in Africa and to Constantinople, as well as throughout Europe, and his delight in the extremes of experience was matched by his determining attraction to return towards the magnetic north and his Lanarkshire home. A second strand may be found among the descendants of Scots, who recognise the Scottish strain becoming a part of a new identity (John Liddell Kelly in New Zealand, noting the entwinement of the heather and the fern) or perhaps dying out altogether. Les Murray laments this in his 'Elegy for Angus Macdonald of Cnoclinn'. In fiction, one might note the kinship of Murray's poem with Alistair MacLeod's tragic novel of Scots in Canada, *No Great Mischief* (2000). By contrast, a comically fanciful Scotland is evoked in Bob Dylan's ballad, 'Highlands'. Burns supplies the opening line, but the Scotland we are asked to imagine is a whimsical, garbled, yet poignantly unrealisable fantasy:

> Well, my heart's in the highlands, gentle and fair
> Honeysuckle bloomin' in the wildwood air
> Bluebelles blazin' where the Aberdeen waters flow
> Well, my heart's in the highlands, I'm gonna go there when I feel
> good enough to go.

(The full text can found on the internet.)

The most familiar aspect of the theme is the exile's longing for a Scotland that can be reimagined but never fully recaptured: Byron remembering the beauty of his dark loch, Allan Cunningham feeling miserable in the bright French sunshine, or Stevenson pulling himself back from sentimental excess in a letter to Sidney Colvin of June 1893, when he writes home from the South Pacific:

> I was standing on the little verandah in front of my room this morning, and there went through me or over me a wave of extraordinary and apparently baseless emotion. I literally staggered. And then the explanation came, and I knew that I had found a frame of mind and body that belonged to Scotland... highland huts, and peat smoke, and the brown swirling rivers, and wet clothes, and whisky, and the romance of the whole thing, and that indescribable bite of the whole thing at a man's heart...

Nostalgia seems about to become unjustifiable (baseless) when that 'bite' restores a profound (baseless) realisation of the significance, strength and real presence of such feeling.

Yet if national vision within Scotland, in the fullest sense of political and cultural consideration, virtually disappeared in the nineteenth century, and if Scottish poetry seems dominated by either lugubriously pious epics such as Robert Pollok's *The Course of Time* (1827), on the one hand, or more fantastic and less ambitious visions such as William Tennant's *Anster Fair* (1812) or Hogg's *Kilmeny* (1813) on the other, there were intriguing signs of change. Hogg's 'Sir Morgan O'Doherty's Farewell to Scotland' and his 'Village of Balmaquhapple' showed that Scots could at last begin to laugh at themselves. Later in the century, poets like James ('B.V.') Thomson (*The City of Dreadful Night*, 1875), James Young Geddes, Robert Buchanan and John Davidson would, through a mixture of despair and mordant humour, begin the deconstruction of so many of Scotland's religious and cultural totems, clearing away Victorian side-issues and preparing the way for the second Scottish Renaissance that began with Hugh MacDiarmid. And while it is true that industrial change had to wait until that Renaissance to be fully explored in literature, there were occasional signs that Scottish poets were willing to face up to some nasty realities. Surprisingly, the once-great, now forgotten, Thomas Campbell was one: here, his atypical 'Lines on Revisiting a Scottish River' opens with the challenging 'And call they this Improvement?' as he sees his beloved Clyde where, now 'unsightly brick lanes smoke, and clanking engines gleam'. Such antipathy towards the industrialisation of Scotland was echoed in the mid-century poetry of Elizabeth Hamilton and William Thom. Scotland had to await Alexander Smith's 'Glasgow' (1857) and the poetry of the neglected James Young Geddes later in the century to find any recognition that industry could possess its own strange beauty and worth. All these poets, however, were absorbed in local, if momentous, events; the late nineteenth century holds little if any affirmative national poetry of any real worth.

The themes of Scotland and Empire were often expressed in unattractive, jingoistic, braggart assertions of national militarism. This was accompanied by an increasing sense of disengagement from history and a withdrawal to the consolations of romantic tradition, landscape, local culture and language. These qualities were combined with a pride in supposed peasant simplicity and strength, and the pseudo-reassurances of Kailyard and Celtic Twilight.

The Scottish Literary Renaissance

Following the Great War, the central concept of the resurgent literature of Scottish nationhood may be summarised as a core belief in the contrasting value and ideals of an ancient past. As Edwin Muir puts it, in 'Scotland 1941': 'We were a tribe, a family, a people / A simple sky roofed in that rustic day' or as novelist Neil Gunn writes in *Highland River* (1937), 'our river took a wrong turning somewhere, but we haven't forgotten the source'.

The 'Scottish Renaissance' of the period between the two world wars forms our sixth period. The Great War changed poets' perspectives utterly and fundamentally. Simmering national awareness became urgent questioning, exacerbating curiosity about what Scotland might yet be. Roots, tradition, the recovery of older languages as a means of recovering lost national consciousness and character, and an underlying belief in an ancient golden age were the hallmarks of this movement. MacDiarmid's Drunk Man studying the national emblem appreciates its stubborn persistence, but the awfulness of wasted potential is the poem's deepest theme. The poetry which speaks of Scotland at this time is not, therefore, necessarily celebratory; MacDiarmid and Muir and others still felt they had to clear away much debris in terms of outworn respect for establishment values and reactionary beliefs. But the tensions between pessimism and optimism, exemplified here in Muir's 'Scotland 1941' and William Soutar's 'Birthday', and in the fiction of the time by writers like Lewis Grassic Gibbon, Gunn and Eric Linklater, were expressed with an energy and innovation which can only be read as positive statements regarding the need for recognition of realities and change. Soutar typically represents his positive vision of Scotland not so much by the lion as by the emblem of the unicorn, symbol of ideal beauty – but haunted always by the delusive cuckoo/gowk representing that recurrent failure of nerve which so often is seen as cheating Scotland of a finer destiny.

This was not merely wishful thinking. All the writers associated with the Renaissance movement held to the idea of Scotland as a small nation where political self-determination might develop in co-ordination with cultural self-expression. When the National Party of Scotland was constituted in 1928, MacDiarmid was among the founding members.

Post-War Revival

Following the Second World War, our seventh period saw many of the ideals of the Renaissance undermined. Ideas of essentialism, or racial purity, and the assertion of unalloyed national identity, had become deeply suspect. As G.S. Fraser puts it in 'Meditation of a Patriot', since he has 'no islands and no ancient stone' to rely on as spiritual resources, 'With Byron and Lermontov / Romantic Scotland's in the grave'.

MacDiarmid continued to write poems explicitly dealing with the state of the nation (there are no fewer than fifteen listed in the index to the *Complete Poems* whose titles begin with 'Scotland', 'Scots' or 'Scottish'). However, the most important of his later poems simply *assume* Scottish national identity and address other issues more centrally. 'On a Raised Beach', in its intense, meditative concentration, *The Kind of Poetry I Want* and *In Memoriam James Joyce* in their open-ended expansiveness, are almost entirely unconcerned with the question of Scottish national character, although the sensitivity to multi-linguistic difference in the Joyce poem has a clear application ('All dreams of imperialism must be exorcised / Including linguistic imperialism, which sums up all the rest'). However, the three *Dìreadh* poems (from which 'Scotland Small?' is an extract) return to the theme emphatically. Perhaps it is best defined in the short poem 'Separatism':

If there's a sword-like sang
That can cut Scotland clear
O' a' the warld beside
Rax me the hilt o't here,

For there's nae jewel till
Frae the rest o' earth it's free,
Wi' the starry separateness
I'd fain to Scotland gi'e.

The worst implications of exceptionalism are challenged here by the dazzling appeal of language and metaphor: both the energy of 'Rax' and the beauty of 'starry separateness' are verbally persuasive beyond the clodbound correctnesses upon which mundane politics insists. Again, the continuity may be felt in the vision of an independent and self-determined

nation in which there is room for difference and dialogue and no enforce-
ment of sterile uniformity. But more generally, however the terms might
be defined, MacDiarmid's work crosses from Modernism into Post-
Modernism and in this, perhaps, he is not as unusual as he might appear.

Arguably, Scottish poetry's early recognition of its fragmented heritage
and competing identities, its Cleared Highlands and blighted Lowlands, its
cultural and linguistic uncertainties, renders the separation of Modernism
and Post-Modernism tenuous. What is clear is that from the 1960s on, with
Norman MacCaig and Crichton Smith's dissections of the relationship
between the observer of Scotland and the materials which are conven-
tionally identified as constituting Scotland's territory, history and ideology,
followed by Edwin Morgan's dazzling exploitations of real and imagined,
possible and impossible variations on a theme of Scotland, all the old values
and ideals were under inquisition.

Towards the Third Millennium

MacDiarmid died in 1978. A majority of Scottish voters demonstrated their
approval of devolution in the Referendum of 1979 but the Westminster
government did not permit this development. Far from being a failure, this
became an inspiration to Scottish writers to look towards a better solution.
The affirmation of the 1997 Referendum led to the re-opening of the
Scottish Parliament in 1999. In this period, the diversity of identities
contained within Scotland has found increasingly varied expression. Edwin
Morgan is the herald and chief exemplar of this era.

National identity can now be accommodated in literary discourse as a
concept encompassing diversity and pluralism. This inclusiveness,
however, presents new problems. Poets might believe in little and inter-
rogate everything. Douglas Dunn's 'Here and There' sets up an exemplary
dialogue which is ultimately impossible of resolution. Duncan Glen's 'The
Hert o Scotland' expresses the impossibility of really belonging to even a
part of diverse Scotland, while in 1987, Liz Lochhead's poetic opening to
Mary Queen of Scots Got Her Head Chopped Off refuses to say what Scotland
is, but after a series of contrasting images, qualified by 'mibbe' and 'or' and
'it depends' admits that 'Ah dinna ken whit like *your* Scotland is...'.

This poetic drama, together with Morgan's exploration of Scotland
from the beginning into the unimaginable future in his 1984 *Sonnets from
Scotland*, and Alasdair Gray's surreal epic novel of 1981, *Lanark*, marks the
beginning of the latest period in Scottish literature – our eighth period –
in which magic realism and the use of myth have returned in style, allowing
Scottish writers to expand immeasurably the limits of imagination
regarding their country. Scotland can now be treated in an endless variety
of modes and genres; it has become recognised – or is being treated – as

entirely a subjective experience, endlessly variable, repeatedly uncivilised and disappointing, and yet somehow still desirable. Yet while the cultural disjunction and social inadequacies of the country are increasingly criticised, contemporary poets are not confined simply to a loyalty to local Scottish upbringing. What remains in the work of these writers, however, is a tangible *address* to what 'Scotland' might mean. Horizons may shift, yet the idea of the nation is still there, presented across the spectrum from hope to despair.

What emerges is a continuing paradox. The nation is castigated for its failures and shames, its warts and wants, in a generally reductive and sceptical idiom which nevertheless allows a message of insistence on national identity and a developing national future. The Edinburgh Parliament has not been used as an inspiration to triumphal national assertion. Perhaps both the spirit of Post-Modernism's distrust of imagined and constructed nationhoods (with all they imply of fixed identity and closure), together with a weary sense of having failed so often before when hopes were high, has left Scottish culture both more suspicious of apparent positive change, and with a tendency to become more eclectic and outward-looking, seeking supportive value in webs of national and international expression. And yet, national identity is undoubtedly *present* in Scotland. It is current, whether as a given, or an unanswered question, or a matter of unfinished business. The worst excesses of banal nationalist chauvinism are all too familiar anywhere but the most lively enquiries into the national agenda exercise a critique and enact an affirmation we would not wish to abandon, even if we could.

In his poems commemorating the great poets of late twentieth-century Scotland, the Irish Nobel Laureate Seamus Heaney registers this singularity of national identity in its various forms. In '"Would They Had Stay'd"' from *Electric Light* (2001), he laments the passing of Norman MacCaig, Iain Crichton Smith, Sorley MacLean and George Mackay Brown, writing from the vantage-point of Ireland: 'they were there / Before we noticed them, all eyes and evening... A match for us. And watching.' And in 'An Invocation' from *The Spirit Level* (1996), he notes that for him, MacDiarmid stood for an accent, an idiom and an idea, 'like a thistle in the wind, / A catechism worth repeating always.' Although Heaney's poems are not specifically about Scotland, the nationality of their subjects is inevitably, implicitly and beautifully woven into his tones of lament and affirmation.

★ ★ ★ ★ ★

Individual readers will of course feel that we have omitted important poems. Henryson is not here and there is no representation of traditional ballads. Fine poets such as George Mackay Brown are only briefly represented, where their vision opens a perspective into the national question. Surprisingly, perhaps, there are relatively few contemporary poetic commentaries on major issues and periods, such as the Scottish Covenanters and the Killing Times, the ill-fated Darien Scheme at the end of the seventeenth century, or the Highland Clearances. Most often, poets deal with such matters specifically, rather than extrapolating them into national symbols. Tendentious as it may appear, however, we decided to include Sorley MacLean's 'Hallaig' as a key poem that does in fact represent the specific in a way that is both unsentimentally universalised and uniquely national.

Taken as a whole, the chronology of the making of Scottish iconography does not coincide with actual historical events. The hagiography of William Wallace had to wait almost two hundred years after Wallace's death in 1305 for its main exponent, in Blind Harry's epic and often very fanciful poem and the popular appeal of Wallace's symbolism was renewed in the eighteenth century with Hamilton of Gilbertfield's English translation of 1722, which was powerfully to inspire Burns and Hogg. And – as the anthology shows – Wallace's ideological significance continues to resurface in response to political feeling throughout the nineteenth and twentieth centuries. It was there again, prior to the 1997 referendum, in Mel Gibson's celluloid version, *Braveheart*. Popular and mass media culture express ideas of Scottish nationality, contemporary with the more recent poems, for an overlapping but distinct readership.

In terms of historical events, popular songs and oral storytelling may constitute a more immediately responsive medium for contemporary comment. Certainly, popular Scottish songs on national identity are abundant and we have included a few merely to indicate that the national question is much more widespread and popular than MacDiarmid at his most scornfully élitist might suggest. 'Scotland the Brave', 'The Scottish Soldier' and 'Flower of Scotland' are so well known they might have been missed among such company as Dunbar, Byron or Liz Lochhead. Yet it would be mistaken to think of these songs as outwith the scope of the anthology: their Scotland is Scotland too.

And there is another significant area of Scottish verse which does in fact deal with many of the above events and icons of Scottish history and culture. The popular chapbooks of Scotland, slight publications of a few pages, produced to be sold at fairs and public events, highly topical and ephemeral, do indeed comment continually on important political and popular events from the sixteenth century on. Thus, street songs rejoiced in the golden promise of the Darien Scheme, seeing Scotland as proclaiming liberty and content amongst savages and colonists. After its failure, the Jacobite publisher William Watson produced a popular ballad rejoicing in Scottish hanging of English pirates as a kind of revenge for English repression of the Scheme:

Then England for its treachery should mourn,
Be forced to truckle in its turn:
Scots pedlars you no longer durst upbraid
And DARIEN should with interest be repaid...

Such street songs and chapbooks were created in response to the Glencoe massacre, 'Bonnie Prince Charlie', Culloden and the celebrated visit to Edinburgh of George IV in 1822. In this anthology we have included the pasquils on the Union of 1707 and an example of the popular broadside ballad commentary, John Skelton's 'A Ballade of the Scottyshe Kynge' (thought to be the oldest printed broadside ballad, its rough rhyming couplets produced after the battle of Flodden in 1513). These texts are mere samples of this kind of commentary. The challenge of surveying the chapbook treatment of Scotland is quite simply too huge for our present collection, and must await its doughty surveyor.

But perhaps one simple point may be emphasised about the number of poems referring critically to the Union of 1707. On the day the treaty was signed, the carilloner at St Giles's Kirk in Edinburgh's Royal Mile rang out a tune that would have been heard and recognised all through the city: 'Why Should I Be So Sad On My Wedding Day?' The poets who attack the Union carry the weight of both popular moral force and their own individual judgement. Their poems register an abhorrence of the hypocrisy of political expediency and money-driven motivation. When political expediency and economic viability (on the one hand) and romantic iden- tification of self and nation and transcendent idealism (on the other) are separated and polarised, the exaggerations and contradictions may lead to political disablement and a sense of disenfranchisement. The Union, like the 1560 Reformation, may well have brought about a number of 'disso- ciations' in Scottish sensibility.

In such a context, kitsch might be a strategy of preservation, and irony might be a saving grace. When the extremes are reunited, though, the full human consequence of both celebration and tragedy may be reimagined, and no one can foresee the consequences of such an event. This is why we have chosen to include MacDiarmid's most famous, strange and unsettling lyric from *A Drunk Man Looks at the Thistle*, 'O wha's the bride?' It is not inconceivable that, whatever else she might represent, the bride with her bouquet of thistles is an image of Scotland. To read the poem in this way brings a difficult, unsentimental and profound affirmation to its conclusion.

★ ★ ★ ★ ★

We have supplied translations for the Gaelic, Latin and more densely Scots poems, but we have not provided notes or glossary. The chronology supplies an essential reference list of dates and events to which poems refer, and the chronological arrangement of the book should make clear the unfolding story of Scotland and the unfinished business of the national ideal of self-determination. More modern poems in Scots are easily understood by English-speaking readers and occasional obscure words can be quickly inferred. The interested reader is referred to the excellent *Concise Scots Dictionary* (ed. Mairi Robinson, Aberdeen, 1985) while many fine histories of Scotland and its literature are generally available. These include the four-volume *History of Scottish Literature* edited by Cairns Craig (Aberdeen, 1987–8), Marshall Walker's *Scottish Literature since 1707* (London and New York, 1996) and Gifford, Dunnigan and MacGillivray's extensive *Scottish Literature* (Edinburgh, 2002). These will readily supply broad historical contexts.

The fragments with which the selection opens include the celebration of the wedding of Margaret, daughter of Alexander III, to Erik of Norway in 1281. The theme of the nation as partner in union echoes through poetic commentaries, from Dunbar's celebration in 'The Thrissel and the Rois' to George Buchanan's hope that Henry Darnley will prove a fit monarch and consort to Mary, or the many less favourable views of the 1707 Union. Our selection comes towards an end with Anne Frater's striking and powerful cry for Scotland's divorce from that Union, a choice which leaves the selection posing an implicit question regarding the third millennium's response to that view of the nation. Whither now? And what kind of perspectives will our future poets give?

These questions remain, yet a new beginning is promised at the close of the anthology, with the resumption and opening of the new Scottish Parliament and the start of this third millennium. Thus we have concluded with two poems forming an 'Envoi and Prelude': Anne Frater's passionate call for a clean break from Scotland's old enemy and long-term partner, and the poem commissioned from Iain Crichton Smith which was read by Tom Fleming as part of the opening of Parliament in 1999. Along with Burns's secular hymn to egalitarianism, 'A Man's a Man', which was sung by Sheena Wellington on the occasion, Crichton Smith's secular prayer for a multi-vocal identity suggests the essential co-ordinates we might begin to work from if we wish to affirm Alasdair Gray's famous invocation to his readers, to work as if we live in the early days of a better nation.

★ ★ ★ ★ ★

On 16 February 2004, the First Minister of Scotland appointed Edwin Morgan as the first ever National Poet for Scotland, effectively Scotland's first poet laureate. Morgan immediately pointed out that the British poet laureate, appointed by the Crown, was traditionally English and it was only fair that Scotland should have a post of its own. We are delighted to begin our book, and end our introduction, with an extract from Morgan's translation of Robert Baston's 'The Battle of Bannockburn'. Here is Morgan's note on the poem:

Robert Baston's *Metrum de Praelio apud Bannockburn* is one of a number of poems included in *Scotichronicon*, Walter Bower's Latin history of Scotland, written in the 1440s. Baston, a Carmelite friar, is to us a fairly shadowy figure, though various works have been attributed to him, and Bower claims that he was 'the most famous poet in England' at the beginning of the fourteenth century. This may not seem too absurd if we remember that he antedated Hoccleve and Gower, Lydgate and Langland: what rivals could he have in 1314? At any rate, the headlong drive of his post-classical Latin has vigour and commitment; the intricate interlace of his rhyme-scheme is at times irregular but could hardly be otherwise, even in Latin, in such a long poem; he scatters alliteration and onomatopoeia sometimes recklessly but often most effectively. The poem was, above all, a remarkable achievement if we consider its origin. Edward II of England was so confident of beating the Scots in his invasion of 1314 that he sent Baston with the army as its official bard, who would compose a paean of victory at the close of the battle. But the English got neither victory nor paean. Baston was captured, and would be ransomed only if he produced a poem celebrating England's defeat. It is impossible not to sympathize with him, and indeed we must admire the way in which he set about his task, not hesitating to criticize the English for their lack of unity but making it overall a 'horrors of war' poem rather than one which was in any sense partisan. Its end is elegiac, dark, wry, self-deprecating. Baston strikes the perfect note. If the work is neither English nor Scottish, it is a part of Scottish history, and deserves to be known. 'If others can do better, let them go ahead.'

> This is a double realm: each itches to dominate:
> Neither hands over the helm for the other to subjugate.
> England and Scotland – which one is the Pharisee?
> Each one has to stand guard, and not fall into the sea!
> Hence those pumped-up factions dyed with crimson blood,
> Squads in battle-actions slaughtered crying in the mud,
> Hence this waste of men, crossed out by war's black pen,
> Whole peoples sunk in the fen, still fighting, again and again,
> Hence white faces in the ground, hence white faces of the
> > drowned,
> Hence huge grief is found, cries with which the stars are crowned,

Hence wars that devastate field and farm and state.
How can I relate each massacre that lies in wait?

It is June Thirteen Fourteen, and here I set the scene,
The Baptist's head on a tureen, the battle on Stirling green.
Oh I am not glued to ancient schism and feud,
But my weeping is renewed for the dead I saw and rued.
Who will lend me the water I need to baptize these forays?
Already torrents and springs overwhelm my heart-strings
And break the rings of my singing of better things.

The governor of the land has that land's domination
At his slightest command a great force is in full formation
Huzzas from English throats; Scots in eager armour;
Soldiers with high notes may not live up to their clamour!
See how the English king, consulting and considering,
Asks boldest men to bring fear to the Scots, penetrating
Chivalry with chivalry, country into country!
Charging with the nobility to draw on every ability,
What a brilliant band of magnates mustering and swerving!
They want you bowing and serving! Scotland, take sword in hand!

The poem describes the battle in flashing, vivid images and poignant, bitter
tones, then draws to its memorable conclusion:

What is truth worth? How can I sing about so much blood?
Could even tragedy bare its breast to show such cut and thud?
The names may be famous but I do not know them all.
I cannot number the humblings and tumblings of hundreds that
fall.

Many are mown down, many are thrown down,
Many are taken in chains for a stated ransom.
So some are rising, riding rich high and handsome
Who before the war were poor and threadbare souls.
The battlefield is barren but piled with spoils.
Shouts and taunts and vengeful cuts and brawls –
I saw, but what can I say? A harvest I did not sow!
Guile is not my style. Justice and peace are what I would show.
Anyone who has more in store, let him write the score.
My mind is numb, my voice half-dumb, my art a blur.

I am a Carmelite, and my surname is Baston.
I grieve that I survive a happening so harrowing and ghastly.
If it is my sin to have left out what should be in,
Let others begin to record it, without rumour or spin.

If this opens up many of the questions about national identity and self-determination, the value of poetic interpretation, personal commitment, faith in human potential and sorrow at the waste of so much of it, questions that the poems in our anthology explore in various ways and from many different points of approach, it is time to let their authors now begin to speak for themselves.

Douglas Gifford
Alan Riach
Department of Scottish Literature,
University of Glasgow
2004

563	St Columba arrives in Scotland
840s	Kenneth MacAlpin King of Scots
1040–1057	Reign of Macbeth
1057–1093	Reign of Malcolm Canmore
1263	Battle of Largs
1281	Marriage of Princess Margaret
1286	Death of Alexander III
1296–1314	The Wars of Independence
1305	Death of William Wallace
1314	Bannockburn
1503	King James IV marries Margaret Tudor
1513	Flodden
c. 1560	The Reformation
1587	Execution of Mary Queen of Scots
1603	The Union of the Crowns: James VI of Scotland becomes James I of England
1660	Restoration of Charles II
1680–1687	'The Killing Times': Charles II and persecution of Scottish Covenanters
1692	Massacre of Glencoe
1696–1700	The Darien Scheme
1707	The Union of the Parliaments
1715	The First Jacobite Rising
1736	The Porteous Riots in Edinburgh
1745	The Second Jacobite Rising
1746	Prince Charles defeated at Culloden
c. 1750–1830	The Scottish Enlightenment
1770s, 1780s	First wave of large-scale Highland Clearances
1776	4 July, American Declaration of Independence
1789	French Revolution; Storming of the Bastille
1812	Napoleon retreats from Moscow
1820s	Second wave of Highland Clearancess
1820	Rising of radical weavers crushed
1837–1901	Reign of Queen Victoria
1840s	Third wave of Highland Clearances
1843	The Disruption of the Church of Scotland
1848	Year of European Revolutions
1882	Battle of the Braes in Skye

1914–1918	World War I
1916	The Easter Rising in Ireland
1917	The Russian Revolution
1922	BBC founded
1924	First British Labour Government
1928	National Party of Scotland founded
1932	Hunger marches in Britain
1939–1945	World War II
1947	First Edinburgh International Festival
1949	Apartheid regime begins in South Africa
1953	Coronation of Queen Elizabeth II
1956	Suez crisis
1957	Campaign for Nuclear Disarmament march to Aldermaston
1960	Oil discovered in the North Sea
1962	Cuban missile crisis
1979	Failure of First Devolution Referendum
1997	Success of Second Devolution Referendum
1999	Scottish Parliament resumed

Deirdre's Farewell to Alba
(from the Gaelic)

A beloved land is that land in the east, Scotland with its wonders;
I should not have come hither out of it if I had not come with Noìse.

Beloved are Dún Fidhgha and Dún Finn, beloved is the stronghold
                                                    above them,
beloved is Inis Draighen, and beloved is Dún Suibhne.

The wood of Cuan, to which Ainnle used to go, alas!
Short we thought the time, I and Noìse on the shores of Scotland.

Glenn Laìgh, I used to sleep beneath the shapely rock;
fish and venison and badger's fat, that was my food in Glenn Laìgh.

Glen Massan, tall was its wild garlic, bright its grasses;
we used to have a broken sleep above the wooded rivermouth of Massan.

Glen Etive, there I raised my first house; lovely is its wood,
and when it rises a cattle-fold of the sun is Glen Etive.

Glenn Urchaìn, that was a straight glen of fair ridges;
no man of his age was prouder than Noìse in Glenn Urchaìn.

Glen Daruel, happy is any man who is its native;
sweet is the voice of the cuckoo on the bending bough on the peak
                                                    above Glen Daruel.

Beloved is Draighen with its firm beach, beloved is its water in the pure
                                                    sand;
I should not have come out of it from the east if I had not come with
                                                    my beloved.

In Praise of Colum Cille
(from the Gaelic)

Colum Cille, Alba's head,
keen for fierce fame over rough seas,
matchless barque of bards' rewards,
eager author, high heaven's noble seal.

Our high apostle of Aran,
unhindered by the world's gold;
blameless sun, fine stride of Cualann,
shoulder bird of the flood's God.

From Conall, Christ brought desire,
sorrowless, for fervent free knowledge,
the son of Heaven's King – he broke great chains:
chief of Conn's household is Colum.

ANONYMOUS (PARTLY 14TH CENTURY)

from the Inchcolm Antiphoner
(from the Latin)

Hymn

Dawn shines red–gold, daylight's herald
stirs us up in joy from sleep,
glad to keep this famous feast
of venerable Columba.

Humble he was, gentle and kind,
a man of joyful face, and worthy of honour,
a man of noble birth, steadfast demeanour,
chaste his body and his mind.

Columba's merits and the wonders he worked,
his prophetic deeds, his famous miracles –
of all these no one can fully know how
to write in script or speak in words.

Leaving behind his beloved Irish home,
by Christ's grace he came to Britain.
Through him, the king of Britain's race
received life's proper new beginning.

Our nation's father, excellent pastor,
grant us, Columba, hope of forgiveness,
and from the stain of all our sins
cleanse us, holy Columba.

May you bring us forgiveness of sin,
wash clean the guilty, endow the land,
and us your servants and all catholic folk
commend to the glorious King.

Praise perpetual may there always be, glory always
to the Father, the Son, and the Holy Paraclete,
to the one and only Lord who rules over us all,
for ever, for all ages.
                    Amen.

Memorial of St Columba

Mouth of the dumb,
light of the blind,
foot of the lame,
to the fallen stretch out your hand.
Strengthen the senseless,
restore the mad.
O Columba, hope of Scots,
by your merits' mediation
make us companions
of the blessed angels.
                    Alleluia.

Responsory

O Columba, our glorious leader,
cleanse our minds, lest the noxious deceiver
harm your servants by the sea's danger,
    that around you they may gladly sing.
For you, above all others, it is right that you should hear
voices raised in joy. To this place bend your ear,
    that around you may they gladly sing.

ANONYMOUS (c. 761 and c. 858)

Verses on Kings of the Picts

On Oengus, Son of Fergus
(from the Gaelic)

Good the day when Oengus took Alba,
  hilly Alba, with its strong chiefs;
He brought battle to towns, with boards,
  with feet and hands, and with broad shields.

On the Death of Cinead, son of Ailpin
(from the Gaelic)

That Cinead with his hosts is no more
  brings weeping to every home:
No king of his worth under heaven
  is there, to the bounds of Rome.

from the Scotichronicon of Walter Bower (1383–1437)

Advice to Mael Coluim from MacDuib
(from the Latin)

Would you bring safety to helpless faithful folk,
those who till today have lacked all help?
For fifteen years the enemy has oppressed them, so
come kindly, relive the wretched for the love of God.
Waste no time in idle speculation, but with ready strength
cast down our foe, relieve your still devoted people.
Let your sword be girded on your thigh, take up your arms,
for the strength of every fibre of your frame is clear.

You are a Scot, born of the line of kings of old,
and so advance in triumph, take up your father's rule.
I promise you, the kingdom's crown will be rightly yours,
for every right belongs to you, and none to him are owed.
Bold in your rights, therefore, be always battle-ready,
but do not reckon warfare to be entered into lightly.
And, barring ill-chance, let you not rush headlong into strife,
for every man may fall through that for which he's unprepared.
But when about to fight, do not let your foe precede you on the field,
but be there first yourself, in the place where the arms will meet.

ANONYMOUS (c. 1113)

A Verse on David, Son of Mael Coluim
(from the Gaelic)

It's bad, what Mael Coluim's son has done,
dividing us from Alexander;
he causes, like each king's son before,
the plunder of stable Alba.

from Macbeth, IV, iii, 163–73

'Stands Scotland where it did?'

MacDuff: Stands Scotland where it did?

Ross: Alas, poor country!
Almost afraid to know itself! It cannot
Be called our mother but our grave, where nothing
But who knows nothing is once seen to smile;
Where sighs and groans, and shrieks that rent the air,
Are made, not marked; where violent sorrow seems
A modern ecstasy. The dead man's knell
Is there scarce asked for who, and good men's lives
Expire before the flowers in their caps,
Dying or ere they sicken.

ANDREW OF WYNTOUN (c. 1355–c. 1425)

Macbeth

In till this tyme that I of tell,
That this tressoune in Ingland fell,
In Scotland fell neire the like cais
Be Fynlaw Makbeth that than was,
Quhen he had mutherist his aune eme
Throu hope at he had of a dreme,
That he saw forow that in sleping,
Quhen he wes dwelland with the king,
That tretit him fairely and weill
In all that langit him ilk deill;
Becaus he wes his sister sone,
His yarnying of she gert be done.
   A nycht him thocht in his dremyng
That he wes sittand neire the King,
At a seit in hunting swa,
And in a lesche had grewhundis twa.
Him thocht, till he wes sa sittand,
He saw thre women by gangand,

And thai thre women than thocht he
Thre werd sisteris like to be.
The first he herd say gangand by:
'Lo, yonder the thayne of Crumbaghty!'
The tother sister said agane:
'Off Murray yonder I see the thayne.'
The thrid said: 'Yonder I se the king.'
All this herd he in his dremyng.
Sone efter that, in his youth heid,
Off thai thayndomes he thayne wes maid;
Than thocht he nixt for to be king,
Fra Duncanis dais had tane ending.
   And thus the fantasy of this dreme
Muffit him for to sla his eme,
As he falsly in deid,
As ye have herd befor this reid;
Syne with his awne emys wif
He lay, and with hir led his lif,
And held hir baith his wif and quene,
Rycht as scho forouth that had bene
Till his eme the king liffand,
Quhen he wes king with croune regnand
For litill taill that tyme gaif he
Off the greis of affinite.
And thusgatis quhen his eme wes dede,
He succedit in his steid,
And winter wes regnand
As king with croune in till Scotland.
Yit in his tyme thar wes plente
Off gold and silver, catall and fee.
He wes in justice rycht lauchfull,
And till his liegis rycht awfull.
Quhen Leo the tend wes pape of Rome,
In pilgrimage thidder he come,
And in almus he sew silver
To pure folkis that had gret mistere;
Yit usit he oftsys to wirk
Proffitably till haly kirk...

Macbeth

*In this time as I have told / Of treason that befell in England, / In Scotland
nearly the same / Was done by Macbeth-Fynlaek. / When he murdered his own*

uncle / *Because of a hope he had from a dream,* / *That he had before, when he* *was sleeping,* / *Dwelling in the same house as the King* / *That treated him* *fairly and well* / *In everything that belonged to him, in every part;* / *For he was* *his sister's son,* / *His every wish was granted.* / *One night he dreamed* / *That* *he was beside the King* / *On a seat while out hunting.* / *In a leash he had two* *greyhounds,* / *And he thought while he was so sitting,* / *He saw three women* *going by,* / *And these women he thought* / *Most like three weird sisters they* *must be.* / *The first he heard saying as she went by* / '*Lo, yonder is the Thane* *of Cromarty.*' / *The other sister said again* / '*Yonder I see the Thane of* *Moray.*' / *The third then said,* '*I see the King.*' / *All this he heard in his* *dreaming.* / *Soon after that as a young man,* / *Of these thanedoms he was then* *made,* / *Then next he thought to be king.* / *The fantasy thus from his dream* / *Made him think of slaying his uncle,* /*As he thereafter falsely did indeed,* / *As* *before you heard me tell.* /*And then with his uncle's wife* / *He lay, and* / *led* *his life with her,* / *And held her as his wife and queen,* / *As she had been* *before,* / *The living queen of his uncle* / *When he was the crowned and reigning* *king.* / *For little heed had her* / *of the grace of affinity.* / *And thus when his* *uncle was dead* / *He succeeded in his stead,* / *And seventeen winters was he full* *reigning king* / *In Scotland.* / *In all his time there was great plenty* / *Of gold* *and silver, beasts and lands.* / *In justice he was right lawful,* / *And held his* *subjects in awe.* / *When Leo the tenth was Pope of Rome* / *He came as a* *pilgrim to his court,* / *And he gave alms and scattered silver* / *To all the needy* *poor folk;* / *And all that time he worked hard* / *And profitably for the Holy* *Church.*

ANONYMOUS (C. 1249)

from the Scotichronicon of Walter Bower (1383–1437)
(from the Latin)

On the Death of Alexander II, King of the Scots

Church's shield, the people's peace, leader of the wretched,
an upright king, stern and wise, honest, well-advised,
a pious king, a mighty king, the best of kings and wealthy.
He was the second to bear his name, the name of Alexander.

For three decades he was king, and five years more,
but now the isle we call Kerrera has taken him away.
His spirit seeks the high places, joined with heavenly beings,
but Melrose here on earth now guards his buried bones.

Song for the Wedding of Margaret of Scotland and Eirik, King of Norway
(from the Latin)

From you arises, sweet Scotland, a light
whose brightness is seen shining in Norway;
how you will sigh when she is borne across the sea,
when the daughter of your king is taken away.

When the flame of peace is kindled, its grace
proclaimed to the nations, gladness makes reply.
Every nation's length and breadth now celebrates,
but above all England shares your joy.

To Eirik the king the royal maid is sent,
and with highest honour there received;
everyone breaks out in wild applause,
the people dancing while they sing her praise.

A crowd of clergy solemnly comes forth,
and wholesomely the holy priesthood prays.
Swiftly now come every class of folk,
men and likewise women, joy resounding.

The king leads forth the maid – a cause of joy
throughout the world is their sweet union.
May the God of all pour blessings on this bond
and of their marriage grant them children

One flesh with the king, the queen now sits
upon the kingdom's throne and wears the crown,
worthy to preside and guide the nation's life.
Praise be to him who make it so, God's Son.

How to praise this partner of the king,
so gentle, kindly, full of prudence?
Humble, she gives to all, strong in her speech,
Made lovelier yet by noble continence.

May she be loving to her man as was Rachel;
may she be pleasing to the king, as Esther was.
As Leah begot, may she be fertile in offspring,
and like Susannah may she live in steadfastness.

Living conjoined with the services of God,
may they in happiness grow old
that when the race is run of this, their passing life,
they may be worthy of a lasting reward.

From you, sweet Scotland, there comes forth
a cause to sing your praise across the earth.

ANONYMOUS (c. 1300)

from the Origynale Cronikle of Andrew of Wyntoun (c.1355–c.1425)

'Qwhen Alexander our kynge was dede'

Qwhen Alexander our kynge was dede,
  That Scotlande lede in lauche and le,
Away was sons of alle and brede,
  Off wyne and wax, of gamyn and gle.
Our golde was changit in to lede.
  Christ, borne in virgynyte,
Succoure Scotlande, and ramede,
  That stade is in perplexite.

'When Alexander our king was dead'

When Alexander our king was dead, / That led Scotland in law and peace, / Gone was plenty of ale and bread, / Of harvest and abundance, of play and pleasure. / Our gold was turned into lead. / Christ, born in virginity, / Succour and save Scotland, / That is lost in perplexity.

from the Scotichronicon of Walter Bower (1383–1437)

On the Death of Edward I
(from the Latin)

One thousand you will count, three hundred years and seven more,
on the Translation of ever blessed Thomas the Martyr,
in Burgh by Sands, where end the kingdom's borders,
there Edward fell, by whose evil Scots were slaughtered.

In Holm his brain and his entrails lie buried in the earth,
war-monger who lashed the English with his dire scourge.
He trampled underfoot the necks of their haughty men,
corrupted all the world, betrayed the Holy Land.

He invaded the Scots, broke up the realm by fraud,
laid waste our churches, shut up our prelates in prison,
he slew Christ's folk and seized the gold of the tithe.
His sins are well known in all the world.

England will weep when at last it lies in ruin.
Scotland, clap your hands at the death of a greedy king.
Give thanks to God now Robert has been crowned
and guided in virtue's strength by the staff of salvation.
God will make his state on earth a blessed one.

ANONYMOUS

from the Scotichronicon of Walter Bower (1383–1437)

William Wallace's Uncle's Proverb
(from the Latin)

This is the truth I tell you:
of all things freedom's most fine.
Never submit to live, my son,
in the bonds of slavery entwined.

from the Scotichronicon of Walter Bower (1383–1437)

Scotland's Strategy of Guerrilla Warfare
(from the Latin)

Let Scotland's warcraft be this: footsoldiers, mountain and marshy ground;
and let her woods, her bow and spear serve for barricades.
Let menace lurk in all her narrow places among her warrior bands,
and let her plains so burn with fire that enemies flee away.
Crying out in the night, let her men be on their guard,
and her enemies in confusion will flee from hunger's sword.
Surely it will be so, as we're guided by Robert, our lord.

ANONYMOUS (c. 1297)

from the Scotichronicon of Walter Bower (1383–1437)

On the Battle of Stirling Bridge
(from the Gaelic)

The aforesaid man, Wallace his name, rallies the Scots;
gathers them like grains, because in French he is 'Valais'.
He gives hot pursuit to the English, to carry on the war,
that Scotland's precious freedom by arms might be restored.
Then England's overthrow was great, of such a kind
as northern lands had never known before.
Even as far as Newcastle, Northumbria was all destroyed,
and thus, their aims achieved, the Scots pressed on for Stainmore.
In that same year of Our Lord the English return again,
I tell you, to do battle with us for Berwick town,
determined on the feast of Cuthbert, in the time of spring.
While Scots looked on, thinking they'd fight on the field,
the English failed to act as they had once agreed,
but all without delay they turned their tails and fled.
When they saw this the Scots in sadness went their way,
but England, backing off, mark their king's shield with shame.
The assembled Scots for these latest gifts give praise,
as those in need give thanks, though the gifts were not complete.
Rising in praise, rejoicing, every house resounds,
but the king takes flight, and in sorrow England groans.

from The Wallace, Book 1, lines 1–16

Our Forebears

Our antecessowris, that we suld of reide,
And hald in mynde thar nobille worthi deid,
We lat ourslide, throw werray sleuthfulnes;
And castis ws euir till vthir besynes.
Till honour ennymys is our haile entent,
It has beyne seyne in their tymys bywent;
Our ald ennymys cummyn of Saxonys blud,
That neuyr yeit to Scotland wald do gud,
Bot euir on fors, and contrar haile thair will,
Quhow gret kyndes thar has beyne kyth thaim till.
It is weyle knawyne on mony diuerss syde,
How thai haff wrocht in to thair mychty pryde,
To hald Scotlande at wndyr euirmar.
Bot God abuff has maid thar mycht to par:
Yhit we suld thynk one our bearis befor.
Of thair parablyss as now I say no mor.

Our Forebears

*Our ancestors, whom we should read about, / And keep in mind their noble,
worthy deeds, / We neglect through laziness / And because we are taken up
with other business. / It is our intention to honour our enemies. / This has been
seen in bygone times. / Our old enemies come from Saxon blood / That never
has done Scotland any good / Except when forced, and then entirely against their
will, / How great kindness has been shown to them. / It is well known on many
and various sides / How they have wrought, in their great pride, / To hold
Scotland under their authority forever. / But God above has made their power
diminish: / So now we should think of our forebears. / Of their stories now I say
no more.*

from The Wallace, Book 11, lines 1109–27

Wallace

Allace, Scotland, to quhom sall thow compleyn!
Allace, fra payn quha sall the now restreyn!
Allace, thi help is fasslie brocht to ground,
Thi bests chyftane in braith bandis is bound!
Allace, thow has now lost thi gyd off lycht!
Allace, quha sall defend the in thi rycht?
Allace, thi payn approchis wondyr ner,
With sorrow sone thow mon bene set in feyr!
Thi gracious gyd, thi grettast gouernour,
Allace, our neir is cumin his fatell hour!
Allace, quha sall the beit now off thi baill?
Allace, quhen sall off harmys thow be haill?
Quha sall the defend? quha sall the now mak free?
Allace, in wer quha sall the helpar be?
Quha sall the help? quha sall the now radem?
Allace, quha sall the Saxons fra the flem?
I can no mar, bot besek God off grace
The to restor in haist to rychtwysnace;
Sen gud Wallace may succour the no mar.
The loss of him encressit mekill cair.

Wallace

*Alas, Scotland, to whom shall you complain? / Alas, who shall pull you back
from pain now? / Alas, your help is falsely brought down, / The best chieftain is
bound in strong bonds! / Alas, now you have lost the guide of light! / Alas, who
shall defend you in the right? / Alas, the pain approaches awfully close, / You
must soon be burning with sorrow! / Your gracious guide, your greatest governor,
/ Alas, his fatal hour is approaching too close! / Alas, who shall help you now
in your torment? / Alas, when shall you be whole again, recovered from your
wounds? / Who will defend you? Who will make you free now? / Alas, in war,
who shall be your helper? / Who shall help you? Who shall redeem you now? /
Alas, who shall drive the Saxons off from you now? / I can no more, but beseech
the God of grace, / To restore you quickly to righteousness / since good Wallace
may succour you no more. / The loss of him increases much concern.*

JOHN BARBOUR (C. 1320–1395)

from The Bruce, Book 1, lines 11–36

A Soothfast Story

...I wald fain set my will,
Gif my wit micht suffice theretil,
To put in writ a soothfast story
That it last aye furth in memory,
Sa that na time of length it let,
Na gar it wholly forget.
For auld storyis that men readis
Representis to them the deedis
Of stalwart folk that livit ere,
Richt as they in presence were
And, certis, they suld weill have pryss
That in their time were wicht and wise,
And led their life in great travail,
And oft in hard stour of battail
Wan richt great pryss of chivalry,
And were voidit of cowardye,
As was King Robert of Scotland
That hardy was of heart and hand;
And gude Sir James of Douglas
That in his time sa worthy was
That of his pryss and his bounté
In far landis renownit was he.
Of them I think this buke to ma:
Now God give grace that I may sa
Treat it and bring it till ending
That I say nocht bot soothfast thing!

A True Story

I would wish to set my will / If I have sufficient intelligence to do so / To put in writing a true story / So that it will stay in the memory, / So that it will last a long time / And will never be entirely forgotten. / For old stories that people read / Represent to them the deeds / Of stalwart folk that lived a while ago / Fully present in their own time / And certainly they should be prized, / Those who, in their time, were strong and wise / And led their lives in great trouble, / And often in the hard dark world of battle / Who won the true and great prize of chivalry / And abjured cowardice, / Such was King Robert of Scotland, / Who was hardy of heart and hand / And good Sir James Douglas / Who was so worthy in his time / That his prized character and quality / Was famed afar in distant lands. / Now God give me grace that I may so / Present this story and bring it to its ending / And that I should say nothing that is not true!

from The Bruce, Book 1, lines 225–40

Freedom

A! fredome is a noble thing!
Fredome mayss man to haiff liking;
Fredome all solace to man giffis
He levys at ess that frely levys
A noble hart may haiff nane ess,
Na ellys nocht that may him pless,
Gyff fredome failye: for fre liking
Is yharnyt our all othir thing.
Hasna he that ay bass levyt fre,
May nocht knaw weill the propyrte,
The angyr, na the wrechyt dome,
That is cowplyt to foule thyrldome.
Bot gyff he had assayit it,
Than all perquer he suld it wyt;
And suld think fredome mar to pryss,
Than all the gold in warld that is.

Freedom

Ah, Freedom is a noble thing! / Freedom makes people have liking. / Freedom helps people to live. / He lives easefully who lives freely. / A noble heart may have no rest / Nor anything else that might please, / If freedom fails; for freedom to choose / Is valued above all other things. / He that has always lived free / Might not know well the property of freedom; / [Or] the anger, the wretched fate / That is coupled to slavery / But if he has tried it / Then he should prize it accordingly, / And should consider freedom more valuable / Than all the gold in the world.

ROBERT FABYAN (d. 1513)

from The Concordance of Histories, 1516

Song on the Battle of Bannockburn

Maidens of England, sore may ye mourn,
For your lemans ye have lost Bannockisbourn,
  With heave-a-lowe.
What, weeneth the King of England
So soon to have won Scotland?
  With rumbylowe.

JOHN OF FORDUN (c. 1320–1384)

from the Scotichronicon of Walter Bower (1383–1437)

King Robert's Testament

On fute should be all Scottis weir,
By hill and moss themselves to were.
Let wood for walls be bow and spear,
That enemies do them nae deir.
In strait places gar keep all store,
And burn the plain land them before;
Then shall they pass away in haste,
When that they find naething bot waste.
With wiles and wakening of the nicht,
And meikle noyis made on heicht,
Then shall they turn with great affray,
As they were chasit with sword away.
This is the counsel and intent
Of gude King Robert's testament.

from the Scotichronicon of Walter Bower (1383–1437)

The Epitaph of Robert Bruce
(from the Latin)

Robert Bruce, the nation's virtue, lies in the earth;
bold and righteous prince of joy, in all his ways most sure.
A Paris he was in shapeliness, a Hector renowned for his sword,
royal rose of soldiery, a Socrates, Maro or Cato in his words.

Begotten of Priam, like Achilles the leader of Greeks,
praiseworthy as Ajax, many-talented like Ulysses,
beloved as the Macedonian, like Arthur a jewel among men,
a leader of the peoples, a Maccabeus for intelligence.

Upright like Aeneas, like Pompey's his total command,
gentle as Saint Andrew, like Jonathan his might was admired.
This Saturn gives nobility to the Cretan shores, while rain
which crossed the Aegean flees, and summer flowers again.

He was a Julius Caesar, in hope he was like Simeon,
outstanding king like Charles, with the wisdom of a Solomon.
A law-giver like Gaius, leader in the power of Dido's love,
a Jason at heart, honest as Sejus, spirited spring of Helicon.

His was the strength of Samson and the blood of Bartholomew,
firm his faith like Simon's, a casket of Sabaean incense.
Always gracious in his gifts, born of royal ancestors
under Juno's Jupiter, he was the very bright daystar.

Lamenting the loss of the royal rights of Scots-born men,
postponing idle pleasures, he left his old sweet life for a bitter regimen.
Cold he suffered, and for sleep he lay in dens of wild beasts,
while for his food he did not refuse the fruit of acorn-laden trees.

For the protection of his rights he placed his only hope in Christ,
hiding himself in the thorny bush, drinking water, never wines.
With his strong comrades in the assault, he seemed a fierce wild boar,
and thus he earned his royal throne, wore down the enemy's spear.

At this man's warrior-thrust a host of evil-doers falls;
on the iron-armoured backs of men his wounds are cruel.
He sharpens the weapons of war, sword raging at a host of knights:
this one falls, that one dies, and their king is put to flight.

In good order the king of Scots brings his standard forth,
fighting mightily he bears it through a thick-packed host.
To boundless praise he triumphs mightily over the foe,
and sent him homewards, the English king, as our new lyric goes.

When he is made lord of Byland, joyful victory is prepared,
the host in flight is ravaged, and the slaughter multiplied.
A solemn truce is covenanted, but the peace agreed is false.
After the death of the reverend king, peace suffers a reverse.

O what grief among the people! Alas, our grief is doubled.
Every eye is given to weeping while disorder multiplies.
He who in the royal roll was counted flower of kings,
now in a muddy little place is laid as food for worms.

He himself was a shining light before the darkness of our eyes,
the glory which gave fragrant variance to the buds of flowers,
a mirror spread before the people, a rose, a moral guide,
sating men's hearts with sweetness, he was their holy food.

This outstanding king was like a bracelet on our arms,
a precious ring or a jewel in the ear of noble men,
a twisted torque which folk may wear around their throats –
now he lies below, stripped of towering glory's robes.

What is worldly reward or honour? Where is the glory of things?
What worth has the kingdom's throne, or the lovely savour of beauty?
What worth have all our talents? – I speak the truth, for sure –
at the end of a man's days, high office has meaning no more.

WILLIAM DUNBAR (1460–1520)

The Thrissil and the Rois

Quhen Merche wes with variand windis past,
And Appryll had, with hir silver schouris,
Tane leif at nature with ane orient blast;
And lusty May, that muddir is of flouris,
Had maid the birdis to begyn thair houris
Amang the tendir odouris reid and quhyt,
Quhois armony to heir it wes delyt;

In bed at morrow, sleiping as I lay,
Me thocht Aurora, with hir cristall ene,
In at the window lukit by the day,
And halsit me, with visage paill and grene;
On quhois hand a lark sang fro the splene,
Awalk, luvaris, out of your slomering,
Se how the lusty morrow dois up spring.

Me thocht fresche May befoir my bed upstude,
In weid depaynt of mony divers hew,
Sobir, benyng, and full of mansuetude,
In brycht atteir of flouris forgit new,
Hevinly of color, quhyt, reid, broun, and blew,
Balmit in dew and gilt with Phebus bemys,
Quhill all the hous illumynit of hir lemys.

'Slugird,' scho said, 'awalk annone for schame,
And in my honour sum thing thow go wryt;
The lork hes done the mirry day proclame,
To rais up luvaris with confort and delyt,
Yit nocht incresis thy curage to indyt,
Quhois hairt sum tyme hes glaid and blisfull bene,
Sangis to mak undir the levis grene.'

'Quhairto,' quod I, 'sall I uprys at morrow,
For in this May few birdis herd I sing?
Thai haif moir caus to weip and plane thair sorrow,
Thy air it is nocht holsum nor benyng;
Lord Eolus dois in thy sessoune ring;
So busteous ar the blastis of his horne,
Amang thy bewis to walk I haif forborne.'

With that this lady sobirly did smyll,
And said, 'Uprys, and do thy observance;
Thow did promyt, in Mayis lusty quhyle,
For to discryve the Ros of most plesance.
Go se the birdis how thay sing and dance,
Illumynit our with orient skyis brycht,
Annamyllit richely with new asur lycht.'

Quhen this wes said, depairtit scho, this quene,
And enterit in a lusty gairding gent;
And than, me thocht, full fresche and weill besene,
In serk and mantill, full haistely I went
In to this garth, most dulce and redolent
Off herb and flour and tendir plantis sueit,
And grene levis doing of dew doun fleit.

The purpour sone, with tendir bemys reid,
In orient bricht as angell did appeir,
Throw goldin skyis putting up his heid,
Quhois gilt tressis schone so wondir cleir,
That all the world tuke confort, fer and neir,
To luke upone his fresche and blisfull face,
Doing all sable fro the hevynnis chace.

And as the blisfull sone of cherarchy
The fowlis song throw confort of the licht;
The birdis did with oppin vocis cry,
'O, luvaris fo, away thow dully nycht,
And welcum day that confortis every wight;
Haill May, haill Flora, haill, Aurora schene!
Haill princes Natur, haill Venus, luvis quene.'

Dame Nature gaif ane inhibition thair
To fers Neptunus, and Eolus the bawld,
Nocht to perturb the wattir nor the air,
And that no schouris, nor blastis cawld,
Effray suld flouris nor fowlis on the fold;
Scho bad eik Juno, goddes of the sky,
That scho the hevin suld keip amene and dry.

Scho ordand eik that every bird and beist
Befoir hir hienes suld annone compeir,
And every flour of vertew, most and leist,
And every herb be feild fer and neir,
As thay had wont in May, fro yeir to yeir,
To hir thair makar to mak obediens,
Full law inclynnand with all dew reverens.

With that annone scho send the swyft Ro
To bring in beistis of all conditioun;
The restless Suallow commandit scho also
To feche all fowll of small and greit renown;
And, to gar flouris compeir of all fassoun,
Full craftely conjurit scho the Yarrow,
Quhilk did furth swirk als swift as ony arrow.

All present wer in twynkling of ane e,
Baith beist, and bird, and flour, befoir the quene,
And first the Lyone, gretast of degre,
Was callit thair, and he, most fair to sene,
With a full hardy countenance and kene,
Befoir dame Natur come, and did inclyne,
With visage bawld and curage leonyne.

This awfull beist full terrible wes of cheir,
Persing of luke, and stout of contenance,
Rycht strong of corpis, of fassoun fair but feir,
Lusty of schaip, lycht of deliverance,
Reid of his cullour, as is the ruby glance;
On feild of gold he stude full mychtely,
With flour delycis sirculit lustely.

This lady liftit up his cluvis cleir,
And leit him listly lene upone hir kne,
And crownit him with dyademe full deir
Off radyous stonis, most ryall for to se;
Saying, 'The King of Beistis mak I the,
And the cheif protector in woddis and schawis;
Onto thi leigis go furth, and keip the lawis.

Exerce justice with mercy and conscience,
And lat no small beist suffir skaith na skornis
Of greit beistis that bene of moir piscence;
Do law elyk to aipis and unicornis,
And lat no bowgle, with his busteous hornis,
The meik pluch ox oppress, for all his pryd,
Bot in the yok go peciable him besyd.'

Quhen this was said, with noyis and soun of joy,
All kynd of beistis in to thair degre,
At onis cryit lawd, 'Vive le Roy!'
And till his feit fell with humilite,
And all thay maid him homege and fewte;
And he did thame ressaif with princely laitis,
Quhois noble yre is *parcere prostratis*.

Syne crownit scho the Egle King of Fowlis,
And as steill dertis scherpit scho his pennis,
And bawd him be als just to awppis and owlis,
As unto pacokkis, papingais, or crennis,
And mak a law for wycht fowlis and for wrennis;
And lat no fowll of ravyne do efferay,
Nor devoir birdis bot his awin pray.

Than callit scho all flouris that grew on feild,
Discirnyng all thair fassionis and effeiris;
Upon the awful Thrissill scho beheld,
And saw him kepit with a busche of speiris;
Concedring him so able for the weiris,
A radius croun of rubeis scho him gaif,
And said, 'In feild go furth, and fend the laif;

And, sen thow art a king, thow be discreit;
Herb without vertew thow hald nocht of sic pryce
As herb of vertew and of odor sueit;
And lat no nettil vyle, and full of vyce,
Hir fallow to the gudly flour delyce;
Nor latt no wyld weid, full or churlichenes,
Compair hir till the lilleis nobilnes.

Nor hald non udir flour in sic denty
As the fresche Ros of cullour reid and quhyt;
For gife thow dois, hurt is thyne honesty,
Conciddering that no flour is so perfyt,
So full of vertew, plesans, and delyt,
So full of blissfull angellik bewty,
Imperiall birth, honour and dignite.'

Than to the Ros scho turnyt hir visage,
And said, 'O lusty dochtir most benyng,
Aboif the lilly, illustare of lynnage,
Fro the stok ryell rysing fresche and ying,
But ony spot or macull doing spring;
Cum blowme of joy with jemis to be cround,
For our the laif thy bewty is renownd.'

A coistly croun, with clarefied stonis brycht,
This cumly quene did on hir heid inclois,
Quhill all the land illumynit of the licht;
Quhairfoir me thocht all flouris did rejos,
Crying attonis, 'Haill be, thow richest Ros!
Haill, hairbis empryce, haill, freschest quene of flouris,
To thee be glory and honour at all houris.'

Thane all the birdis song with voce on hicht,
Quhois mirthfull soun wes mervelus to heir;
The mavys song, 'Haill, Rois most riche and richt,
That dois up flureis undir Phebus speir;
Haill, plant of yowth, haill, princes dochtir deir,
Haill, blosome breking out of the blud royall,
Quhois pretius vertew is imperiall.'

The merle scho sang, 'Haill, Rois of most delyt,
Haill, of all flouris quene and soverane!'
The lark scho song, 'Haill, Rois, both reid and quhyt,
Most plesand flour, of michty cullouris twane!'
The nychtingaill song, 'Haill, naturis suffragene,
In bewty, nurtour, and every nobilnes,
In riche array, renown, and gentilnes.'

The commoun voce uprais of birdis small,
Apone this wys, 'O blissit be the hour
That thow wes chosin to be our principall;
Welcome to be our princes of honour,
Our perle, our plesans, and our paramour,
Our peax, our play, our plane felicite,
Chryst the conserf frome all adversitie.'

Than all the birdis song with sic a schout,
That I annone awoilk quhair that I lay,
And with a braid I turnyt me about
To se this court, bot all wer went away:
Than up I lenyt, haiflingis in affrey,
And thus I wret, as ye haif hard to forrow,
Off lusty May upone the nynt morrow.

The Thistle and the Rose

*When March was, with varying winds, past / and April had, with her silver
showers, / taken leave of nature with a blast from the east, / and lusty May,
that is the mother of flowers, / had made the birds begin their songs at the proper
hours / among the tender, fragrant, red and white flowers / to hear whose
harmony was delightful, //*

*In bed at sunrise, sleeping as I lay, / I thought the Dawn with her crystal eyes,
/ looked in the window with daylight / and greeted me with a pale, wan face /
on whose hand a lark sang from the heart: / 'Awake, lovers, out of your slum-
bering, / See how the lusty morrow springs up!' //*

*I thought fresh May before my head was standing / dressed in various aspects, /
sober, benign, and full of gentleness and mildness / in bright clothes of new-
sprung flowers / heavenly of colour, white, red, dark violet and blue, / balmy
with dew and all lit up with sunbeams / while all the house was illuminated by
her rays of light. //*

*'Sluggard,' she said, 'Wake up right now for shame / and go and write some-
thing in my honour; / the lark has proclaimed the merry day / to raise up lovers
with encouragement and delight / yet nothing seems to inspire you to go and
compose, / whose heart, once upon a time, was glad and blissful / [enough] to
make songs under the green leaves.' //*

*'Why,' said I, 'should I get up at sunrise, / for in this May I heard few birds
singing? / They have more cause to weep and complain of their sorrow; / your
air is not wholesome nor benign / the lord of the winds rules in your season, /
the blasts of his horn are so blustery / that I have forborne to walk among your
branches.' //*

*With that this lady smiled soberly, / and said, 'Get up, and do your duty; /
you promised, in the lusty time of May, / to describe the most delightful Rose. /
Go and see how the birds sing and dance, / illuminated overall with bright
easterly skies, / enamelled richly with new azure light.' //*

*When this was said, she departed, this queen, / and went into a beautiful,
elegant garden, / and then, I thought, freshly and well dressed, / in shirt and
cloak, I hastily followed / into this most gracious and redolent garden, / of
herbs and flowers and tender, sweet plants, / and green leaves flowing down with
dew. //*

*The bright sun with tender red beams, / appeared in the east, bright as an angel,
/ through golden skies, lifting his head, / whose gilt tresses shone so wondrously
clear / that all the world took comfort, far and near, / to look upon his fresh and
blissful face, / chasing from the heavens all sable colours. //*

*And like the blissful sun of the angelic hierarchies / the birds were singing
through the comfort of the light; / the birds with open voices cried / O, lovers'
enemy, away with you, dismal Night / and welcome Day that pleases every
person; / Hail, May! Hail, Flora! Hail, Dawn, beautiful and bright! / Hail,
Princess Nature! Hail, Venus, Queen of Love! //*

*Dame Nature set out a prohibition there / to fierce Neptune, God of the Sea,
and bold Aeolus, God of the Winds, / not to stir up the water or the air / and
that no showers or cold blasts / should flourish, alarming the birds upon the
earth; / she instructed Juno, Goddess of the Sky, / to keep the heavens mild and
dry. //*

*She ordained also that every bird and beast / before her Highness should at once
come forward / and every flower possessing medicinal or magical properties, the
greatest and the smallest, / and every herb in the fields both far and near, / as
they were accustomed to be, in May each year, / to make clear their obedience to
her, their maker, / bowing low with all due reverence. //*

*With that, immediately, she sent the swift roe deer / to bring in the animals of
every kind; / the restless swallow she also commanded / to fetch all the birds,
of small or great renown; / and to order flowers of all sorts to step forward; /
very craftily, she conjured the milfoil herb, / which darted forth as quick as an
arrow. //*

*In the twinkling of an eye, all were present, / both beasts and birds and flowers,
before the Queen. / And first the Lion, greatest of rank, / the fairest to be seen,
was called there, / and with a very bold and keen look about him, / came before
Dame Nature, and bowed, / with courageous features and the manly spirit to be
expected of a lion. //*

*This awful beast was awe-inspiring to look at: / his gaze was piercing and his
countenance brave, / his body strong, his build was beautiful and incomparable, /
shaped lustily, yet of a light deportment; / his colour was red as the gleams from
a ruby. / He stood mightily on a field of gold / attractively encircled by heraldic
lilies. //*

*This lady lifted up his bright claws / and let him gracefully lean upon her knee /
and crowned him with a precious diadem / of radiant gems, most royal to behold,
/ saying, 'The King of Beasts I make thee, / and the Chief Protector in forests
and groves. / To your subjects go forth and keep the laws. //*

*Exercise justice with mercy and conscience / and let no small beast suffer harm or
insults / from the great beasts that are more powerful. / Enforce the law alike to
apes and unicorns / and let no wild ox with his powerful horns / oppress the
meek ox that pulls the plough, for all his pride / he should go peaceably beside
him in the yoke.'*

*When this was said, with noise and sounds of joy / all kinds of beasts in their
various stations / at once cried out loud, 'Long live the King!' / and the Lion
fell to his feet with humility / and all the other animals paid him homage and
gave loyal salutation / and he received them with princely manners / whose noble
anger is tempered, fair and just. //*

*Then she crowned the Eagle King of Birds / and she sharpened his talons like
steel darts / and instructed him to be as fair to bullfinches as to owls / and as
to peacocks, parrots or cranes / and to make one law for powerful birds as for
wrens, / and let no bird of prey cause alarm / nor eat other birds, except his own
prey. //*

*Then she called all the flowers that grew on the field, / examining all their
shapes and manners; / her gaze fell upon the awe-inspiring Thistle / and saw
him protected by a bush of spears. / Considering how ready he was for warfare, /
she gave him a radiant crown of rubies / and said, 'Go forth into the field and
defend all others. //*

*And since you are a King, you should be discreet, / do not hold plants without
virtue at the same value / as those of virtue and sweet fragrance / and let no vile
and evil nettle / associate as an equal with goodly and delightful flowers / and let
no wild churlish weed / compare herself to the lily's nobility. //*

*Nor hold other flowers in such high esteem / as the fresh Rose, of colour red and
white / for if you do, your honour will be compromised / considering that no
flower is so perfect, / so full of virtue, pleasance and delight, / so full of blissful,
angelic beauty, / of exalted birth, honour and dignity.' //*

*Then to the Rose she turned and looked / and said, 'O beautiful daughter most
benign, / even more than the lily, of illustrious descent, / arising from the royal
stock, fresh and young, / spotless and unblemished, / come, bloom of joy, with
gems to be crowned, / for above the others your beauty is renowned.' //*

*A costly crown with clear bright stones / this lovely Queen placed upon her head,
/ while all the land was illuminated by the light; / and thus, I thought, all the
flowers rejoiced, / crying at once, 'Hail to you, richest Rose! / Hail, Empress of
Plants! Hail, freshest Queen of Flowers! / To thee be glory and honour at all
hours!' //*

*Then all the birds sang with voices in the heights / whose mirthful sound was
marvellous to hear / The song-thrush sang, 'Hail, Rose most rich and right /*

that blossoms in the sunlight! / Hail, plant of youth! Hail, dear daughter of the
prince! / Hail, blossom budding from royal blood! / Whose precious virtue is
imperial!' //
The blackbird sang, 'Hail, Rose of most delight! / Hail, of all flowers Queen
and Sovereign!' / The lark sang, 'Hail, Rose both red and white, / Most
pleasant flower of two powerful colours!' / The nightingale sang, 'Hail, Nature's
deputy / in beauty, nourishment and every nobleness / in rich clothes, reputation
and gentleness.' //
The common voice of small birds rose up / like this: 'O blessed be the hour /
that you were chosen to be our Principal! / Welcome to be our Princess of
Honour, / our pearl, our pleasance and our beloved, / our peace, our delight, our
simple happiness. / May Christ protect you from all adversity.' //
Then all the birds sang with such a shout / that I woke up at once where I was
lying / and with a start, I turned around / to see this court, but all had gone
away. / Then up I got, half-frightened, / and thus I wrote, as you have already
heard, / upon the ninth morning of the cheerful month of May.

ANONYMOUS (c. 1513)

bho Ar Sliocht Gaodhal

Is dú éirghe i n-aghaidh Gall,
nocha dóigh éirghe udmhall;
faobhair claidheamh, reanna ga,
cóir a gcaitheamh go h-aobhdha.

Ré Gallaibh adeirim ribh,
sul ghabhadar ar ndúthaigh;
ná léigmid ar ndúthaigh dhínn,
déinmid ardchogadh ainmhín,
ar aithris Gaoidheal mBanbha,
caithris ar ar n-athardha.

★ ★ ★ ★ ★

Ghill-easbuig nach d'eitigh d'fhear,
is tú an Lugh fá dheireadh;
a Iarla Oirir Ghaoidheal,
bí id churaidh ag commaoidheamh.

Cuir th'urfhógra an oir 's an iar
ar Ghaoidhlibh ó Ghort Gáilian;
cuir siar thar ardmhuir na Goill,
nach biadh ar Albain athroinn.

Na fréamha ó bhfuilid ag fás,
díthigh iad, mór a bhforfhás,
nach faighthear Gall beó dot éis,
ná Gaillseach an ré h-aisnéis.

Loisg a mbantracht nach maith mín,
loisg a gclannmhaicne ainmhín,
is loisg a dtighe dubha,
is coisg dhínn a n-anghutha.

Léig le h-uisge a luaithre sin,
i ndiaidh loisgthe dá dtaisibh;
ná déan teóchroidhe a beó Gall,
a eó bheóghoine anbhfann.

Cuimhnigh féin, a ghruaidh mar shuibh,
go bhfuil orainn ag Gallaibh
annsmacht réd linn agus pléid
'nar chinn gallsmacht [   ].   [original text missing]

Cuimhnigh Cailéin th'athair féin,
cuimhnigh Gill-easbuig ainnséin,
cuimhnigh Donnchadh 'na ndeaghaidh,
an fear conchar cairdeamhail.

Cuimhnigh Cailéin eile ann,
cuimhnigh Gill-easbuig Arann;
's Cailéin na gceann, mór a chlí,
lér gabhadh geall an [   ].

Cuimhnigh nach tugsad na fir
umhla ar uamhan do Ghallaibh;
cia mó fá dtugadh tusa
umhla uait an dula-sa?

Ó nach mair acht fuidheall áir
do Ghaoidhlibh ó ghort iomgháidh,
teagair lé chéile na fir,
's cuir th'eagal féine ar náimhdibh.

Saigh ar Ghallaibh 'na dtreibh féin:
bí id dúsgadh, a Mheic Cailéin:
d'fhear cogaidh, a fholt mar ór,
ní maith an codal ramhór.

from To the Earl of Argyll
(before Flodden)

To fight the Saxons is right,
no rising followed by flight;
edge of sword, point of spear,
let us ply them with good cheer.

Against Saxons, I say to you,
lest they rule our country too;
fight roughly, like the Irish Gael,
we will have no English Pale.

★ ★ ★ ★ ★

I know one who'd fight like Lugh:
Archibald, to honour true,
Earl of the Coastland of the Gael
exultant warrior, do not fail!

Send your summons east and west,
let Ireland come at your behest;
drive Saxons back across the sea,
let Scotland not divided be.

Destroy the roots from which they grow –
too great their increase – and lay low
each Saxon, robbing him of life;
give the same treatment to his wife.

Burn their women, coarse, untrue,
burn their uncouth children too,
and burn down their black houses:
rid us of their grouses.

Send their ashes down the flood
when you've burnt their flesh and blood;
show no rue to living Saxon,
death-dealing salmon-hero — tax them!

Remember, cheek of raspberry hue,
that Saxons lord it over you;
keep in memory their spite
as Saxon power has grown in might.

Remember Colin, your own father,
remember Archibald, your grandfather,
remember Duncan after them,
a man who loved both hounds and men.

Remember the other Colin then,
and Archibald of Arran,
and Colin of the Heads, who won
the hero's stakes, ere he was done.

Remember these men did not yield,
for fear of Saxon in the field;
why should you make submission now
and bend before them your proud brow?

Since of the Gael there now remain
but scant survivors of the slain,
together gather all your men;
strike fear into the foe again.

Attack the Saxons in their land,
awake! MacCailein, understand,
O golden-haired one, that a fighter
profits much by sleeping lighter.

Jok Upalland

Now is our king in tendir aige:
Christ conserf him in his eild
to do justice bath to man and pege
that garris our land ly lang onteild.
Thocht we do double pay thair wege,
pur commonis presently now ar peild,
thay ryd about in a sic a rege
be firth, forrest and feild,
with bow, buklar and brand.
'Lo, quhair thay ryd in till our ry.
The divill mot sane yone company
I pray fro many hairt trewly.'
Thus said Jok Upalland.

He that wes wont to beir the barrowis
betwix the baikhous and the brewhous,
on twenty schilling now he tarrowis
to ryd the he gait by the plewis.
'Bot wer I king bund haif gud fallowis,
in Norroway thay suld heir of newis:
I suld him takand all his marrowis
and hing thame heich upoun yone hewis,
and tharto plichtis my hand.
Thair lordis and barronis grit
upoun ane gallowis suld I knit
that this doun treddit hes our quhit.'
This said Johine Uponland.

Wald the lordis the lawis that leidis
to husbandis do gud ressone and skill,
to chiftanis thair chiftanis be the heidis
and hing thame heich upoun ane hill.
Than micht husbandis lawbor thair steidis
and preistis mycht pattir and pray thair fill,
for husbandis suld nocht haif sic pleidis:
bayth scheip and nolt mycht ly full still,
and stakis still mycht stand.
'For sen thay red amang our durris
with splent on spald and rousty spurris,

thair grew no fruct in till our furris.'
Thus said Johine Uponland.

Tak a pure man a scheip or two
for hungir or for falt or fude
to five or sex bairnis or mo,
thay will him hing with raipis rud.
Bot and he tak a flok or two,
a bow of ky and lat thame blud,
full falsly may he ryd or go.
'I wait nocht gif thir lawis be gud.
I schrew thame first thame fand.
Jesu, for thy holy passioun,
thou grant him grace that weiris the croun
to ding thir mony kingis doun.'
Thus said Johine Uponland.

Jock the Peasant

*Now our king is a young man / Christ support him in his age / to do justice
upon the men / who make our land lie long untilled. / Though we pay double
taxes / the poor commonfolk are plundered / they ride about in such fury / by
firths, forests and fields / with bows, bucklers and brands. / 'Look, where they
ride into our rye / the devil curse such company / I pray from my heart truly.' /
Thus said Jok Upalland. //*
*He who used to bear the barrow / between the bakehouse and the brewhouse /
for twenty shillings now he tarries / to ride the high road by the fields. / 'But if I
were king with a band of good men / in Norway they would hear some news: / I
would take him and all his fellows / and hang them high upon yon hillside / and
thereto I pledge my hand. / These lords and barons great / I would tie upon a
gallows / who have so downtrodden our wheat.' / This said Johine Uponland. //*
*Would that the lords who lead the laws / be reasonable and do well to
husbandmen / be chief of the chieftains / and hang them high upon a hill. /
Then might husbandmen labour on their steadings / and priests might pray and
patter their fill, / for husbandmen need not such troubles: / both sheep and cattle
might lie in peace, / and fences still might stand. / 'For since they rode among
our doors / with armoured limbs and rusty spurs / no fruitfulness is in our
furrows.' / Thus said Johine Uponland. //*
*If a poor man takes a sheep or two / for hunger or for want of food / for five or
six or more of bairns / they will hang him with rough ropes. / But if another
take a flock or two / a herd of cattle for slaughter / against all that is right he
may freely ride. / 'I know not if these laws be good. / I curse them who first*

made them. / *Jesus, for thy holy passion,* / *grant him grace who wears the crown* / *to cast these many upstarts down'* / *Thus said Johine Uponland.*

SIR DAVID LYNDSAY (c. 1490–c. 1555)

from The Dreme of Schir David Lyndsay

Of the Realme of Scotland

Quhen that I had oversene this Regioun,
The quhilk, of nature, is boith gude and fair,
I did propone ane lytill questioun,
Beseikand hir the sam for to declare.
Quhat is the cause our boundis bene so bair?
Quod I: or quhate dois mufe our Miserie?
Or quhareof dois proceid our povertie?

For, throw the supporte of your hie prudence,
Off Scotland I persave the properteis,
And, als, considderis, be experience,
Off this countre the gret commoditeis.
First, the haboundance of fyschis in our seis,
And fructual montanis for our bestiall;
And, for our cornis, mony lusty vaill;

The ryche Ryveris, plesand and proffitabyll;
The lustie lochis, with fysche of sindry kyndis;
Hountyng, halkyng, for nobyllis convenabyll;
Forrestis full of Da, Ra, Hartis, and Hyndis;
The fresche fontanis, quhose holesum cristel strandis
Refreschis so the fair fluriste grene medis:
So laik we no thyng that to nature nedis.

Off euery mettell we have the ryche Mynis,
Baith Gold, Sylver, and stonis precious.
Howbeit we want the Spyces and the Wynis,
Or uther strange fructis delycious,
We have als gude, and more neidfull for us.
Meit, drynk, fyre, clathis, thar mycht be gart abound,
Quhilkis als is nocht in al the Mapamound;

More fairer peple, nor of gretar ingyne,
Nor of more strength gret dedis tyll indure.
Quharefor, I pray yow that ye wald defyne
The principall cause quharefor we ar so pure;
For I marvell gretlie, I yow assure,
Considderand the peple and the ground,
That Ryches suld nocht in this realme redound.

My Sonne, scho said, be my discretioun,
I sall mak answeir, as I understand.
I say to the, under confessioun,
The falt is nocht, I dar weill tak on hand,
Nother in to the peple nor the land.
As for the land, it lakis na uther thing
Bot laubour and the pepyllis governyng.

Than quharein lyis our Inprosperitie?
Quod I. I pray yow hartfullie, Madame,
Ye wald declare to me the veritie;
Or quho sall beir of our barrat the blame?
For, be my treuth, to se I thynk gret schame
So plesand peple, and so fair ane land,
And so few verteous dedis tane on hand.

Quod scho: I sall, efter my Jugement,
Declare sum causis, in to generall,
And, in to termes schorte, schaw myne intent,
And, syne, transcend more in to speciall.
So, this is myne conclusion fynall:
Wantyng of Justice, polycie, and peace,
Ar cause of thir unhappynes, allace!

It is deficill Ryches tyll incres,
Quhare Polycie makith no residence,
And Policey may never have entres,
Bot quhare that Justice dois delygence
To puneis quhare thare may be found offence.
Justice may nocht have Dominatioun,
Bot quhare Peace makis habitatioun.

Quhat is the cause, that wald I understand,
That we sulde want Justice and policie
More than dois France, Italie, or Ingland?
Madame, quod I, schaw me the veritie:
Sen we have Lawis in to this countre,
Quhy want we lawis Exersitioun?
Quho suld put Justice tyll exicutioun?

Quhare in dois stand our principall remeid?
Or quha may mak mendis of this myschief?
Quod scho: I fund the falt in to the heid;
For thay in quhome dois ly our hole releif,
I fynd thame rute and grund of all our greif,
For, quhen the heddis ar nocht delygent,
The membris man, or neid, be necligent.

So I conclude, the causis principall
Off al the trubyll of this Natioun
Ar in to Prencis, in to speciall,
The quhilkis hes the Gubernatioun,
And of the peple Dominatioun,
Quhose contynewall exersitioun
Sulde be in Justice exicution.

from The Dream of Sir David Lyndsay

On the Realm of Scotland

When I had looked over this region, / Which in nature is both good and fair, / I put forward a small question, / Beseeching her [Dame Remembrance] to answer the same. / 'What is the reason that our bounds are so bare?' / Said I: 'Or what is the cause of our misery? / From what proceeds our poverty? //

For, supported by your high wisdom / I perceive the properties of Scotland / And also I know from experience, / the great commodities of this country.' / First, the abundance of fish in our seas, / And fertile hills for our beasts; / And many fruitful valleys for our corn: //

The rich rivers, pleasing and profitable; / The lochs teeming with fish of sundry kinds; / Hunting and hawking, for nobles agreeable; / Forests full of the doe, the roe, harts and hinds; / The fresh fountains, whose wholesome crystal strands / So refresh the fair flourishing green meadows: / So we lack nothing needful to Nature. //

We have rich mines of every metal, / Both gold and silver, and precious stones /

Although we lack spices and wines, / Or other strange and delicious fruits, / We have as good, and more necessary for us. / Food, drink, fire, clothes that might be made abundant, / The like of which is not to be found in all the world; // More fair people, nor of greater wit, / nor of greater strength to achieve great deeds. / Therefore I pray you that would define / the main cause why we are so poor; / For I marvel greatly, I assure you, / Considering the people and the country, / That riches should not abound in this land.' //

'My son,' she said, 'with discretion, / I shall answer as best I understand. / I confess to you / The fault is neither, I say assuredly, / In the people or the land. / As for the land, it lacks nothing else / But labour and the governing of the people.' //

'Then wherein lies our lack of prosperity?' / Said I. 'I pray you from my heart, Madam, / You would declare to me the truth / Or who shall bear the blame for our misery? / For truthfully I think it great shame to see / Such pleasing people, and so fair a land, / And so few virtuous undertakings in hand.' //

Said she: 'I shall in my judgement, / declare some general causes, / And in brief, show my intent, / And then move to detail. / So, this is my final conclusion: / Lacking justice, policy and peace / Causes such unhappiness, alas! //

It is difficult to increase wealth, / Where policy has no home, / And policy may never have entrance, / Unless to where justice diligently / Punishes where there is offence. / Justice may not predominate, / Unless peace makes habitation.' //

'What is the cause, I would understand, / That we lack justice and policy / More than France, Italy, or England? / Madam,' said I, 'show me the truth: / Since we have laws in this country, / Why is the law not exercised? / Who should execute justice? //

Where stands our principal remedy? / Or who can amend this mischief?' / Said she: 'I find the fault at the head; / For those in whom our whole relief lies, / I find to be the root and ground of all our grief, / For when the heads are not diligent, / The members must needs be negligent. //

So I conclude, the principal cause / Of all the trouble of this nation, / Are in its princes, and especially / Those who have the governance / and domination of the people, / Whose continual exercise / Should be in execution of justice.'

The Compleynt of the Comoun Weill of Scotland

And, thus as we wer talking to and fro,
We saw a busteous berne cum ower the bent,
But hors, on fute, als fast as he mycht go,
Quhose rayment wes all raggit, riven, and rent,
With visage leyne, as he had fastit lent:
And forward fast his wayis he did advance,
With ane rycht malancolious countynance,

With scrip on hip, and pyikstaff in his hand,
As he had purposit to passe fra hame:
Quod I: gude man, I wald faine understand,
Geve that ye plesit, to wyt quhat wer your name:
Quod he: my Sonne, of that I think gret schame;
Bot, sen thow wald of my name have ane feill,
Forsuith, thay call me Jhone the Comoun Weill.

Schir Commoun Weill, quho hes yow so disgysit?
Quod I: or quhat makis yow so miserabyll?
I have marvell to se yow so supprysit,
The quhilk that I have sene so honorabyll.
To all the warld ye have bene proffitabyll,
And weill honorit in everilk Natioun:
How happinnis, now, your tribulatioun?

Allace, quod he, thow seis how it dois stand
With me, and quhow I am disherisit
Off all my grace, and mon pass of Scotland,
And go, afore quhare I was cherisit.
Remane I heir, I am bot perysit.
For thare is few to me that takis tent,
That garris me go so raggit, rewin, and rent.

My tender friendis ar all put to the flycht;
For Polecey is fled agane in France:
My Syster, justice, almaist haith tynt hir sycht,
That scho can nocht hald evenly the ballance.
Plane wrang is plane capitane of Ordinance,
The quhilk debarris Lawtie and Reassoun,
And small remeid is found for oppin treassoun.

In to the south, allace, I was neir slane:
Over all the land I culd fynd no releiff;
Almoist betwix the Mers and Lochmabane
I culde nocht knaw ane leill man be ane theif.
To schaw thare reif, thift, murthour, and mischeif,
And vicious workis, it wald infect the air:
And, als, langsum to me for tyll declair.

In to the Hieland I could fynd no remeid,
Bot suddantlie I wes put to exile:
Tha sweir swyngeoris thay tuke of me non heid,
Nor amangs thame lat me remane ane quhyle.
Als, in the oute Ylis, and in Argyle,
Unthrift, sweirnes, falset, povertie, and stryfe
Pat Polecey in dainger of hir lyfe.

In the Lawland I come to seik refuge,
And purposit thare to mak my residence:
Bot singulare proffit gart me soune disluge,
And did me gret Injuris and offence,
And said to me: swyith, harlote, hy the hence;
And in this countre se thow tak no curis,
So lang as my auctoritie induris.

And now I may mak no langer debait;
Nor I wate nocht quhome to I suld me mene;
For I have socht throw all the Spirituall stait,
Quhilkis tuke na compt for to heir me complene.
Thare officiaries, thay held me at disdane;
For Symonie, he rewlis up all that rowte;
And Covatyce, that carle, gart bar me oute.

Pryde haith chaist far frome thame Humilitie;
Devotioun is fled unto the freris;
Sensuale Plesour hes baneist Chaistitie;
Lordis of Religioun, thay go lyke Seculeris,
Taking more compt in tellyng thare deneris
Nor thay do of thare constitutioun,
Thus ar thay blyndit be ambitioun.

Oure gentyll men ar all degenerate;
Liberalitie and Lawoe, baith, ar liste;
And Cowardyce with Lordis is laureate;
And knychtlie curage turnit to brag and boste;
The Civil Weir misgydis everilk oist.
Thare is nocht ellis bot ilk man for hym self,
That garris me go, thus baneist lyke ane elf.

Tharefor, adew; I may no langer tarye.
Fair weill, quod I, and with Sanct Jhone to borrow.
Bot, wyt ye weill, my hart was wounder sarye,
Quhen Comoun Weill so sopit was in sorrow.
Yit, efter the nycht cumis the glaid morrow;
Quharefor, I pray yow, schaw me, in certane,
Quhen that ye purpose for to cum agane.

That questioun, it sall be soon desydit,
Quod he: thare sall na Scot have comfortyng
Of me, tyll that I see the countre gydit
Be wysedome of ane gude auld prudent kyng,
Quhilk sall delyte hym maist, abone all thyng,
To put justice tyll exicutioun,
And on strang tratouris mak puneisioun.

Als yit to the I say ane uther thyng:
I see, rycht weill, that proverbe is full trew,
Wo to the realme that hes ouir young ane king.
With that, he turnit his bak, and said adew.
Ouer firth and fell rycht fast fra me he flew,
Quhose departyng to me was displesand.
With that, Remembrance tuk me be the hand.

And sone, me thocht, scho brocht me to the roche,
And to the cove quhare I began to sleip.
With that, ane schip did spedalye approche,
Full plesandlie saling apone the deip,
And syne did slake hir sailis, and gan to creip
Towart the land, anent quhare that I lay:
Bot, wyt ye weill, I gat ane fellown fraye.

All hir Cannounis sche leit craik of at onis:
Down schuke the stremaris frome the topcastell;
Thay sparit nocht the poulder, nor the stonis;
Thay schot thare boltis, & doun thare ankeris fell;
The Marenaris, thay did so youte and yell,
That haistalie I stert out of my dreme,
Half in ane fray, and spedaye past hame,

And lychtlie dynit, with lyste and appityte,
Syne efter, past in tyll ane Oritore,
And tuke my pen, and thare began to wryte
All the visioun that I have schawin afore.
Schir, of my dreme as now thou gettis no more,
Bot I beseik God for to send the grace
To rewle thy realme in unitie and peace.

The Complaint of the Commonweal of Scotland

And thus, as we were walking to and fro, / We saw a rough fellow come over the
moor, / Without a horse, on foot, as fast as he might go, / Whose raiment was
all ragged, riven and rent, / With a lean visage, as if he had fasted for Lent: /
And forward fast his ways did he advance, / With a right melancholy
countenance. //
With a pouch on his hip and a pikestaff in his hand, / As if he meant to
journey from home. / Said I: 'Good man, I would gladly understand, / If you
please, what is your name?' / Said he: 'My son, I am ashamed of that; / But
since you would have knowledge of my name,/ Forsooth, they call me John the
Commonweal.' //
'Sir Commonweal, who has so disguised you?' / Said I: 'or what makes you so
miserable? / I marvel to see you so ill-fared / Whom I have seen before so
honourable. / You have been profitable to all the world, / And well honoured in
every nation: / How happens now your tribulation?' //
'Alas,' said he, 'you see how it stands / With me, and how I am disinherited /
Of all my grace, and must pass from Scotland, / And go from where I was once
cherished. / If I remain here, I am dead. / For there are few who care about me,
/ Which makes me go so ragged, riven, and rent. //
My tender friends are all put to flight; / For policy is fled again to France. / My
sister, Justice, has almost lost her sight, / So that she cannot hold the balance
evenly. / Plain wrong is captain in authority, / Which shuts out loyalty and
reason, / And there is small remedy for open treason. //
In the south, alas, I was nearly slain! / Over all the land I could find no relief; /
Almost between the Merse and Lochmaben / I could not tell a loyal man from a
thief / To show their thieving, murder and mischief, /And vicious works, it
would infect the air: / And also, too long for me to tell. //
In the Highlands I could find no remedy, / But suddenly I was put to exile. /
These lazy villains took no heed of me, / Nor would they let me remain there a
while. / Also, in the outer isles, and in Argyll, / Thriftlessness, laziness,
falsehood, poverty and strife, / Put policy in danger of her life. //
In the Lowlands I came to seek refuge, / And purposed there to make residence.
/ But unnatural greed forced me soon to shift, / And did me great injury and

*offence, / And said to me: quickly, villain, hie thee hence; / And in this country
you see you have no rights, / As long as my authority endures. //*

*And now I may no longer argue any more; / Nor know I to whom I should
complain; / For I have sought through all the spiritual state, / Which took no
occasion to hear me complain. / Their officials, they all held me in disdain; / For
Simony, he rules over all that crowd; / And that fellow Covatice had me put
out. //*

*Pride has chased humility far from them; / Devotion is fled to friars; / Sensual
pleasure has banished Chastity; / Lords of religion have become secular, /
Taking more care in counting their money / Nor do they as their constitution
requires, / Thus are they blinded by ambition. //*

*Our gentlemen are all degenerate; / Liberality and Loyalty both are lost; / And
Cowardice with lords is first / And knightly courage empty in brag and boast; /
Internal war misguides each army. / There is nought else but each man for
himself, / Which forces me to leave, thus banished like the elves. //*

*Therefore, adieu; I may no longer tarry.' / 'Farewell,' said I, 'and may Saint
John bless you.' / But know well that my heart was sorely wounded, / When
Commonweal was so steeped in sorrow. / Yet, after the night comes the glad
morrow; / 'Therefore, I pray you, show me for sure, / When you intend to come
again?' //*

*'That question will soon be decided,' / Said he: 'No Scot shall have comfort /
From me, until I see the country guided / By the wisdom of a good old prudent
king. / What will delight him most, above all things, / Will be to put Justice
into execution, / And make punishment on guilty traitors. //*

*I say to you also another thing: / I see well that the proverb is really true, / Woe
to the realm has too young a king.' / With that he turned his back and said
adieu. / Over rivers and hills so swiftly from me he flew, / Whose departure was
so displeasing to me. / With that, Remembrance took me by the hand, //*

*And soon, I thought, she brought me to the rocks, / And to the cove where I
began to sleep. / With that, a ship speedily approached, / Pleasantly sailing on
the deeps, / And soon she slacked her sails, and slowly / moved towards land, /
Close by where I lay: / But, know you well, I got a fiercesome fright. //*

*All cannons she let fire at once: / Down shook the pennants from the topcastle; /
They spared neither gunpowder nor cannonballs; / They shot their bolts and
down the anchors fell; / The mariners did so shout and yell, / That hastily I
started out my dream, / Half-frighted, and speedily passed home, //*

*And cheerfully dined, with hearty appetite. / Soon after passing into a study, /
And took my pen, and there began to write / All of the vision that I have shown
before. / Sir, now of my dream you get no more, / But I beseech God to send
thee grace / To rule thy realm in unity and peace.*

GEORGE BUCHANAN (1506–1582)

To Henry Darnley, King of Scots
(from the Latin)

The marigold nowhere turns from the sun.
Opening at dawn, it closes in the dusk.
We too depend on you, our sun. To all
Your turns of fortune we are left exposed.

JOHN SKELTON (c. 1460–c. 1529)

A Ballade of the Scottyshe Kynge
(after Flodden)

King Jamy, King Jamy your joye is all go
Ye sommoned our kynge why dyde ye so?
To you nothing it dyde accorde
To sommon our kynge your soverayne lorde.
A kynge a somner it is wonder
Knowe ye not salt and sugar asonder?
In you sommynge ye were to malaperte
And your harolde no thynge experte.
Ye thought ye dyde it sull valyauntolye
But not worth thre skippes of a pye.
Syr quyer galyarde ye were to swyfte
Your wyll renne before your wytte.
To be so scornfull to your alye
Your counseyle was not worth a flye.
Befor the frensshe kynge, danes, and other
Ye ought to honour your lorde and brother.
Trowe ye syr James his noble grace
For you and your scottes of gelawaye
For your kynge may synge welawaye.
Now you must knowe our kynge for your regent
Your soverayne lorde and precedent
In hym is figured melchisedeche
And ye be so desolate as armeleche.
He is our noble champyon.
A kynge anoynted and ye be non,
Thrugh your counseyle your fader was slayne

Wherfore I fere ye wyll suffre payne
And ye proude scottes of dunbar
Parde ye be his homager
And suters to his parlyment
Ye dyde not your dewty therin.
Wyerfore ye may it now repent
Ye bere yourselfe som what to holde
Therfore ye have lost your copholde
Ye bounde tenauntes to his estate
Gyve up your game ye playe chekmate
For to the castell of norham
I understonde to soone ye cam.
For your prysoner now ye be
Eyther to the devyll or the trinite
Thanked be saynte Gorge our ladyes knythe
Your pryd is paste adwe good nyght.
Ye have determyned to make a fraye
Our kynge than beynge out of the waye
But by the power and myght of god
Ye were beten with your owne rod.
By your wanton wyll syr at a worde
Ye have lost spores, cote armure, and sworde
Ye had better to have busked to huntey bankes
Than in England to playe ony suche prankes
But ye had som wyle sede to sowe
Therefore ye be layde now full lowe,
Your power coude no longer atteyne
Warre with our kynge to meyntayne
Of the kyng of naverne ye may take hede
How unfortunately he doth now spede,
In double welles now he doeth dreme.
That is a kynge witou a realme
At hym example ye wolde none take
Experyence hath brought you in the same brake
Of the out yles ye rough foted scottes
We have well eased you of the bottes
Ye rowe rank scottes and dronken danes
Of our englysshe bowes ye have fette your banes
It is not syttynge in tour or towne
A somner to were a kyngs crowne
That noble erle the whyte Lyon,
Your pompe and pryde hath layde a downe
His sone the lord admyrall is full good

His swerd hath bathed in the scottes blode
God save kynge Henry and his lordis all
And sende the frensshe kynge suche an other fall
   Amen/for saynt charyte
   And god sav enoble
      Kynge/Henry/
      The VIII.

ALEXANDER CRAIG (1567–1627)

Scotlands Teares
(in response to the Union of Crowns, 1603)

When fabling *Æsop* was at fatall *Delphos* tane,
And there by doome condemd to be precipitat & slane
He like a woman weep't, and tooke delight in teaires,
Cause they alleviat and made lesse the conscience of his caires.
But *Solon* when he spid his deerest sonne was dead,
He weepd the more, because his teaires to grief gave no remead:
Yet neither he nor he by teaires could salve his ill,
Though of those salt and fruitles flouds impetuus spaits they spil
Then maymed *Scotland* thou made Orphane from delight,
Whom all the hosts of heavens abhor with undeserv'd delight.
With deeing *Æsop* mourne, or wofull *Solon* weepe:
And tho as they, thou weepe in vaine let not thy sorrow sleepe:
With frustrat *Æsau* shout, curse life and wish to dee,
Since *Jacob* with his mothers helpe thy blessing steals from thee:
Now rivall *England* brag, for now, and not till now
Thou has compeld unconquered harts & sturdy necks to bow.
What neither wits, nor wars, nor force afore could frame,
Is now accomplisht by the death of thy Imperiall Dame.
Eliza faire is gone, into the land of rest,
To that *Elisium* predecried and promis'd to the blest;
And *England* for her sake now weaires the sabill weepe,
But *Scotland* if thou rightly looke thou has more cause indeede.
They for a *Dian* dead, Apolloes beames enioy,
And all their straying steps allace, our Titan dooth tonnoy.
Now dawn's their glorious day with *Phoebus* rayes bespred,
And we are but *Cymmerian* slaves with gloomy clouds ou'rcled.
Rich neighbour nation then, from thy complayning cease:
Not thou, but we should sigh, & so to our complaints give place.

Our Garland lacks the Rose, our chatton tins the stone,
Our Volier wants the *Philomel*, we left allace alone.
What art thou *Scotland* then? no Monarchie allace,
A oligarchie desolate, with stay and onkow face,
A maymed bodie now, but shaip some monstrous thing,
A reconfused chaos, a countrey, but a King.
When *Paris* fed his flockes among the *Phrigian* plaines,
Ænone's love was his delights, his death were her disdaynes.
But when allace he knew that *Priam* was his Sire,
He left *Ænone* sweet, and syne for *Helene* would aspire.
Proud pellux *England* so thou art the adulterat brid,
Who for *Ænone* thinkes no shame to lye by *Paris* sid.
Who knowes ere it be long, but our your happy King,
With *Belgic*, *Celtic*, *Aquitan*, to his Empire may bring?
And he (why should he not) your *Troynauant* shall leave,
And unto *Parise* spurre the post, his right for to receave?
Then, then shall *England* weepe, and shed abounding teaires,
And we shall to our comfort find companions in our caires.
And till it so befall, with pitie, not with scorne,
Upon this confinde Kingdome looke, as on a land forlorne:
Wise *Plato* would not once admit it in his minde,
He lov'd *Xenocrates* so well, he could become unkinde,
And no more can we thinke dread Leige, though thou be gone,
Thou will ungratly leave us thus disconsolat allone,
By Contrars Contrars plac'd, no dout most clearely kith,
And now thy absence breedes our bale, whose biding made us blith.
O were thou not both wise and good, we should not mourne,
We would not for thy absence weepe, nor wish for thy returne.
Long sleepe made *Rufus* loose the use of both his eene.
O do not thou sweet Prince make stay, lest thou forget us cleene
Like *Epimenides* when thou returns againe:
The shapp of al things shal be chaing't, thine own sheepe shalbe slaine,
Democrit rather choose no King at all to bee,
Then over wicked men to rule, and such allace are wee:
Our Jewell *England* joyes, & yet no way dooth wrong us;
The world may see we were not worth, that thou shuld be among us:
But since it must be thus, and thou art forc'd to flitt:
Now like a Heart on to the mids of thy great body fitt:
And from thy *Troynaunant,* which pleasures store impairts,
Behold thy Kingdom's round about thy hand in all the Airts;
Examples old thou taks, and layis before thy face,
The famous *Numids* thoght the midst to be most honored place
Thus by *Hyempsals* side *Adherbal Salust* sets,

And so *Iugurtha* in the midst wee reed no intrance gets.
Grave *Maro* marks likway, the Queene of *Cartage* brave,
Betwix *Ascaniud* and the wife *Æneas*, place to have,
Dooth not *Apollo* too in proudest pompe appere,
With bright and day-adorning beames in his meridian sphere?
So thou hast choos'd the midst, of all thy Kingdom's knowne;
For looke about thee where thou list, thou looks but on thine owne
And since the Gods decree (Great King) that so shall bee,
Since Peace must florish in thy time, & Wars must cease & die,
But competition too, since thou has *Englands* Crowne,
Which was a *Heptarchie* of old, of uncontrould renowne,
Let Us and *Al-bi-on*, that wee with one consent,
One God, one King, one Law, may be t'adore, serve, keepe, content.
In *Rome* the *Sabins* grew, with *Tyrians Trojans* mixt,
And *Juda* joyned with *Israel*, but least wee seeme prolixt,
And that our loving plaint's, and teares may now take end,
Thee to thy Crowns, thy Crowns to thee, the great good God defend.

WILLIAM LITHGOW (1582–1645)

from The Totall Discourse of the Rare Adventures
& Painfull Peregrinations

To thee sweete Scotland first

I wander in exile,
    As though my Pilgrimage:
Were sweete Comedian scænes of love
    Upon a golden Stage.
Ah I, poore I, distres'd,
    Oft changing to and fro,
Am forc'd to sing sad Obsequies
    Of this my Swan-like wo.
A vagabonding Guest,
    Transported here and there,
Led with the mercy-wanting winds
    Of feare, griefe, and dispaire
Thus ever-moving I,
    To restlesse journeys thrald,
Obstaines by Times triumphing frownes
    A calling, unrecal'd:

Was I præordain'd so
                    Like Tholos Ghost to stand.
Three times foure houres, in twenty foure
                    With Musket in my hand.
Ore-blasted with the stormes
                    Of Winter-beating Snow,
And frosty pointed haile-stones hard
                    On me poore wretch to blow.
No Architecture Lo
                    But whirling-windy Skyes.
Or'e-syld with thundring claps of Clouds,
                    Earths center to surprise.
I, I, it is my fate,
                    Allots this fatall crosse,
And reckons up in Characters,
                    The time of my Times losse.
My destiny is such,
                    Which doth predestine me,
To be a mirrour of mishaps,
                    A Mappe of misery.
Extreamely doe I live,
                    Extreames are all my joy,
I finde in deepe extreamities,
                    Extreames, extreame annoy.
Now all alone I watch,
                    With Argoes eyes and wit.
A Cypher twixt the Greekes and Turkes
                    Upon this Rocke I sit.
A constrain'd Captive I,
                    Mongst incompassionate Greekes,
Bare-headed, downeward bowes my head,
                    And liberty still seekes.
But all my sutes are vaine,
                    Heaven sees my wofull state:
Which makes me say, my worlds eye-sight
                    Is bought at too high rate.
Would God I might but live,
                    To see my native Soyle:
Thrice happy in my happy wish,
                    To end this endlesse toyle:
Yet still when I record,
                    The pleasant bankes of Clide:
Where Orchards, Castles, Townes, and Woods,

Are planted by his side:
And chiefly Lanerke thou,
     Thy Countries Laureat Lampe:
In this bruised body now
     Did first receive the stampe.
Then doe I sigh and sweare,
     Till death or my returne,
Still for to weare the Willow wreath,
     In sable weed to mourne.
Since in this dying life,
     A life in death I take,
Ile sacrifice in spight of wrath,
     These solemne vows I make,
To thee sweete Scotland first,
     My birth and breath I leave:
To Heaven my soule, my heart King James,
     My Corpes to lye in grave.
My staffe to Pilgrimes I,
     And Pen to Poets send;
My haire-cloth roabe, and halfe-spent goods,
     To wandering wights I lend.
Let them dispose as though
     My treasure were of Gold,
Which values more in purest prise,
     Then drosse ten thousand fold.
These Trophees I erect,
     Whiles memory remaines:
An epitomiz'd Epitaph,
     On Lithgows restlesse paines:
My will's inclos'd with love,
     My love with eartly bliss:
My blisse in substance doth consist,
     To crave no more but this.
Thou first, is, was, and last,
     Eternall, of thy grace,
Protect, prolong, great Britanes King,
     His Sonne, and Royall Race.

The Scottish Kirke
(on the General Assembly, 1638)

The scottish kirke the English church doe name,
The english church the Scotes a kirke doe call;
Kirke and not church, church and not kirke, O shame!
Your kappa turne in chi, or perishe all:
Assemblies meet, post Bishopes to the court;
If these two Nationes fight, its strangers sport.

ANONYMOUS (c. 1603)

The Lion and The Unicorn

The lion and the unicorn
Were fighting for the crown;
The lion beat the unicorn
All round about the town.

Some gave them white bread,
And some gave them brown;
Some gave them plum cake
And drummed them out of town.

IAIN LOM / JOHN MACDONALD (c. 1620–c. 1707)

Oran an Aghaidh an Aonaidh

Ge bè dh'èireadh san lasair
    An am fadadh na smùide,
Thèid an cuibhreach mun chapall
    Mar bhiodh fada fo glùinibh;
Ach fhir a dh'èirich le gradachd
    Chur fastadh nan taod rith',
Spàrr thu 'n gòisnein mu ladhar
    Mar eun chladhach an rùcain.

Bhris thu lairg anns a' chrann sin
   'S chaidh an seanndamh am mearachd,
Le beuc nan damh òga
   Chaidh an Dròbhair am mearal;
Fhir a b'àbhaist an ceannsach'
   'S an tionndadh le h-ainiochd,
'S e Diùc Atholl le dùrachd
   A bhris do lùban a dh'aindeoin.

Ge bè leanadh gu dìreach
   Diùc fìrinneach Atholl,
'S raghainn chruthaicht' thar sluagh e
   Bhuidhneadh buaidh mar rinn athair;
Bha thu 'n aghaidh luchd cìse
   Ghabh na mìltean mar raghainn,
Ach fàgaidh mis' iad gu h-ìseal
   'Nan laighe shìos anns na spleadhan.

'S mòr tha ghliocas na rìoghachd
   Deagh sgrìobht' ann ad mheamhail,
Bha thu foghlam as t'òige
   Chur na còrach air adhart.
'N aghaidh Banndairean misgeach
   Bha ri bristeadh an lagha,
Nam biodh iad uile gu m'òrdugh
   Gheibheadh iad còrd agus teadhair.

Na biodh ortsa bonn airtneil –
   Tha fir Atholl nan seasamh,
Luchd nan gormlanna geura
   Dhèanadh feum dhuit gad fhreasdal;
Mar siud 's do dheagh bhràithre,
   Luchd nan sàrbhuillean sgaiteach,
Fir a chaitheadh nan saighead
   'S a ro-ghleidheadh na cartach.

Na biodh ort-sa bonn mìghean –
   Tha fir do thìre glè ullamh,
Còrr mòr is deich mìle
   Ged a lìbhinn a thuille;
Mheud 's a bhuinnig e phrìs duit
   Chaidh e sgrìobhte do Lunnain
Na chuireadh dragh air an Alba
   Gu robh nan armaibh glè ullamh.

Là randabù 'n t-slèibhe
   Bha mi fhèin ann is chunnaic,
Bha na trupanna srèin' ann,
   Bha na ceudan a' cruinneach';
Ge bè ghabhadh air anam
   Gu robh mnathan mar dhuin' ann,
Gu rachadh saighead 'nan àrnaibh
   Gus an teàrrail i 'n fhuil ast'.

Mhorair *Duplin* gun fhuireach
   Dh'fhosgail uinneag do sgòrnain,
Dh'èirich rosgal ad chridhe
   Nuair chual' thu tighinn an t-òr ud;
Shluig thu 'n aileag den gheanach,
   Dh'at do sgamhan is bhòc e,
Dh'fhosgail teannsgal do ghoile
   'S lasaich greallag do thòna.

Cha b'iongnadh siud duit a thachairt,
   Ogha baigeire Liunnsaidh,
'S a liuthad doras mòr caisteil
   Ris 'n do stailc e chnàimh tiompain;
Cha d'fhàg e baile gun siubhal
   O Chill-a-rubha gu Grainse,
Mar ghabhas sin 's an t-Òrd Gallach
   Gu ruige baile Iarl Aondram.

Ogha baigeir na lùirich,
   Ciod e do chùis an Taigh-Phàrla?
Mur deach thu dh'fhoghlam a' gheanaich
   Mar bha an seanair on d'fhàs thu;
Cha d'fhàg e ursainn gun locradh
   Eadar Ros is Cinn t-Sàile;
Bhiodh a dhiosg-san glè ullamh
   An am cromadh fon àrd'ras.

Tha *Queensberry* 'n tràth-sa
   Mar fhear-stràice cur thairis,
Eis' a' tarraing gu dìreach
   Mar ghearran dian ann an greallaig;
Is luchd nam putagan anairt
   Làn smear agus geire,
'S nam bu mhise an ceannair'
   Bhiodh 'n ceann dan amall air deireadh.

Tha Diùc Atholl 's Diùc Gòrdon
    Glè chlòiste 's iad dùinte,
Air an sgrìobhadh gu daingeann,
    Ach tha *Hamilton* dùbailt;
Iarla Bhrathainn bhiodh mar ris,
    Cha bhiodh mealladh sa chùis ac',
Toirt a' chrùin uainn le ceannach
    An ceart fhradharc ar sùilean.

Tha Mèinnearach Uaimh ann
    Glè luaineach na bhreathal,
'S e mar dhuine gun sùilean
    'G iarraidh iùil air feadh ceathaich;
Ach thig e fathast le h-ùmhlachd
    Chum an Diùc mas i bheatha,
'S bidh a shannt 's a mhì-dhùrachd
    Anns an smùr gun aon rath air.

Iarla Bhrathainn a Sìoford,
    Cha bhi sìothshaimh ri d' bheò dhuit,
Gum bi ortsa cruaidh fhaghaid
    Thall a-staigh den Roinn Eòrpa;
Ach nam faighinn mo raghainn
    Is dearbh gu leaghainn an t-òr dhuit,
A-staigh air faochaig do chlaiginn
    Gus an cas e do bhòtainn.

Song Against the Union

In the reek of the kindling
    will arise from the flames,
what will hobble the mare
    round her fetlocks for sure;
but you who rushed forward
    to fasten her binding,
looped a rope on her hooves
    like a snare for a buzzard.

You broke the plough-stilt there,
    the old ox went straying;
at the roar of young bullocks
    the drover went witless;

the man who once drove them
  and turned at the head-rig,
'twas the goodwill of Atholl
  broke your fetters despite you.

Who would follow the Duke
  the true lineage of Atholl
finest leader of armies
  wins the day like his father;
how you hated the tax-men
  who skimmed off the thousands,
but I'll leave them humbled
  laid low in their writhing.

Great the wisdom of ruling
  in your mind written strongly,
you were taught from your boyhood
  advancement of justice
against mad Covenanters
  the breakers of laws, they'd
get tethers and tying
  were they under my orders.

Let no cloud come upon you –
  Men of Atholl hold firmly
folk of sharpened blue blades
  who shall rescue and serve you;
at their side your true bretheren
  of the sharp-smiting buffets
who will shower their arrows
  that find a true target.

Let no gloom come upon you –
  for your comrades are ready,
ten thousand and more
  should I leave out some others;
there's respect for your name
  in dispatches to London
that the Scots are in arms
  that will give them some trouble.

At yon moorland rally
  I was present and saw it,

troops of cavalry there
  in their hundreds assembled;
who swear there were women
  in disguise there as men,
may a shaft in the kidneys
  drain all their blood from them.

Lord Duplin, there straightly
  your maw opened widely,
and your heart wildly beat
  when you heard gold was coming;
but you stifled greed's breath
till your lungs swelled and hiccuped,
till you could not contain it
and set light to your arsehole.

Small wonder that mishap
  to the Lundy tramp's grandson,
many a door of a castle
  he braced with his backside;
not a mansion he passed by
  from Grange to Kilarrow,
the whole lot from Caithness
  to the Earl's place in Antrim.

What, ragged tramp's grandson,
is your case in the Council?
Unless to learn greed
  like the grandad who bred you;
no threshold left scraped
  between Ross and Kintail;
set the floorboards to creaking
  as he bowed at the lintel.

And Queensberry there
  taking fistful from bagful,
as he draws tight the string
  as a gelding pulls traces;
they who like clootie dumplings
  well marrowed and larded,
if I harnessed that team
  I'd yoke last in the traces.

Dukes of Atholl and Gordon
  make agreement in secret,
though their names firm in writing,
  but Hamilton's two-faced;
but with Brathan his crony,
  their minds were united,
to trade in full view
  crown and sovereign rights.

And Menzies of Weem there
  his brains in a swither,
like a man of poor sight
  seeking guidance through mist;
but he'll come up there creeping
  to the Duke if he's welcome,
though his malice and greed
  get an answer in dust.

No peace, Seaforth of Brahan,
  you'll get in your lifetime,
hot pursuit you will find
  on your tail throughout Europe;
but if I had my way
  I would melt your gold payment,
pour it into your skull
  till it reached to your boots.

Òran Cumhaidh air Cor na Rìoghachd

Mi gabhail Sraith Dhruim Uachdair,
'S beag m' aighear anns an uair so:
Tha an latha air dol gu gruamachd
  'S chan e tha buain mo sproc.

Ge duilich leam 's ge dìobhail
M'fhear cinnidh math bhith dhìth orm,
Chan usa learm an sgrìob-s'
  Thàinig air an rìoghachd bhochd.

Tha Alba dol fo chìoschain
Aig farbhalaich gun fhìrinn
Bhàrr a' chalpa dhìrich –
  'S e cuid de m' dhìobhail ghoirt.

Tha Sasannaich gar fairgneadh,
Gar creach, gar murt 's gar marbhadh;
Gun ghabh ar n-Athair fearg ruinn –
    Gur dearmad dhuinn 's gur bochd.

Mar a bha Cloinn Israel
Fo bhruid aig rìgh na h-Èiphit,
Tha sinn air a' chor cheudna:
    Chan èigh iad ruinn ach 'Seoc'.

Ar rìgh an dèidh's a chrùnadh
Mun gann a leum e ùrfhas,
Na thaisdealach bochd rùisgte
    Gun gheàrd gun chùirt gun choist.

Ga fharfhuadach as àite
Gun duine leis de chàirdean,
Mar luing air uachdar sàile,
    Gun stiùir gun ràimh gun phort.

Cha tèid mi do Dhùn Èideann
O dhòirteadh fuil a' Ghreumaich,
An leòghann fearail treubhach
    Ga cheusadh air a' chroich.

B'e siud am fìor dhuine uasal
Nach robh den linne shuarach,
Bu ro mhath rudhadh gruadhach
    'N àm tarraing suas gu troid.

Deud chailc bu ro mhath dlùthadh
Fo mhala chaoil gun mhùgaich,
Ge tric do dhàil gam dhùsgadh
    Cha rùisg mi chàch e nochd.

Mhic Nèill à Asaint chianail,
Nan glacainn an mo lìon thu
Bhiodh m'fhacal air do bhìnne
    Is cha dìobrainn thu on chroich.

Thu fèin is t'athair cèile,
Fear taighe sin na Lèime,
Ged chrochta sibh le chèile
    Cha b'èiric air mo lochd.

Craobh rùisgt' den abhall bhreugach
Gun mheas gun chliù gun cheutaidh
Bha riamh ri murt a chèile,
    Nur fuidheall bheum is chorc.

Marbhaisg ort fèin, a dhìmheis,
Mar olc a reic thu an fhìrinn
Air son na mine Lìtich
    Is dà thrian dith goirt.

A Lament for the State of the Country

As I travel the Strath of Drumochter,
little my joy at this season:
the day has turned out grimly
    and that does not help my gloom.

Though I feel it a hard deprivation
to be lacking my good kinsman,
no easier borne is this mishap
    that has overcome the poor land.

Scotland is under tribute
to foreigners without justice
above the right taxation –
    that is part of my sore plight.

We are plundered by the English,
despoiled, slain and murdered;
we must have caused our Father anger –
    for we are neglected and poor.

Like the children of Israel
in bondage to the King of Egypt,
we have the same standing:
    they call us only 'Jock'.

Our king after his crowning,
barely before he was adult,
turned into a poor stripped vagrant
    without guard or parliament or court.

Expelled from his rightful position
without any of his friends with him,
like a ship on the top of the ocean
 without rudder or oar or port.

I will go no more to Edinburgh
since Graham's blood was spilled there,
the lion valiant and mighty
 tortured on the gallows tree.

He was a nobleman truly
of no paltry lineage,
his cheek's flushing was prodigious
 when drawing up to fight.

Chalk-white teeth set closely
under a slim unfrowning eye-brow,
though often your lot kept me wakeful
 I will not make it public tonight.

Son of Niall from dismal Assynt,
if in my net I could but trap you,
I would not banish you from the gallows,
 my word would seal your doom.

You yourself and your wife's father,
that householder on Lemlair,
even were you hanged together
 that would not compensate my loss.

Of the perjured apple-tree a bare offshoot
without fruit or fame or decorum
you were forever murdering each other,
 the leftovers of knives and blows.

A curse on you, you disgraced one,
for wickedly have you sold justice
for the sake of a boll of Leith-meal
 with two-thirds of it gone sour.

DANIEL DEFOE (1660–1731)

from The True-Born Englishman (1701)

The Romans first with Julius Caesar came,
Including all the Nations of that Name,
Gauls, Greeks, and Lombards; and by Computation
Auxiliaries or Slaves, of ev'ry Nation.
With Hengest, Saxons; Danes with Sueno came,
In search of Plunder, not in search of fame.
Scots, Picts, and Irish from th' Hibernian Shore:
And Conqu'ring William brought the Normans o'er.

    All these their Barbarous Offspring left behind,
The Dregs of Armies, they of all Mankind;
Blended with Britains who before were here,
Of whom the Welsh ha' blest the Character.

    From this Amphibious Ill-born Mob began
That vain ill-natur'd thing, an Englishman.

★ ★ ★ ★ ★

    These are the Heroes who despise the Dutch,
And rail at new-come Foreigners so much;
Forgetting that themselves are all deriv'd
From the most Scoundrel Race that ever lived,
A horrid Crowd of Rambling Thieves and Drones,
Who ransack'd Kingdoms, and dispeopled Towns:
The Pict and Painted Britain, Treach'rous Scot,
By Hunger, Theft, and Rapine, hither brought;
Norwegian Pirates, Buccaneering Danes,
Whose Red-hair'd Offspring ev'rywhere remains;
Who join'd with Norman-French compound the Breed
From whence your True-Born Englishmen proceed.

JONATHAN SWIFT (1667–1745)

Verses Said to be Written on the Union

The Queen has lately lost a part
Of her entirely English heart,
For want of which by way of botch,
She pieced it up again with Scotch.
Blessed revolution, which creates
Divided hearts, united states.
See how the double nation lies;
Like a rich coat with skirts of frieze:
As if a man in making posies
Should bundle thistles up with roses.
Whoever yet a union saw
Of kingdoms, without faith or law.
Henceforward let no statesman dare,
A kingdom to a ship compare;
Lest he should call our commonweal,
A vessel with a double keel:
Which just like ours, new rigged and manned,
And got about a league from land,
By change of wind to leeward side
The pilot knew not how to guide.
So tossing faction will o'erwhelm
Our crazy double-bottomed realm.

ANONYMOUS (1706)

Verses on the Scots Peers

Our Duiks were deills, our Marquesses wer mad,
Our Earls were evills, our Viscounts yet more bad,
Our Lords were villains, and our Barons knaves
    Who with our burrows did sell us for slaves.

They sold the church, they sold the State and Nation,
They sold their honour, name and reputation,
They sold their birthright, peerages and places
    And now they leave the House with angrie faces.

And now they frown, and fret, and curse their fate,
And still in vain lost libertie regrate,
And are not these rare merchants nicelie trickt,
    Who were old Peers, but now are deils belikt.

Barons and burrows equally rewarded,
They were cajoled by all, but now by none regarded,
O may our God, who rules both heaven and earth
    Avert sad judgements – from us turn his wrath.

Let all true Scots with God importunat be
That he may yet restore our pristine libertie;
That he who rues the hearts of kings alone
    May settle James at length upon the throne.

ANONYMOUS

A Litanie Anent the Union

From a forced and divided Union
And from the church and kirk communion
Where Lordly prelates have dominion
                        Deliver us, Lord.

From a new transubstantiation
Of the old Scots into ane English nation
And from all the foes to Reformation
                        Deliver us, Lord.

From selling Kingdoms, Kings and Crowns
For groats ill payed by Southeron lowns,
From mitres, surplices, long sleev'd gowns
                        Deliver us, Lord.

From a November powder treason
To blow up Parliament at this season,
Tho without powder, rhyme or reason,
                        Deliver us, Lord.

From Pets, and men of Posts and Pensions,
Sole managers of state conventions,
And from all interest in contentions
                              Deliver us, Lord.

From heavie taxes laid on salt,
On blinkèd ale, on beer or malt,
And herrieing us without a fault
                              Deliver us, Lord.

From trading with ane emptie purse
And meriting the old wife's curse,
And from all changes to the worse
                              Deliver us, Lord.

From paying debts we do not owe,
Equivalents we do not know,
From being mad and still kept low
                              Deliver us, Lord.

From Patriots to Presbytery
Who to it bear antipathy,
And such friends as old Cromarty
                              Deliver us, Lord.

From Patriots who for pious ends
Keep kirks unplanted that the teinds
They may secure to their best friends
                              Deliver us, Lord.

From bartering the ancient nation
For a new trade communication,
From English acts of navigation,
                              Deliver us, Lord.

From Burrows, Barons, and our Peers
Who bring ane old house o'er their ears,
For which thay shall pay, some folk swears
                              Deliver us, Lord.

From Holy Wars and hellish plots,
From faithless Christians, brutish Scots
And the disease that noses rots
                              Deliver us, Lord.

From rebell ruleing corporations
And headless Mobs governing nations
And acting out of their stations,

                    Deliver us, Lord.

From paying us our Darien costs
By laying on cess and new imposts,
From the English ruling the Scots rosts

                    Deliver us, Lord.

From a free trade with prohibitions,
Restriction's heavie impositions,
Union on base unjust conditions

                    Deliver us, Lord.

From Peers whose state's a sepulchre,
Who vote the nation to interre,
And enemies to fast and prayer

                    Deliver us, Lord.

From pillor'd Poets and Scots Pedlars
For souldering kingdoms, busie meddlers,
From Organs and Cathedral Fiddlers

                    Deliver us, Lord.

From old Scots nobles in the rear
Of each new upstart English Peer,
And rouping Parliament robes next year

                    Deliver us, Lord.

From oaths and Tests which bar the just,
From Offices of place and trust
To satisfy the Clergy's lust

                    Deliver us, Lord.

From Esau Merchants and Trustees
Who serve them best, who give best fees,
And men whose heads are full of bees

                    Deliver us, Lord.

From Pride, Poverty and greed
United, and from old Scots feed
From making more haste than good speed

                    Deliver us, Lord.

From all religious compositions
Of old and modern superstitions,
From boots and thumbkin inquisitions
      Deliver us, Lord.

From innocent men laying snares
And killing Glenco-men by pairs,
From sudden death, like the Earl of Stair's
      Deliver us, Lord.

ANONYMOUS (c. 1706)

A Curse Against the Unionists and the Revolutionists

Scotland and England now must be
  United in one nation;
So we again perjur'd must be,
  And taik the abjuration.

The Stuarts, antient true born race,
  We must now all give over;
We must receive into their place
  The mungrells of Hanover.

Curst be the Papists who first drew
  Our King to their persuasion;
Curst be that covenanting crew,
  Who gave the first occasion,
To a stranger to ascend the throne,
  By a Stuart's abdication!

Curst be the wretch who seiz'd his throne,
  And marr'd our Constitution;
Curst be all those who helped on
  Our cursed Revolution!
Curst be those treacherous traitors who,
  By their perfidious knaverie,
Have brought the nation now unto
  Ane everlasting slaverie!

Curst be the Parliament that day
They gave the Confirmation;
And curst for ever be all they
Shall swear the abjuration.

ALLAN RAMSAY (1684–1758)

A Poem

When loud mouth'd Fame the dismal News did sound,
PITCAIRN Was Dead, great Grief was seen around
Fix'd on each Face, for him whose generous Thought,
The good of our ——— and *Scotland* sought.
For like a Noble *Scot* of Antient Race,
He Spurned at our Slavery and Disgrace.
Poor Slaves to England, *Wretched, O ye Gods!*
He'd often cry, *Confound them for such Loads*
Hard to be Born by us, who ne're knew how
To Drudge, or to the proudest Monarchs bow.
But to our Own, Thus He.
But now he's gone Disdaining longer stay,
'Mongst *English* Slaves, his Soul now free'd from Clay
Through Bright Elysium Roams; where he will meet
Heroes, who gladly will his Landing Greet;
There they such Pleasure have, as none can tell,
And Freedom large, which Villains cannot Sell.
   A kindly Genij, who doth oft Relate
To me the hid Concerns of future State,
Of these hid Scenes of Happiness and Wo,
Where Good and Bad, in their own Colours show.
   Said He, I was upon the Stygian Coast,
Just when arriv'd the Doctors Noble Ghost.
Old Charon grumbl'd when he took him in,
For that, *he said in Hell it was a Sin,*
To suffer Good and Loyal Souls to come:
Because such Rays would Brighten the Dark Gloom.
Quickly he past the Smoaky Dark Empire
Of furious Dis, the God of Wrath and Ire,
Who Chains bad Souls in Lakes of liquid Fire,
In which the Brimston Rocks with hideous Crack,
Incessantly fall down from Mountains Black.

There he Observ'd a Pool of Boyling Gold,
On which did float, those who their Country Sold.
They Howl'd and Yell'd, and often Curs'd the Gods,
Who had not made them Vipers, Asps, or Toads.
Here he the Faces of some Traitours knew,
Who at the U—— did their hands embrew,
In the heart Blood of Antient Caledon,
Which Mortal wound makes her dear Children Groan.
They're so well known, it's vain their Names to tell,
But be assur'd thy're firmly Chain'd in Hell.
There in Just Rage he did his Passion Vent,
In Words like these, or to the same Intent.
Those are the Knaves, said he, who oft did strive
To Vye with Hell in Mischief, while alive.
Now let them Roar, and all that gave consent,
To Ruin us ne're have Grace to Repent.
Let black Dispair them to Perdition drive,
And in Eternal Faction let them strive.
Amen said I, Now tell me gentle Friend,
I long to know where did his Journey end?
    Then He Replyed,
    With Nimble Flight he left these Dark Abodes,
Till he Arriv'd, Where dwell th'Immortal Gods;
The Happy Regions of Eternal Light,
Where Loyal Souls do shine with Splendor bright,
And in soft Notes of sublime Matters sing;
Here none dare come, who hate their God and King.
But to *PITCAIRN,* they Joyful welcome sang,
With chearful noise, the high Empyrean Rang.
Those Noble *Scots*, who for their Countrey's Good,
Had Sacrific'd their Fortunes with their Blood.
And those, who for their Learning had their Name,
Wote in the endless bright Records of Fame;
All Joy'd to see him safely Landed there,
Where no Disturbance fills the Mind with care.
    With Grave Majestick Stalk, the Royal shade
Of Valiant *BRUCE* approach'd to him *and said,*
Tell me, how fares it with my Albions *now,*
Can they with Ease to the Proud Saxons *bow?*
O Gods! Is the *Great Soul of* SCOTLAND *fled;*
Or does She Dream on some dark drowzy Bed.
Will she not rise to gain Her Old Renown,
And show She wears an Independent Crown.
    The *Sage* Reply'd, we're plagu'd with *Whig* and *Tory,*

Who mind their Interest more than great *Jove's* Glory,
About meer Triffles they make such a Pother,
Still Damning and Devouring one another.
So when E're ought's propos'd for *SCOTLAND'S* good,
It's by a *Cursed Party* still withstood:
Thus all our best Designs are Ruin'd quite,
Allenarly by *Whig* and *Tory* Spite.

    WALLACE came next with *Aspect Stern*, yet kind;
And ask'd, If there was none of Martial Mind,
Who durst like him, through Blood and Ruin go,
To save Old SCOTLAND *from Her Hated Foe.*
No, no, the *Doctor* said, there's none at all:
Our *Peers* are False, our *Gentry's* Courage Small.
Then did the *HERO* groan and wish tho late,
It might be granted by Eternal Fate,
For him once more to head the Valiant Clans,
SCOTS *should have freedom large as their Demands.*
With Joy he met great *DOUGLAS,* and brave *GRAHAM,*
And many other Worthies of their Name.
There good *BEILHAVEN* did kindly him embrace,
And Thousands others of that happy Place,
Where I him left Penning Harmonious Odes,
In praise of Vertue, and the Immortal Gods.
    FINIS.

from The Vision

Compylit in Latin be a most lernit Clerk in Tyme of our Hairdship and Oppression,
anno 1300, and translatit in 1524.

    Bedoun the bents of Banquo brae,
    Milane I wandert waif and wae,
       Musand our main mischaunce;
    How be thae faes we ar undone,
    That staw the sacred stane frae Scone,
       And lead us sic a daunce;
    Quhyle Ingland's Edert taks our tours,
       And Scotland first obeys;
    Rude ruffians ransak ryal bours,
       And Baliol homage pays:
        Throch feidom, our freedom
        Is blotit with this skore,

Quhat Romans', or no man's,
　　　　　Pith culd eir do before.

The air grew ruch with bousteous thuds;
Bauld Boreas branglit outthrow the cluds,
　　Maist lyke a drunken wicht;
The thunder crakt, and flauchts did rift,
Frae the blak vissart of the lift;
　　The forest shuke with fricht;
Nae birds abune thair wing extenn,
　　They ducht not byde the blast;
Ilk beist bedeen bang'd to thair den,
　　Until the storm was past:
　　　Ilk creature, in nature,
　　　　That had a spunk of sense,
　　　In neid then, with speid then,
　　　　Methocht, cry'd in defence.

To se a morn in May sae ill,
I deimt dame Nature was gane will,
　　To rair with rackles reil;
Quhairfor to put me out of pain,
And skonce my skap and shanks frae rain,
　　I bure me to a beil;
Up ane heich craig that hungit alaft,
　　Out owre a canny cave, –
A curious cruif of nature's craft,
　　Quhilk to me schelter gaif:
　　　There vexit, perplexit,
　　　　I leint me doun to weip;
　　　In brief ther, with grief ther,
　　　　I dottard owre on sleip.

Heir Somnus in his silent hand
Held all my senses at command,
　　Quhyle I forget my cair;
The mildest meid of mortall wichts
Quha pas in peace the private nichts,
　　That wauking finds it rare;
Sae in saft slumbers did I ly,
　　But not my wakryfe mynd,
Quhilk still stude watch, and couth espy
　　A man with aspeck kynd,

Richt auld lyke, and bauld lyke,
    With baird thre quarters skant,
Sae braif lyke, and graif lyke,
    He seemt to be a sanct.

Grit darring dartit frae his ee,
A braid-sword shogled at his thie,
   On his left arm a targe;
A shynand speir fill'd his richt hand,
Of stalwart mak in bane and brawnd,
   Of just proportions, large;
A various rainbow-colourt plaid
   Owre his left spaul he threw:
Doun his braid back, frae his quhyt heid,
   The silver wymplers grew.
     Amaisit, I gaisit,
       To se, led at command,
     A stampant, and rampant,
       Ferss lyon in his hand,

Quhilk held a thistle in his paw,
And round his collar graift I saw
   This poesy pat and plain;
'*Nemo me impune lacess-*
Et:'-(in Scots) 'Nane sall oppress
   Me, unpunist with pain.'
Still shaking, I durst naithing say,
   Till he with kynd accent
Sayd, 'Fere let nocht thy hairt affray,
   I cum to heir thy plaint;
     Thy graneing, and maneing,
       Have a laitlie reich'd myne eir,
     Debar then, affar then,
       All eiryness, or feir;

'For I am ane of a hie station,
The warden of this auntient nation,
   And can nocht do thee wrang.'
I vizyt him then round about,
Syne with a resolution stout,
   Speird, quhair he had been sae lang?
Quod he, 'Althocht I sum forsuke,
   Becaus they did me slicht,

To hills and glens I me betuke,
    To them that loves my richt;
        Quhase mynds yet, inclynds yet,
            To damm the rappid spate,
        Devysing, and prysing,
            Freidom at ony rate.

'Our trechour peirs thair tyranns treit,
Quha jyb them, and thair substance eit,
    And on thair honour stamp;
They, pure degenerate! bend their baks,
The victor, Langshanks, proudly cracks
    He has blawn out our lamp;
Quhyle trew men, sair complainand, tell,
    With sobs, thair silent greif,
How Baliol their richts did sell,
    With small howp of releife;
        Regretand, and fretand,
            Ay at his cursit plots,
        Quha rammed, and crammed,
            That bargin down thair throts.

'Braiv gentrie sweir, and burgers ban;
Revenge is muttert be ilk clan,
    That's to their nation trew;
The cloysters cum, to cun the evil,
Mailpayers wiss it to the devil,
    With its contryving crew;
The hardy wald, with hairty wills,
    Upon dyre vengance fall;
The feckless fret owre heuchs and hills,
    And eccho answers all;
        Repetand, and greitand,
            With mony a sair alace!
        For blasting, and casting,
            Our honour in disgrace.'

'Waes me!' quod I, 'our case is bad,
And mony of us are gane mad,
    Sen this disgraceful paction.
We are felld and herryt now by forse;
And hardly help fort, that's yit worse,
    We are sae forfairn with faction.

Then, has not he gude cause to grumble,
    That's forst to be a slaif?
Oppression dois the judgement jumble,
    And gars a wyse man raif.
        May cheins then, and pains then,
            Infernal be thair hyre,
        Quha dang us, and flang us,
            Into this ugsum myre!'

Then he, with bauld forbidding luke,
And staitly air, did me rebuke,
    For being of sprite sae mein.
Said he, 'It's far beneath a Scot
To use weak curses, quhen his lot
    May sumtyms sour his splein;
He rather sould, mair lyke a man,
    Some braiv design attempt;
Gif its nocht in his pith, what than,
    Rest but a quhyle content,
        Nocht feirful, but cheirful,
            And wait the will of Fate,
        Which mynds to, desygns to,
            Renew your auntient state.

'I ken sum mair than ye do all
Of quhat sall afterwart befall,
    In mair auspicious times.
Far aften far abuve the mune,
We watching beings do convene,
    Frae round eard's utmost climes;
Quhair ev'ry warden represents
    Cleirly his nation's case,
Gif famyne, pest, or sword torments,
    Or vilains hie in place,
        Quha keip ay, and heip ay,
            Up to themselves grit store,
        By rundging, and spunging,
            The leil laborious pure.'

'Say, then,' said I, 'at your hie sate,
Lernt ye ocht of auld Scotland's fate,
    Gif eir schoil be hersell?'
With smyle celest, quod he, 'I can;

But it's nocht fit an mortal man
    Should ken all I can tell.
But part to thee I may unfold,
    And thou may saifly ken,
Quhen Scottish peirs slicht Saxon gold,
    And turn trew heartit men;
      Quhen knaivry, and slaivrie,
        Ar equally dispysd,
      And loyalte, and royaltie,
        Universalie are prysd;

'Quhen all your trade is at a stand,
And cunyie clene forsaiks the land,
    Quhilk will be very sune;
Will preists wothout their stypands preich?
For nocht will lawyers' causes streich?
    Faith thatis nae easy done!
All this and mair maun cum to pass,
    To cleir your glamourit sicht;
And Scotland maun be made an ass,
    To set her judgement richt.
      Theyil jade hir, and blad hir,
        Untill she brak hir tether,
      Thocht auld she 's, yit bauld she 's,
        And teuch like barkit lether.

'But mony a corss sall braithless ly,
And wae sall mony a widow cry,
    Or all rin richt again;
Owre Cheviot prancing proudly north,
The faes sall tak the field near Forth,
    And think the day their ain;
But burns that day sall rin with blude
    Of them that now oppress;
Thair carcasses be Corbys fude,
    By thousands on the gress.
      A king then, sall ring then,
        Of wyse renoun and braif,
      Quhase *pusiens*, and *sapiens*,
        Sall richt restore and saif.'

'The view of freidomis sweit,' quod I.
'O say, grit tennant of the skye,

How neir's that happie tyme?'
'We ken things but be circumstans,
Nae mair,' quod he, 'I may advance,
   Leist I commit a cryme.'
'Quhat air ye pleis, gae on,' quod I,
   'I sall not fash ye more.
Say how, and quhair ye met, and quhy,
   As ye did hint before?'
      With air then, sae fair then,
         That glanst like rayis of glory,
      Sae godlyk, and oddlyk,
         He thus resumit his story.

'Frae the sun's rysing to his sett,
All the pryme rait of wardens met,
   In solemn bricht array,
With vehicles of aither cleir,
Sic we put on quhen we appeir
   To sauls rowit up in clay;
Thair in a wyde and splendit hall,
   Reir up with shynand beims,
Quhais rufe-treis wer of rainbows all,
   And paivt with starrie gleims,
      Quhilk prinked, and twinkled,
         Brichtly beyont compair,
      Much famed, and named,
         A castill in the air.

'In the midst of quhilk a tabill stude,
A spacious oval rede as blude,
   Made of a fyre-flaucht;
Arround the dazling walls were drawn,
With rays, be a celestial haud,
   Full mony a curious draucht.
Inferiour beings flew in haist,
   Without gyd or derectour,
Millions of myles throch the wyld waste,
   To bring in bowlis of nectar:
      Then roundly, and soundly,
         We drank lyk Roman gods,
      Quhen Jove sae, dois rove sae,
         That Mars and Bacchus nods.

'I still support my precedens
Abune them all for sword and sens,
   Thoch I haiv layn richt now lown;
Quhylk was, because I bure a grudge
At sum fule Scotis, quha lykd to drudge
   To princes no their own.
Sum thanes thair tenants pykt and squeist,
   And purst up all thair rent,
Syne wallopt to far courts, and bleist,
   Till riggs and shaws war spent;
      Syne byndging, and whyndging,
        Quhen thus redusit to howps,
      They dander, and wander,
        About, pure lickmadowps.

'But now its tyme for me to draw
My shynand sword against club-law,
   And gar my lyon roir;
He sall or lang gie sic a sound,
The echo sall be hard around
   Europe, frae shore to shore.
Then lat them gadder all their strenth,
   And stryve to wirk my fall,
Tho' numerous, yit at the lenth
   I will owrecum them all;
      And raise yit and blase yit,
        My braifrie, and renown,
      By gracing, and placing,
        Aright the Scottis crown.

'Quhen my braif Bruce the same sall weir
Upon his ryal heid, full cleir
   The diadem will shyne;
Then sall your sair oppression ceise,
His intrest yours he will not fleice,
   Or leiv you eir incline.
Thoch millions to his purse be lent,
   Yell neir the puirer be,
But rather richer, quhyle its spent
   Within the Scottish se:
      The field then, sall yield then,

To honest husbands' welth,
　　Gude laws then, sall cause then,
　　A sickly state haif helth.'

Quhyle thus he talkt, methocht ther came
A wondir fair ethereal dame,
　　And to our warden sayd:
'Gret Callidon, I cum in serch
Of you, frae the hych starry arch,
　　The counsill wants your ayd;
Frae every quarter of the sky,
　　As swift as quhirl-wynd,
With spirits, speid the chieftains hy,
　　Sum gret thing is desygnd.
　　　　Owre mountains, be fountains,
　　　　　And round ilk fairy ring,
　　　　I haif chaste ye; O haist ye,
　　　　　They talk about your king!'

With that my hand methocht he shuke,
And wischt I happiness micht bruke,
　　To eild be nicht and day;
Syne quicker than an arrow's flicht,
He mountit upwarts frae my sicht,
　　Straicht to the Milkie way.
My mynd him followit throw the skyes,
　　Untill the brynie streme
For joy ran trickling frae myne eyes,
　　And wakit me frae dreme:
　　　　Then peiping, half-sleiping,
　　　　　Frae furth my rural beild,
　　　　It eisit me, and pleisit me,
　　　　　To se and smell the field.

For Flora in hir clene array,
New washen with a showir of May,
　　Lukit full sweit and fair;
Quhyle hir cleir husband frae abuve
Shed down his rayis of genial luve,
　　Hir sweits perfumt the air;
The winds war husht, the welkin cleird,
　　The glumand clouds war fled,
And all as saft and gay appeird

As ane Elysion ched;
            Quhilk heisit, and bleisit,
                My heart with sic a fyre,
            As raises these praises,
                That do to Heaven aspire.

Quod AR. Scot.

from The Vision

*Compiled in Latin by a most learned clerk in time of our hardship and oppression, anno
1300, and translated in 1524.*

*Down the fields of the braes of Banquo / On my own I wandered, sad and
lonely, / Musing on our main troubles; / How we are undone by those foes, /
That stole the scared stone from Scone, / And lead us such a dance: / While
England's Edward takes our towers, / And Scotland first obeys, / Rude ruffians
ransack royal bowers, / And Baliol homage pays; / Through endless war our
freedom / Is removed by this score, / What Roman's or no man's / Power could
do before. //*
*The air grew rough with boisterous thuds, / Bold Boreas blasted through the
clouds, / Most like a drunken fellow; / The thunder cracked, and flashes ripped
/ From the black visor of the sky: / The Forest shook with fright; / No birds
above extend their wings, / They dare not endure the blast, / Every beast swiftly
took to its den, / Until the storm was past; Each creature in nature / That had a
spark of sense, / In need then, with speed then, / Methought hid in defence. //*
*To see a morn in May so ill, / I deemed Dame Nature had gone wild, / To
roar with reckless reel; / Therefore to put me out of pain, / And keep my head
and legs from rain, / I took myself to shelter, / Up a high crag that hung aloft, /
Out over a cave at hand, / A curious fold made by nature, / Which gave me
shelter; / There, vexed, perplexed, / I lent me down to weep, / In brief there,
with grief there, / I drifted off to sleep. //*
*Here Somnus in his silent hand / Held all my senses at command, / While I
forgot my care; / The mildest gift to mortal beings / Who pass in peace the
private nights, / That waking finds so rare; / So in soft slumbers did I lie, / But
not my wakeful mind, / Which still stood watch, and could espy / A man with
aspect kind, / Right old-like, and bold-like, / With thin and meagre beard, /
So brave-like and grave-like, / He seemed to be a saint. //*
*Great daring darted from his eye, / A broad sword hung at his thigh, / On his
left arm a shield; / A shining spear filled his right hand, / Of stalwart make, in
bone and brawn, a well-proportioned giant; / A plaid of various rainbow colours
/ Over his left shoulder he threw, / Down his broad back from his white head, /
Silver hair fell in curls; / Amazed, I gazed, / To see, led at command, / A*

stamping and rampant / Fierce lion in his hand. //

Which held a thistle in his paw, / And round his collar engraved I saw / This poetry apt and plain, / Nemo me impune lacess- / -et, – in Scots, none shall oppress / Me, unpunished with pain; / Still shaking, I dared say nothing, / Till he in kind accents / Said, 'Let not thy heart be afraid, / I come to hear your complaint; / Thy groans and moans / Have lately reached my ear, / Banish then afar / All eeriness or fear. //

'For I am of a high station, / The Warden of this ancient nation, / and cannot do thee wrong.' / I gazed all round him, / then with resolution stout, / Asked, where had he been so long? / Said he 'Although I abandoned some / Because they slighted me, / To hills and glens I took myself, / To those who love my cause, / Whose minds yet incline yet / To dam the rapid rush, / Devising, and prizing / Freedom at any cost. //

'Our treacherous peers serve their tyrants, / Who mock them, and consume their goods, / And stamp upon their honour; / They, poor degenerates, bend their backs, / The victor, Longshanks, proudly boasts / He has blown out our lamp: / While true men, sore compalining, tell, / With sobs, their silent grief, / How Baliol has sold their rights, / With small hope of relief; / Regretting, and fretting / Always, at his cursed plot, / Who rammed and crammed / That bargain down their throat. //

'Brave gentry swear, and burgers curse, / Revenge is muttered by each clan / Which is true to its nation; / The church now sees the evil, / Farmers wish it at the devil, / With its contriving crew: / The hardy would with hearty will, / Exact dire vengeance; / The feckless fret on hills and dales, / And Echo answers all, / Repeating and weeping, / With many a sore sighing, / For the blasting and casting / Of our honour in disgrace.' //

'Woe is me!' cried I, 'our case is bad, / And many of us are gone mad, / Since this disgraceful treaty. / We are struck down and harried now by force; / And can hardly help it, which is worse, / We are so worn with faction. / Then has not he good cause to grieve, / Who's forced to be a slave; / Oppression skews all judgement / And makes a wise man rave. / May chains then, and pains then / Infernal be their reward / Who struck us, and flung us / Into this filthy mire.' //

Then he with bold forbidding look, / And stately air, did me rebuke, / For being so mean of spirit; / Said he, 'It's far beneath a Scot / To use weak curses when his lot / May sometimes sour his spleen, / He rather should, more like a man, / Attempt some brave design; / If not within his power, what then, / But rest a while content, / Not fearful, but cheerful, / Waiting the will of fate, / Which minds to, and designs to / Renew your ancient state. //

'I know some more than all of you / Of what shall afterwards befall, / In more auspicious times; / For often far above the moon, / We watching beings do convene, / From round earth's furthest places, / Where every Warden represents / His nation's case clearly, / If famine, pestilence, or sword, torments, / Or villains in high places, / Who always keep and always heap, / Up for them-

selves great store, / By robbing and sponging / Off the laborious poor.' //
'Say then,' I said, 'at your high seat / Learn you anything of old Scotland's fate,
/ If ever she will be herself?' / With celestial smile said he, 'I can, / But it is
not fit that mortal man / Should ken all I can tell: / But part to you I can
unfold, / And you may safely know, / When Scottish peers hate Saxon gold, /
And turn true-hearted men; / When knavery and slavery, / Are equally
despised, / And loyalty and royalty, / Universally are prized. //
When all your trade is at a stand, / And coinage clean forsakes the land, /
Which will be very soon, / Will priests without their stipends preach? / For
nought will lawyers their causes plead? / Faith, that's not easily done. / All this
and more must come to pass, / To clear your enchanted sight, / And Scotland
must be made an ass / To set her judgement right. / They'll goad her and prick
her, / Until she breaks her tether, / Though old yet, she's bold yet, / And
tough like treated leather. //
'But many a corpse shall breathless lie, / And woe shall many a widow cry, / Till all
turns well again; / Over Cheviot, prancing proudly north, / The foes shall take
the field near Forth, / And think the day their own: / But burns that day shall
run with blood, / Of them that now oppress; / Their carcasses will be crow's food,
/ In thousands, on the grass. / A king then shall reign then / Of wise renown,
and brave, / Whose power and wisdom, / Shall right restore and save.' //
'The view of freedom's sweet,' said I, / 'O say, great tenant of the sky, / How
nears that happy time?' / 'We know things but by circumstance, / No more,'
said he, 'May I foretell, / Lest I commit a crime.' / 'Whatever you wish to tell,
go on,' said I, / 'I shall not task you more, / Say how, and where you met, and
why, / As you did hint before.' / With air then so fair then / That glanced like
rays of glory, / So godly, and oddly / He thus resumed his story. //
'From the sun's rising to its setting, / All the first rank of wardens meet, / In
solemn bright array, / With garments of clear ether / Such as we put on when
we appear / to souls wrapped in clay; / There in a wide and splendid hall, /
Raised up with shining beams, / Where the roof-trees are all of rainbows, / And
spread with the gleams of stars, / Which shine and twinkle / Brightly, beyond
compare, / Far-famed and named, / A castle in the air. //
'In the midst of which a table stands, / A spacious oval red as blood, / Made
from a lightning-flash, / Around the dazzling walls are drawn, / With rays, a
celestial hand, / Many curious designs. / Inferior beings fly in haste, / Without
guide or director, / Millions of miles through the wild waste, / to bring in bowls
of nectar: / Then roundly, and soundly, / We drink like Roman gods; / When
Jove so, does rove so, / Then Mars and Bacchus nods.' //

★ ★ ★ ★ ★

'I still maintain my precedence / Above them all, for sword and sense, / Though
I have lain quiet till now, / Which was, because I bore a grudge / At some foul

Scots, who liked to crawl, / To princes not their own; / Then some tormented and squeezed their tenants, / And put their rents in purses, / Gallivanting and showing off in distant courts, / Till fields and woods were spent; / Then complaining and whining, / When thus reduced to hopes, / They uselessly wander / About, poor arselickers. //

'But now it's time for me to draw / My shining sword against injustice, / And make my lion roar; / He shall before long give such a sound / The echo shall be heard around, / Europe, from shore to shore; / Then let them gather all their strength, / And strive to work my fall, / Though numerous, yet in the end, / I will overcome them all, / And raise yet and blaze yet / My bravery and renown, / By gracing and placing / Aright, the Scottish Crown. //

'When my brave Bruce the crown shall wear, / On his royal head, full clear / The diadem will shine; / Then shall your sore oppression cease, / Your interests he will not harm, / Or ever think to leave you; / Though millions to his purse be lent, / You'll never be the poorer; / But rather richer, while it's spent, / Within Scotland. / The fields then will yield then / To honest husband's wealth, / Good laws then shall cause then / A sick state to have health.' //

While thus he talked, methought there came / A wondrous fair ethereal dame, / And to our Warden said / 'Great Caledonian, I come in search / Of you, from the high starry arch. / The council wants your aid; / From every quarter of the sky, as swift as the whirl-wind, / With spirits speed the chieftains move, / Some great thing is designed / Over mountains, by fountains, / And round each fairy ring, / I've chased ye, / O haste ye, / They talk about your king.' //

With that my hand methought he shook, / And wished that I might happiness enjoy, / In age, both night and day. / Then quicker than an arrow's flight, / He mounted upwards from my sight, / Straight to the Milky Way; / My mind followed him through the skies, / Until salty tears / For joy from my eyes then ran / And wakened me from dream. / Then peeping, half sleeping, / From out of my rural shelter, / It eased me and pleased me / To see and smell the fields. //

For Flora in her clean array, / New-washed with showers of May, / Looked out full sweet and fair; / While her bright husband from above / Shed down his rays of genial love, / Her sweets perfumed the air; / The winds were hushed, the sky was clear, / The gloomy clouds had fled, / And all as soft and gay appeared, / As though Elysian fields; / Which lifted and blessed / My heart, with such a fire, / As raises these praises, / That to heaven now aspire.

Said AR. Scot.

JAMES THOMSON (1700–1748) and DAVID MALLET (1705–1765)

Rule Britannia

When Britain first, at heaven's command,
Arose from out the azure main,
This was the charter of the land,
And guardian angels sung this strain –
'Rule, Britannia, rule the waves;
Britons never will be slaves.'

The nations, not so blest as thee,
Must in their turns to tyrants fall;
While thou shalt flourish great and free,
The dread and envy of them all.
'Rule, Britannia, rule the waves;
Britons never will be slaves.'

Still more majestic shalt thou rise.
More dreadful from each foreign stroke;
As the loud blast that tears the skies
Serves but to root thy native oak.
'Rule, Britannia, rule the waves;
Britons never will be slaves.'

Thee haughty tyrants ne'er shall tame;
All their attempts to bend thee down
Will but arouse thy generous flame,
But work their woe and thy renown.
'Rule, Britannia, rule the waves;
Britons never will be slaves.'

To thee belongs the rural reign;
Thy cities shall with commerce shine;
All thine shall be the subject main,
And every shore it circles thine.
'Rule, Britannia, rule the waves;
Britons never will be slaves.'

The Muses, still with freedom found,
Shall to thy happy coast repair:
Blest isle! with matchless beauty crowned,
And manly hearts to guard the fair.
'Rule, Britannia, rule the waves;
Britons never will be slaves.'

Albania

O Loved Albania! hardy nurse of men!
Holding thy silver cross, I worship thee,
On this thy old and solemn festival,
Early, ere yet the wakeful cock has crowed.
    Hear! goddess hear! that on the beryl flood,
Enthroned of old, amid the waters sound,
Reign'st far and wide o'er many a sea-girt spot.
Oh smile! whether on high Dunedin thou
Guardest the steep and iron-bloted rock
Where trusted lie the monarchy's last gems,
The sceptre, sword, and crown, that graced the brows,
Since father Fergus, of an hundred kings:
Or if, along the well-contested ground,
The warlike Border-land, thou marchest proud,
In Teviotdale, where many a shepherd dwells,
By lovely winding Tweed, or Cheviot brown.
Nor ween I now in Durham's lofty spire
To seek thee, though thy loved St David's work;
Nor where Newcastle opes her jetty mines
Of coal; nor in strong Berwick; nor in Man,
That never dreaded plague; nor in the wilds
Of stony Westmorland: all once thy own.
    Hail, land of bowmen! seed of those who scorned
To stoop the neck to wide imperial Rome.
O dearest half of Albion, sea-walled!
Hail! state unconquered by the fire of war,
Red war, that twenty ages round thee burned!
To thee, for whom my purest raptures glow,
Kneeling with filial homage, I devote
My life, my strength, my first and latest song.
    Shall I forget thy tenderness? shall I
Thy bounty, thy parental cares forget,
Hissing with viper's tongue? – who born of thee,
Now twice twelve years have drawn thy vital air,
And eat thy fruit, protected with thy sons;
Though stronger far and holier is the tie
By which are knit my heart-strings to thy love;
Thou gav'st me, yet an infant unbaptised,
Immortal wealth, the seeds of better life.

Thou goddess! by the softening sun beloved,
Rejoicest, he with unfulfilled desire
Delights not only on thy face to dwell
In amorous smile the live-long summer's day,
But, looking back from the Atlantic brine,
Eyes thy glad slumbers with reflected beam,
And glitters o'er thy head the clear night long.

Neglect not thou the sea, that yields thee salt,
Salt, origin of tastes, with which we eat
The well-fed ox, and bread by labour earned.
Thence too the coal its nitrous spirit draws –
Coal such as dug from firy Elphingston,
Or Winton's level land that smiles with wheat,
Brings back bright ore, reward of industry,
Or such as in Montrose, fair harboured town,
They burn; or in Alectum, lofty domed,
And dims, Edina, thy aspiring brow.
No other fuel claimeth Glasgow blue,
Watery Linlithgow's royal seat, or Perth,
Whose evening bells the roving Highlander
Hears sweet, though far descending Stenton hill,
Nor Fife, well-peopled in her sea-towns tiled.
Such also we in high Devana burn,
Glancing on marble heath, the oily jet
Crackling full fast makes mild the bitter air
With sulphured steam, and thaws with grateful warmth
The frozen pilgrim, while the glowing grate
Doubles the heat, and gay the enlivened hall
Laughs wide, illumined with the pleasing gleam.

Ere since of old the haughty thanes of Ross –
So to the simple swain tradition tells –
Were wont with clans and ready vassals thronged
To wake the bounding stag or guilty wolf,
There oft is heard at midnight, or at noon,
Beginning faint, but rising still more loud
And nearer, voice of hunters and of hounds
And horns hoarse-winded, blowing far and keen.
Forthwith the hubbub multiplies, the gale
Labours with wilder shrieks and rifer din
Of hot pursuit – the broken cry of deer
Mangled by throttling dogs, the shouts of men,

And hoofs thick beating on the hollow hill.
Sudden the grazing heifer in the vale
Starts at the noise, and both the herdsman's ears
Tingle with inward dread. Aghast he eyes
The mountain's height and all the ridges round;
Yet not one trace of living wight discerns,
Nor knows o'erawed and trembling as he stands,
To what or whom he owes his idle fear –
To ghost, to witch, to fairy, or to fiend;
But wonders, and no end of wondering finds.

Albania dear, attend! behold I seek
Thy angel night and day with eager feet
On peopled coast and western mountain lone,
In city paved and well-aired village thatched,
From end to end of Scotland many-minded.
Oft too I dare the deep, though winter storms
Rage fierce, and round me mad Corbrecho roar,
Wafted with love to see Columba's isles.

There view I winged Skye, and Lewes long,
Resort of whales; and Wyste where herrings swarm;
And talk, at once delighted and appalled,
By the pale moon, with utmost Hirta's seers,
Of beckoning ghosts and shadowy men that bode
Sure death. Nor there doth Jura's double hill
Escape my sight; nor Mull, though bald and bare;
Nor Ilay, where erewhile Macdonalds reigned.
Thee too, Lismore! I hail St Moloch's shrine;
Inchgall, first conquered by the brand of Scots;
And, filled with awe of ancient saints and kings,
I kiss, O Icolmkill! thy hallowed mould.

Thus, Caledonia, many-hilled! to thee,
End and beginning of my ardent song,
I tune the Druid's lyre, to thee devote
This lay, and love not music but for thee.

HENRY ERSKINE (1720–1765)

In the Garb of Old Gaul

Such our love of liberty, our country and our laws,
That like our ancestors of old, we'll stand in Freedom's cause;
We'll bravely fight like heroes bold, for honor and applause,
And defy the French, with all their art, to alter our laws.

In the garb of old Gaul, wi' the fire of old Rome,
From the heath-covered mountains of Scotia we come,
Where the Romans endeavoured our country to gain,
But our ancestors fought, and they fought not in vain.

No effeminate customs our sinews unbrace,
No luxurious tables enervate our race;
Our loud-sounding pipe bears the true martial strain,
So do we the old Scottish valor retain.

We're tall as the oak on the mount of the vale,
Are swift as the roe which the hound doth assail,
As the full moon in Autumn our shields do appear,
Minerva would dread to encounter our spear.

As a storm in the ocean when Boreas blows,
So are we enraged when we rush on our foes.
We sons of the mountains, tremendous as rocks,
Dash the force of our foes with our thundering strokes.

Quebec and Cape Breton, the pride of old France,
In their troops fondly boasted till we did advance;
But when our claymores they saw us produce,
Their courage did fail, and they sued for a truce.

In our realm may the fury of faction long cease,
May our councils be wise, and our commerce increase;
And in Scotia's cold climate may each of us find
That our friends still prove true, and our beauties prove kind.

Then we'll defend our liberty, our country, and our laws,
And teach our late posterity to fight in freedom's cause,
That they like our ancestors bold, for honor and applause,
May defy the French, with all their art, to alter our laws.

TOBIAS SMOLLETT (1721–1771)

The Tears of Scotland
(after Culloden)

Mourn, hapless Caledonia, mourn
Thy banish'd peace, thy laurels torn!
Thy sons, for valour long renown'd,
Lie slaughter'd on their native ground;
Thy hospitable roofs no more
Invite the stranger to the door;
In smoky ruins sunk they lie,
The monuments of cruelty.

The wretched owner sees afar
His all become the prey of war;
Bethinks him of his babes and wife,
Then smites his breast and curses life.
Thy swains are famish'd on the rocks,
Where once they fed their wanton flocks;
Thy ravish'd virgins shriek in vain;
Thy infants perish on the plain.

What boots it then, in every clime,
Through the wide spreading waste of time,
Thy martial glory, crown'd with praise,
Still shone with undiminish'd blaze?
Thy tow'ring spirit now is broke,
Thy neck is bended to the yoke.
What foreign arms could never quell,
By civil rage and rancour fell.

The rural pipe and merry lay
No more shall cheer the happy day;
No social scenes of gay delight
Beguile the dreary winter night;
No strains but those of sorrow flow,
And nought be heard but sounds of woe,
While the pale phantoms of the slain
Glide nightly o'er the silent plain.

O baneful cause, oh! fatal morn,
Accurs'd to ages yet unborn!
The sons against their father stood,
The parent shed his children's blood.
Yet, when the rage of battle ceas'd
The victor's soul was not appeas'd;
The naked and forlorn must feel
Devouring flames, and murd'ring steel!

The pious mother, doom'd to death,
Forsaken, wanders o'er the heath;
The bleak wind whistles round her head,
Her helpless orphans cry for bread;
Bereft of shelter, food, and friend,
She views the shades of night descend;
And stretch'd beneath th' inclement skies,
Weeps o'er her tender babes, and dies.

While the warm blood bedews my veins,
And unimpair'd remembrance reigns,
Resentment of my country's fate
Within my filial breast shall beat;

And, spite of her insulting foe,
My sympathizing verse shall flow:
'Mourn, hapless Caledonia, mourn
Thy banish'd peace, thy laurels torn.'

JOHN HOME (1722–1808)

Epigram

Firm and erect the Caledonian stood;
Old was his mutton, and his claret good.
'Let him drink port!' an English statesman cried;
He drank the poison, and his spirit died.

JEAN ELLIOTT (1727–1805)

The Flowers of the Forest

I've heard them lilting at our ewe-milking,
Lasses a-lilting before the dawn o' day;
But now they are moaning on ilka green loaning;
'The Flowers of the Forest are a' wede away.'

At buchts, in the morning, nae blythe lads are scorning;
The lasses are lonely, and dowie, and wae;
Nae daffin', nae gabbin', but sighing and sabbing:
Ilk ane lifts her leglen, and hies her away.

In hairst, at the shearing, nae youths now are jeering,
The bandsters are lyart, and runkled and grey;
At fair or at preaching, nae wooing, nae fleeching:
The Flowers of the Forest are a' wede away.

At e'en, in the gloaming, nae swankies are roaming
'Bout stacks wi' the lasses at bogle to play,
But ilk ane sits drearie, lamenting her dearie:
The Flowers of the Forest are a' wede away.

Dule and wae for the order sent our lads to the Border;
The English, for ance, by guile wan the day:
The Flowers of the Forest, that foucht aye the foremost,
The prime o' our land, are cauld in the clay.

We'll hear nae mair lilting at our ewe-milking,
Women and bairns are heartless and wae;
Sighing and moaning on ilka green loaning:
'The Flowers of the Forest are a' wede away.'

ALEXANDER GEDDES (1737–1802)

from The Epistle to the President, Vice-Presidents, and Members of the Scottish Society of Antiquaries: On Being Chosen a Correspondent Member

... Let bragart England in disdain
Ha'd ilka lingo, but her a'in:
Her a'in, we wat, say what she can,
Is like her true-born Englishman,
A vile promiscuous mungrel seed
Of Danish, Dutch, an' Norman breed,
An' prostituted, since, to a'
The jargons on this earthly ba'!
Bedek't, 'tis true, an' made fu' smart
Wi' mekil learning, pains an' art;
An' taught to baik, an' benge, an' bou
As dogs an' dancin'-masters do:
Wi' fardit cheeks an' pouder't hair,
An' brazen confidential stare –
While ours, a blate an' bashfu' maid
Conceals her blushes wi' her plaid;
And is unwillan' to display
Her beuties in the face o' day.

    Bot strip them baith – an' see wha's shape
Has least the semblance of an ape?
Wha's lim's are straughtest? Wha can sheu
The whiter skin, an' fairer heu;
An' whilk, in short, is the mair fit
To gender genuine manly wit?
I'll pledge my pen, you'll judgement pass
In favor of the Scottis lass.

ALEXANDER WATSON (1744–1831)

The Kail Brose of Scotland

When our gutchers of auld made a troke wi' the laird
For a wee bit o' grund to be a kailyard,
It was to the brose that they had a regard.
    Oh, the kail brose of auld Scotland,
    And oh, the Scottish kail brose!

When their leal-hearted youngsters were roused frae repose,
Their frien's to defend, or to conquer their foes,
They proved wi' a vengeance what pith there's in brose.
    Oh, the kail brose of auld Scotland,
    And oh, the Scottish kail brose!

When Wallace and Bruce turned the chase on their foes,
They saired them o' fighting wi' very few blows,
The bauldest cried out, 'Let us turn: they've got brose!'
    Oh, the kail brose of auld Scotland,
    And oh, the Scottish kail brose!

Then our sodgers were steel frae the heel to the nose,
Wi' the plaid and the kilt, the claymore, and the hose,
And the bag o' oatmeal at their backs to be brose.
    Oh, the kail brose of auld Scotland,
    And oh, the Scottish kail brose!

At our annual elections for baillies or mayor,
Nae kickshaws o' puddin's or tarts were seen there;
But a dish o' gude brose was the favourite fare.
    Oh, the kail brose of auld Scotland,
    And oh, the Scottish kail brose!

There was hotch-potch and haggis, a feast for a lord,
And sheep's heads, the fattest our hills could afford;
But a dish o' gude brose was the king o' the board.
    Oh, the kail brose of auld Scotland,
    And oh, the Scottish kail brose!

Whare then were our bucks, and our bloods, and our beaux.
Wi their lang-leggit breeks and their short-leggit hose?
The devil a breek did we wear when we'd brose.
  Oh, the kail brose of auld Scotland,
  And oh, the Scottish kail brose!

Our baby bit lassies buskit up to be shows:
Their white-washen cheeks they would blush like the rose,
Could they see how their grandmothers thrave upon brose.
  Oh, the kail brose of auld Scotland,
  And oh, the Scottish kail brose!

Nae born coopers then sought to gather a pose
By grindin' aff puir bodies faces the nose;
But man, wife, and wean, they got wamefu's o' brose.
  Oh, the kail brose of auld Scotland,
  And oh, the Scottish kail brose!

But now that the thistle is joined to the rose,
And Scotsmen and Englishmen nae mair at blows,
We've lost a great deal of our relish for brose.
  Oh, the kail brose of auld Scotland,
  And oh, the Scottish kail brose!

Yet still wi' the foremost we'll cock up our nose,
And deal out Scots measure to a' our proud foes.
Let the French then beware our beef and our brose.
  Oh, the kail brose of auld Scotland,
  And oh, the Scottish kail brose!

Yet, gi'e but a Scotsman a cog o' kail brose,
A jorum o' whiskey, and prime weel his nose,
Wi' the French, wi' the Dons, wi' the devil he'll close.
  Oh, the kail brose of auld Scotland,
  And oh, the Scottish kail brose!

ROBERT FERGUSSON (1750–1774)

Elegy on the Death of Scots Music

Mark it, Caesario; it is old and plain,
The spinsters and the knitters to the sun,
And the free maids that weave their thread with bond,
Do use to chant it.
                              Shakespeare's Twelfth Night

On Scotia's plains, in days of yore,
When lads and lasses tartan wore,
Saft Music rang on ilka shore,
        In hamely weed;
But harmony is now no more,
        And *music* dead.

Round her the feather'd choir wad wing,
Sae bonnily she wont to sing,
And sleely wake the sleeping string,
        Their sang to lead,
Sweet as the zephyrs of the spring;
        But now she's dead.

Mourn, ilka nymph and ilka swain,
Ilk sunny hill and dowie glen;
Let weeping streams and Naiads drain
        Their fountain-head;
Let echo swell the dolefu' strain,
        Since music's dead.

When the saft vernal breezes ca'
The grey-hair'd Winter's fogs awa,
Naebody then is heard to blaw,
        Near hill or mead,
On chaunter, or on aiten straw,
        Since music's dead.

At gloamin now the bagpipe's dumb,
When weary owsen hameward come;
Sae sweetly as it wont to bum,
        And pibrochs skreed ;
We never hear its warlike hum ;
        For music's dead.

Macgibbon's gane: Ah! wae's my heart!
The man in music maist expert,
Wha could sweet melody impart,
    And tune the reed,
Wi' sic a slee and pawky art;
        But now he's dead.

Ilk carline now may grunt and grane,
Ilk bonny lassie mak great mane,
Since he's awa, I crow there's nane
    Can fill his stead;
The blythest sangster on the plain
        Alake, he's dead!

Now foreign sonnets bear the gree,
And crabbit queer variety
Of sounds fresh sprung frae Italy,
    A bastard breed!
Unlike that saft-tongu'd melody
        Which now lies dead.

Could lav'rocks at the dawning day,
Could linties chirming frae the spray,
Or todling burns that smoothly play
    O'er gowden bed,
Compare wi' *Birks of Invermay*
        But now they're dead.

O Scotland! that could yence afford
To bang the pith of Roman sword,
Winna your sons, wi' joint accord,
    To battle speed?
And fight till Music be restor'd,
        Which now lies dead?

ANN GRANT (1755–1838)

The Bluebells of Scotland

'O where, tell me where, is your Highland laddie gone?
O where, tell me where, is your Highland laddie gone?'
'He's gone with streaming banners, where noble deeds are done,
And my sad heart will tremble till he come safely home.'

'O where, tell me where, did your Highland laddie stay?
O where, tell me where, did your Highland laddie stay?'
'He dwelt beneath the holly trees beside the rapid Spey,
And many a blessing followed him the day he went away.'

'O what, tell me what, does your Highland laddie wear?
O what, tell me what, does your Highland laddie wear?'
'A bonnet with a lofty plume, the gallant badge of war,
And a plaid across his manly breast that yet shall wear a star.'

'Suppose, ah! suppose, that some cruel, cruel wound
Should pierce your Highland laddie and all your hopes confound!'
'The pipe would play a cheering march, the banners round him fly,
And for his king and country dear with pleasure would he die.'

'But I will hope to see him yet in Scotland's bonnie bounds,
But I will hope to see him yet in Scotland's bonnie bounds.
His native land of liberty shall nurse his glorious wounds,
While wide throughout all our Highland hills his warlike name resounds.'

ROBERT BURNS (1759–1796)

Such a Parcel of Rogues in a Nation

Fareweel to a' our Scottish fame,
   Fareweel our ancient glory!
Fareweel ev'n to the Scottish name,
   Sae famed in martial story!
Now Sark rins over Solway sands,
   An' Tweed rins to the ocean,
To mark where England's province stands
   Such a parcel of rogues in a nation!

What force or guile could not subdue
  Thro' many warlike ages
Is wrought now by a coward few
  For hireling traitor's wages.
The English steel we could disdain,
  Secure in valour's station;
But English gold has been our bane
  Such a parcel of rogues in a nation!

O, would, or I had seen the day
  That Treason thus could sell us,
My auld grey head had lien in clay
  Wi' Bruce and loyal Wallace!
But pith and power, till my last hour
  I'll mak this declaration: –
'We're bought and sold for English gold' –
  Such a parcel of rogues in a nation!

Scots, Wha Hae

Scots, wha hae wi' Wallace bled,
Scots, wham Bruce has aften led,
Welcome to your gory bed
    Or to victorie!

Now's the day, and now's the hour:
See the front o' battle lour,
See approach proud Edward's power
    Chains and slaverie!

Wha will be a traitor knave?
Wha can fill a coward's grave?
Wha sae base as be a slave?
    Let him turn, and flee!

Wha for Scotland's King and Law
Freedom's sword will strongly draw,
Freeman stand, or freeman fa',
    Let him follow me!

By Oppression's woes and pains,
By your sons in servile chains,
We will drain our dearest veins
　　But they shall be free!

Lay the proud usurpers low!
Tyrants fall in every foe!
Liberty's in every blow!
　　Let us do, or die!

CAROLINA OLIPHANT, LADY NAIRNE (1766–1845)

Songs of My Native Land

Songs of my native land,
To me how dear!
Songs of my infancy,
Sweet to mine ear!
Entwined with my youthful days,
Wi' the bonny banks and braes,
Where the winding burnie strays
Murmuring near.

Strains of thy native land,
That thrill the soul,
Pouring the magic of
Your soft control!
Often has your minstrelsy
Soothed the pangs of misery,
Winging rapid thoughts away
To realms on high.

Weary pilgrims there have rest,
Their wand'rings o'er;
There the slave, no more oppress'd,
Hails Freedom's shore.
Sin shall then no more deface,
Sickness, pain, and sorrow cease,
Ending in eternal peace,
And songs of joy!

There, when the seraphs sing,
In cloudless day;
There, where the higher praise
The ransom'd pay.
Soft strains of the happy land,
Chanted by the heavenly band,
Who can fully understand
How sweet ye be!

The Attainted Scottish Nobles
(after Culloden)

Oh, some will tune their mournfu' strains,
To tell o' hame-made sorrow,
And if they cheat you o' your tears,
They'll dry upon the morrow.
Oh, some will sing their airy dreams,
In verity they're sportin',
My sang's o' nae sic thewless themes,
But wakin' true misfortune.

Ye Scottish nobles, ane and a',
For loyalty attainted,
A nameless bardie's wae to see
Your sorrows unlamented;
For if your fathers ne'er had fought
For heirs of ancient royalty,
Ye're down the day that might ha'e been
At the top o' honour's tree a'.

For old hereditary right,
For conscience' sake they stoutly stood;
And for the crown their valiant sons
Themselves have shed their injured blood;
And if their fathers ne'er had fought
For heirs of ancient royalty,
They're down the day that might ha'e been
At the top o' honour's tree a'.

JAMES HOGG (1770–1835)

Sir Morgan O'Doherty's Farewell to Scotland

Farewell, farewell, beggarly Scotland,
Cold and beggarly poor countrie!
If ever I cross thy border again,
The muckle deil must carry me.
There's but one tree in a' the land,
And that's the bonnie gallows tree:
The very nowte look to the south,
And wish that they had wings to flee.

Farewell, farewell, beggarly Scotland,
Brose and bannocks, crowdy and kale!
Welcome, welcome, jolly old England,
Laughing lasses and foaming ale!
'Twas when I came to merry Carlisle,
That out I laughed loud laughters three;
And if I cross the Sark again
The muckle deil maun carry me.

Farewell, farewell, beggarly Scotland,
Kiltit kimmers, wi' carroty hair,
Pipers, who beg that your honours would buy
A bawbee's worth of their famished air!
I'd rather keep Cadwaller's goats,
And feast upon toasted cheese and leeks,
Than go back again to the beggarly North,
To herd 'mang loons with bottomless breeks.

The Flowers of Scotland

What are the flowers of Scotland,
   All others that excel –
The lovely flowers of Scotland,
   All others that excel?
The thistle's purple bonnet,
   And bonny heather-bell,
O, they're the flowers of Scotland,
   All others that excel!

Though England eyes her roses
  With pride she'll ne'er forego,
The rose has oft been trodden
  By foot of haughty foe;
But the thistle in her bonnet blue
  Still nods outow'r the fell,
And dares the proudest foeman
  To tread the heather-bell.

For the wee bit leaf o' Ireland,
  Alack and well a-day!
For ilka hand is free to pu'
  An' steal the gem away.
But the thistle in her bonnet blue
  Still bobs aboon them a';
At her the bravest darena blink,
  Or gi'e his mou' a thraw.

Up wi' the flowers o' Scotland,
  The emblem o' the free,
Their guardians for a thousand years,
  Their guardians still we'll be.
A foe had better brave the deil
  Within his reeky cell,
Than our thistle's purple-bonnet,
  Or bonny heather-bell.

Caledonia

Caledonia! thou land of the mountain and rock,
  Of the ocean, the mist, and the wind –
Thou land of the torrent, the pine, and the oak,
  Of the roebuck, the hart, and the hind;
Though bare are thy cliffs, and though barren thy glens,
  Though bleak thy dim islands appear,
Yet kind are the hearts, and undaunted the clans,
  That roam on these mountains so dear!

A foe from abroad, or a tyrant at home,
    Could never thy ardour restrain;
The marshall'd array of imperial Rome,
    Essay'd thy proud spirit in vain!
Firm seat of religion, of valour, of truth,
    Of genius unshackled and free,
The muses have left all the vales of the south,
    My loved Caledonia, for thee!

Sweet land of the bay and the wild-winding deeps,
    Where loveliness slumbers at even,
While far in the depths of the blue water sleeps
    A calm little motionless heaven!
Thou land of the valley, the moor, and the hill,
    Of the storm, and the proud-rolling wave –
Yes, thou art the land of fair liberty still,
    And the land of my forefathers' grave!

SIR WALTER SCOTT (1771–1832)

from The Lay of the Last Minstrel, Canto vi, lines 1–36

Scotland

Breathes there the man with soul so dead,
Who never to himself hath said,
    This is my own, my native land!
Whose heart hath ne'er within him burn'd
As home his footsteps he hath turn'd,
    From wandering on a foreign strand!
If such there breathe, go, mark him well;
For him no minstrel raptures swell;
High though his titles, proud his name,
Boundless his wealth as wish can claim;
Despite these titles, power, and pelf,
The wretch, concentred all in self,
Living, shall forfeit fair renown,
And, doubly dying, shall go down
To the vile dust, from whence he sprung,
Unwept, unhonour'd, and unsung.

O Caledonia! stern and wild,
Meet nurse for a poetic child!
Land of brown heath and shaggy wood,
Land of the mountain and the flood,
Land of my sires! what mortal hand
Can e'er untie the filial band
That knits me to thy rugged strand!
Still, as I view each well-known scene,
Think what is now and what hath been,
Seems as, to me, of all bereft,
Sole friends thy woods and streams were left;
And thus I love them better still,
Even in extremity of ill.
By Yarrow's stream still let me stray,
Though none should guide my feeble way;
Still feel the breeze down Ettrick break,
Although it chill my wither'd cheek;
Still lay my head by Teviot Stone,
Though there, forgotten and alone,
The Bard may draw his parting groan.

ROBERT SOUTHEY (1774–1843)

The Death of Wallace

Joy, joy in London now!
He goes, the rebel Wallace goes to death,
At length the traitor meets the traitor's doom,
    Joy, joy in London now!

    He on a sledge is drawn,
His strong right arm unweapon'd and in chains,
And garlanded around his helmless head
    The laurel wreath of scorn.

    They throng to view him now
Who in the field had fled before his sword,
Who at the name of Wallace once grew pale
    And faltered out a prayer.

Yes, they can meet his eye,
That only beams with patient courage now,
Yes, they can gaze upon those manly limbs
    Defenceless now and bound.

    And that eye did not shrink
As he beheld the pomp of infamy,
Nor did one rebel feeling shake those limbs
    When the last moment came.

    What though suspended sense
Was by their damned cruelty revived;
What though ingenious vengeance lengthened life
    To fell protracted death –

What though the hangman's hand
Graspt in his living breast the heaving heart,
In the last agony, the last sick pang,
    Wallace had comfort still.

    He called to mind his deeds
Done for his country in the embattled field;
He thought of that good cause for which he died,
    And it was joy in death!

    Go, Edward, triumph now!
Cambria is fallen, and Scotland's strength is crush'd;
On Wallace, on Llewellyn's mangled limbs
    The fowls of heaven have fed.

    Unrivalled, unopposed,
Go, Edward, full of glory, to thy grave!
The weight of patriot blood upon thy soul!
    Go, Edward, to thy God!

JOHN LEYDEN (1775–1811)

from Scottish Music: An Ode

To Ianthe

Again, sweet siren! breathe again
That deep, pathetic, powerful strain;
   Whose melting tones, of tender woe,
Fall soft as evening's summer dew
That bathes the pinks and harebells blue
   Which in the vales of Teviot blow.

Such was the song that soothed to rest,
Far in the green isle of the west,
   The Celtic warrior's parted shade;
Such are the lonely sounds that sweep
O'er the blue bosom of the deep,
   Where shipwrecked mariners are laid.

Ah! sure as Hindú legends tell,
When music's tones the bosom swell,
   The scenes of former life return;
Ere, sunk beneath the morning star,
We left our parent climes afar,
   Immured in mortal forms to mourn.

Or if, as ancient sages ween,
Departed spirits, half-unseen,
   Can mingle with the mortal throng;
'Tis when from heart to heart we roll
The deep-toned music of the soul,
   That warbles in our Scottish song.

I hear, I hear, with awful dread,
The plaintive music of the dead!
   They leave the amber fields of day:
Soft as the cadence of the wave,
That murmurs round the mermaid's grave,
   They mingle in the magic lay...

THOMAS CAMPBELL (1777–1844)

Lines on Revisiting a Scottish River

And call they this Improvement? – to have changed,
My native Clyde, thy once romantic shore,
Where Nature's face is banish'd and estranged,
And Heaven reflected in thy wave no more;
Whose banks, that sweeten'd May-day's breath before,
Lie sere and leafless now in summer's beam,
With sooty exhalations cover'd o'er;
And for the daisied green-sward, down thy stream
Unsightly brick-lanes smoke, and clanking engines gleam.

Speak not to me of swarms the scene sustains;
One heart free tasting Nature's breath and bloom
Is worth a thousand slaves to Mammon's gains.
But whither goes that wealth, and gladdening whom?
See, left but life enough and breathing-room
The hunger and the hope of life to feel,
Yon pale Mechanic bending o'er his loom,
And Childhood's self as at Ixion's wheel,
From morn till midnight task'd to earns its little meal.

Is this Improvement? – where the human breed
Degenerates as they swarm and overflow,
Till toil grows cheaper than the trodden weed,
And man competes with man, like foe with foe,
Till Death, that thins them scarce seems public woe?
Improvement! – smiles it in the poor man's eyes,
Or blooms it on the cheek of Labour? – No –
To gorge a few with Trade's precarious prize,
We banish rural life, and breathe unwholesome skies.

Nor call that evil slight; God has not given
This passion to the heart of man in vain,
For Earth's green face, th'untainted air of Heaven,
And all the bliss of Nature's rustic reign.
For not alone our frame imbibes a stain
From fetid skies; the spirit's healthy pride
Fades in their gloom – And therefore I complain,
That thou no more through pastoral scenes shouldst glide,
My Wallace's own stream, and once romantic Clyde!

The Thistle's Grown aboon the Rose

Full white the Bourbon lily blows,
And fairer haughty England's rose.
Nor shall unsung the symbol smile,
Green Ireland, of thy lovely isle.
In Scotland grows a warlike flower,
Too rough to bloom in lady's bower;
His crest, when high the soldier bears,
And spurs his courser on the spears,
O, there it blossoms – there it blows –
The thistle's grown aboon the rose.

Bright like a steadfast star it smiles
Aboon the battle's burning files;
The mirkest cloud, the darkest night,
Shall ne'er make dim that beauteous light;
And the best blood that warms my vein
Shall flow ere it shall catch a stain.
Far has it shone on fields of fame,
From matchless Bruce till dauntless Graeme,
From swarthy Spain to Siber's snows; –
The thistle's grown aboon the rose.

What conquered ay, what nobly spared,
What firm endured and greatly dared?
What reddened Egypt's burning sand?
What vanquished on Corunna's strand?
What pipe on green Maida blew shrill?
What died in blood Barossa hill?
Bade France's dearest life-blood rue
Dark Soignies and dread Waterloo?
That spirit which no terror knows; –
The thistle's grown aboon the rose.

I vow – and let men mete the grass
For his red grave who dares say less –
Men kinder at the festive board,
Men braver with the spear and sword,
Men higher famed for truth – more strong
In virtue, sovereign sense, and song,

Or maids more fair, or wives more true,
Than Scotland's, ne'er trode down the dew.
Round flies the song – the flagon flows, –
The thistle's grown aboon the rose.

The Sun Rises Bright in France

The sun rises bright in France,
And fair sets he;
But he has tint the blithe blink he had
In my ain country.
O, gladness comes to many,
But sorrow comes to me,
As I look oer the wide ocean
To my ain country.

O, it's nae my ain ruin
That saddens aye my e'e,
But the love I left in Galloway,
Wi' bonnie bairnies three.
My hamely hearth burnt bonnie,
An' smiled my fair Marie;
I've left my heart behind me
In my ain country.

The bud comes back to summer,
And the blossom to the bee;
But I'll win back – O never,
To my ain country.
I'm leal to the high heaven,
Which will be leal to me,
An' there I'll meet ye a' soon
Frae my ain country.

Lachin y Gair

Away, ye gay landscapes, ye gardens of roses!
In you let the minions of luxury rove;
Restore me the rocks where the snow-flake reposes,
Though still they are sacred to freedom and love:
Yet, Caledonia, beloved are thy mountains,
Round their white summits though elements war;
Though cataracts foam stead of smooth-flowing fountains,
I sigh for the valley of dark Loch na Garr.

Ah! there my young footsteps in infancy wandered;
My cap was the bonnet, my cloak was the plaid;
On chieftains long perished my memory pondered,
As daily I strode through the pine-covered glade;
I sought not my home till the day's dying glory
Gave place to the rays of the bright polar star;
For fancy was cheer'd by traditional story,
Disclosed by the natives of dark Loch na Garr.

'Shades of the dead! have I not heard your voices
Rise on the night-rolling breath of the gale?'
Surely the soul of the hero rejoices
And rides on the wind o'er his own highland vale.
Round Loch na Garr while the stormy mist gathers,
Winter presides in his cold icy car:
Clouds there encircle the forms of my fathers;
They dwell in the tempests of dark Loch na Garr.

'Ill-starred, though brave, did no visions foreboding
Tell you that fate had forsaken your cause?'
Ah, were you destined to die at Culloden,
Victory crowned not your fall with applause:
Still were you happy in death's earthly slumber,
You rest with your clan in the caves of Braemar:
The pibroch resounds to the piper's loud number,
Your deeds on the echoes of dark Loch na Garr.

Years have rolled on, Loch na Garr, since I left you,
Years must elapse ere I tread you again:
Nature of verdure and flowers has bereft you,
Yet still are you dearer than Albion's plain.
England! thy beauties are tame and domestic
To one who has roved o'er the mountains afar:
Oh for the crags that are wild and majestic!
The steep frowning glories of dark Loch na Garr.

JOHN KEATS (1795–1821)

from A Song About Myself
(from a letter to Fanny Keats, 2 July 1818)

There was a naughty Boy,
And a naughty Boy was he,
He ran away to Scotland
The people for to see –
Then he found
That the ground
Was as hard,
That a yard
Was as long,
That a song
Was as merry,
That a cherry
Was as red –
That lead
Was as weighty,
That fourscore
Was as eighty,
That a door
Was as wooden
As in England –
So he stood in his shoes
And he wonder'd,
He stood in his
Shoes and he wonder'd.

HENRY SCOTT RIDDELL (1798–1870)

Scotia's Thistle

Scotia's thistle guards the grave,
Where repose her dauntless brave;
Never yet the foot of slave
    Has trod the wilds of Scotia.

Free from tyrant's dark control –
Free as waves of ocean roll –
Free as thoughts of minstrel's soul,
    Still roam the sons of Scotia.

Scotia's hills of hoary hue,
Heaven wraps in wreathes of blue,
Watering with its dearest dew
    The healthy locks of Scotia.

Down each green-wood skirted vale,
Guardian spirits, lingering, hail
Many a minstrel's melting tale,
    As told of ancient Scotia.

When the shades of eve invest
Nature's dew-bespangled breast,
How supremely man is blest
    In the glens of Scotia!

There no dark alarms convey
Aught to chase life's charms away;
There they live, and live for aye,
    Round the homes of Scotia.

Wake, my hill harp! wildly wake!
Sound by lee and lonely lake,
Never shall this heart forsake
    The bonnie wilds of Scotia.

Others o'er the oceans foam
Far to other lands may roam,
But for ever be my home
    Beneath the sky of Scotia!

Canadian Boat Song

Fair these broad meads – these hoary woods are grand;
But we are exiles from our fathers' land.

Listen to me, as when you heard our father
Sing long ago the song of other shores –
Listen to me, and then in chorus gather
All your deep voices, as ye pull your oars.

From the lone sheiling of the misty island
Mountains divide us, and the waste of seas –
Yet still the blood is strong, the heart is Highland,
And we in dreams behold the Hebrides.

We ne'er shall tread the fancy-haunted valley,
Where 'tween the dark hills creeps the small clear stream,
In arms around the patriarch banner rally,
Nor see the moon on royal tombstones gleam.

When the bold kindred, in the time long vanished,
Conquered the soil and fortified the keep, –
No seer foretold the children would be banished
That a degenerate lord might boast his sheep.

Come foreign rage – let discord burst in slaughter.
O then for clansmen true, and stern claymore –
The hearts that would have given their blood like water,
Beat heavily beyond the Atlantic roar.

JOHN IMLAH (1799–1846)

Farewell to Scotland

Loved land of my kindred, farewell – and forever!
    Oh! what can relief to the bosom impart;
When fated with each fond endearment to sever,
    And hope its sweet sunshine withholds from the heart!
Farewell, thou fair land! which, till life's pulse shall perish,
    Though doom'd to forego, I shall never forget;
Wherever I wander, for thee will I cherish
    The dearest regard and the deepest regret.

Farewell, ye great Grampians, cloud-robed and crested!
    Like your mists in the sunbeam ye melt in my sight;
Your peaks are the king-eagle's thrones – where have rested
    The snow-falls of ages – eternally white.
Ah! never gain shall the falls of your fountains
    Their wild murmur'd music awake on mine ear;
No more the lake's lustre that mirrors your mountains,
    I'll pore on with pleasure – deep, lonely, yet dear.

Yet – yet Caledonia! when slumber comes o'er me,
    Oh! oft will I dream of thee, far away;
But vain are the visions that rapture restore me,
    To waken and weep at the dawn of the day.
Ere gone the last glimpse, faint and far o'er the ocean,
    Where yet my heart dwells – where it ever shall dwell,
While tongue, sigh, and tear, speak my spirit's emotion,
    My country – my kindred – farewell, oh, farewell!

WILLIAM AIR FOSTER (1801–1864)

Fareweel to Scotia

Fareweel to ilka hill where the red heather grows,
To ilk bonnie green glen whaur the mountain stream rows,
To the rock that re-echoes the torrent's wild din,
To the graves o' my sires, and the hearths o' my kin.

Fareweel to ilk strath an' the lav'rock's sweet sang –
For trifles grow dear whan we've kenn'd them sae lang;
Round the wanderer's heart a bright halo they shed,
A dream o' the past when a' others ha'e fled.

The young hearts may kythe, though they're forced far away,
But its dool to the spirit when haffets are grey;
The saplin' transplanted may flourish a tree,
Whar the hardy auld aik wad but wither and dee.

They tell me I gang whaur the tropic suns shine
Owre landscapes as lovely and fragrant as thine;
For the objects sae dear that the heart had entwined
Turn eerisome hame-thoughts, and sicken the mind.

No, my spirit shall stray whaur the red heather grows!
In the bonnie green glen whaur the mountain stream rows,
'Neath the rock that re-echoes the torrent's wild din,
'Mang the graves o' my sires, and the hearths o' my kin.

HUGH MILLER (1802–1856)

Ode to My Mither Tongue

I loe the tones in mine ear that rung
In the days when care was unkind to me;
Ay, I loe thee weel, my mither tongue,
Though gloom the sons o' lear at thee.
Ev'n now, though little skilled to sing,
I've raxed me doun my simple lyre;
O, while I sweep ilk sounding string,
Nymph o' my mither tongue, inspire.

I loe thee weel, my mither tongue,
An' a' thy tales, or sad or wild;
Right early to my heart they clung,
Right soon my darkening thoughts beguiled –
Ay, aft to thy sangs o' a langsyne day,
That tell o' the bluidy fight sublime,
I've listened, till died the present away,
An' returned the deeds o' departed time.

An' gloom the sons o' lear at thee?
An' art thou reckoned poor an' mean?
Ah, could I tell as weel's I see,
Of a' thou art, an' a' thou'st been.
In thee has sung the enraptured bard
His triumphs over pain and care;
In courts and camps thy voice was heard –
Aft heard within the house o' prayer.

In thee, whan came proud England's might,
Wi' its steel to dismay and its gold to seduce,
Blazed the bright soul o' the Wallace wight,
And the patriot thoughts o' the noble Bruce.
Thine were the rousing strains that breathed
Frae the warrior bard ere closed the fray;
Thine, whan victory his temples wreathed,
The sang that arose oer the prostrate fae.

An' loftier still, the enraptured saint,
When the life o' time was glimmering awa',
Joyful o' heart, though feeble and faint,
Tauld in thee o' the glories he saw
O' the visions bright o' a coming life,
O' angels that joy oer the closing grave,
An' o' Him that bore turmoil an' strife,
The children o' death to succor and save.

An' aft, whan the bluid hounds tracked the heath,
Whan followed the bands o' the bluidy Dundee,
The sang o' praise, an' the prayer o' death,
Arose to Heaven in thee.
In thee, whan Heaven's ain sons were called
To sever ilk link o' the papal chain,
Thundered the ire o' that champion bauld
Whom threat'nins and dangers assailed in vain.

Ah, mither tongue, in days o' yore,
Fu' mony a noble bard was thine;
The clerk o' Dunkeld, and the coothy Dunbar,
An' the best o' the Stuart line;
An' him wha tauld o' Southron wrang
Cowed by the might o' Scottish men;
Him o' the Mount and the gleesome sang,
And him the pride o' the Hawthornden.

Of bards were thine in latter days
Sma need to tell, my mither tongue.
Right bauld and slee were Fergie's lays,
An' roared the laugh when Ramsay sung;
But wha without a tear can name
The swain this warl' shall ne'er forget?
Thine, mither tongue, his sangs o' fame,
'Twill learning be to ken thee yet.

HORATIUS BONAR (1808–1889)

The Martyrs of Scotland

There was gladness in Zion, her standard was flying,
Free o'er her battlements glorious and gay.
All fair as the morning shone forth her adorning,
And fearful to foes was her godly array.

There is mourning in Zion, her standard is lying
Defiled in the dust, to the spoiler a prey;
And now there is wailing, and sorrow prevailing,
For the best of her children are weeded away.

The good have been taken, their place is forsaken –
The man and the maiden, the green and the gray;
The voice of the weepers wails over the sleepers –
The martyrs of Scotland that now are away.

The hue of her waters is crimsoned with slaughters,
And the blood of the martyrs has reddened the clay;
And dark desolation broods over the nation,
For the faithful are perished, the good are away.

On the mountains of heather they slumber together.
On the wastes of the moorland their bodies decay.
How sound is their sleeping, how safe is their keeping,
Though far from their kindred they molder away.

Their blessing shall hover, their children to cover,
Like the cloud of the desert, by night and by day.
Oh, never to perish, their names let us cherish,
The martyrs of Scotland that now are away.

JOHN STUART BLACKIE (1809–1895)

Hail, Land of My Fathers!

Hail, land of my fathers! I stand on thy shore,
'Neath the broad-fronted bluffs of thy granite once more;
Old Scotland, my mother, the rugged, the bare,
That reared me with breath of the strong mountain air.
No more shall I roam where soft indolence lies
'Neath the cloudless repose of the featureless skies,
But where the white mist sweeps the red-furrowed scaur,
I will fight with the storm and grow strong by the war!

What boots all the blaze of the sky and the billow,
Where manhood must rot on inglorious pillow?
'Tis the blossom that blooms from the taint of the grave,
'Tis the glitter that gildeth the bonds of the slave.
But Scotland, stern mother, for struggle and toil
Thou trainest thy children on hard, rocky soil;
And thy stiff-purposed heroes go conquering forth,
With the strength that is bred by the blasts of the north.

Hail, Scotland, my mother! and welcome the day
When again I shall brush the bright dew from the brae,
And, light as a bird, give my foot to the heather,
My hand to my staff, and my face to the weather;
Then climb to the peak where the ptarmigan flies,
Or stand by the linn where the salmon will rise,
And vow never more with blind venture to roam
From the strong land that bore me – my own Scottish home.

ROBERT LEIGHTON (1822–1869)

from Scotch Words

They speak in riddles north beyond the Tweed.
The plain, pure English they can deftly read;
Yet when without the book they come to speak,
Their lingo seems half English and half Greek.

Their jaws are *chafts*; their hands, when closed, are *neives*;
Their bread's not cut in slices, but in *sheives*;
Their armpits are their *oxters*; palms are *luifs*;
Their men are *cheilds*; their timid fools are *cuiffs*;
Their lads are *callants*, and their women *kimmers*;
Good lasses *denty queans*, and bad ones *limmers*.
They *thole* when they endure, *scart* when they scratch;
And when they give a sample it's a *swatch*.
Scolding is *flytin'*, and a long palaver
Is nothing but a *blether* or a *haver*.
This room they call the *but*, and that the *ben*;
And what they do not know they *dinna ken*.
On keen cold days they say the *wind blaws snell*.
And when they wipe their nose they *dicht their byke*;
And they have words that Johnson could not spell,
As *umph'm*, which means – anything you like;
While some, though purely English, and well known,
Have yet a Scottish meaning of their own: –
To *prig*'s to plead, beat down a thing in cost;
To *coff*'s to purchase, and a cough's a *host*;
To *crack* is to converse; the *lift*'s the sky;
And *bairns* are said to *greet* when children cry.
When lost, folk never ask the way they want
They *speir the gate*; and when they yawn they *gaunt*.
Beetle with them is *clock*; a flame's a *lowe*;
Their straw is *strae*, chaff *cauff*, and hollow *howe*;
A *pickle* means a few; *muckle* is big,
And a piece of crockeryware is called a *pig*.

Speaking of pigs – when Lady Delacour
Was on her celebrated Scottish tour,
One night she made her quarters at the 'Crown',
The head inn of a well-known county town,
The chambermaid, on lighting her to bed,
Before withdrawing curtsied low, and said –
'This nicht is cauld, my leddy, wad ye please,
To hae a pig i' the bed to warm your taes?'
'A pig in bed to tease! What's that you say?
You are impertinent – away, away!'
'Me impudent! no, mem – I meant nae harm,
But just the greybeard pig to keep ye warm.'

★ ★ ★ ★ ★

On the return of Lady Delacour,
She wrote a book about her northern tour,
Wherein the facts are graphically told,
That Scottish gentlefolks, when nights are cold,
Take into bed fat pigs to keep them warm;
While common folk, who share their beds in halves –
Denied the richer comforts of the farm –
Can only warm their sheets with lean, cheap calves.

JOHN LIDDELL KELLY (1850–1926)

from The Heather and the Fern

From this isle in the wide Southern Ocean,
How oft does my swift fancy flee,
On pinions of love and devotion,
Dear home of my father, to thee!
In a land lapped in bright summer weather,
I sigh for one rugged and stern;
I long for the bloom of the Heather
In the Land of the Kauri and Fern.

Though here there is nought to remind me
Of the dark, misty land of my birth,
Not tears and not distance can blind me
To scenes that are dearest on earth.
As I list to the Tui's clear whistle,
I sigh – 'Shall I ever return
To the Land of the Heather and Thistle
From the Land of the Kauri and Fern?'

★ ★ ★ ★ ★

Though dear to my heart is Zealandia,
For the home of my boyhood I yearn;
I dream, amid sunshine and grandeur,
Of a land that is misty and stern;
From the land of the Moa and the Maori
My thoughts to old Scotia will turn;
Thus the Heather is blent with the Kauri
And the Thistle entwined with the Fern.

Blows the Wind Today

To S.R. Crockett

Blows the wind today, and the sun and the rain are flying.
  Blows the wind on the moors today and now,
Where about the graves of the martyrs the whaups are crying,
  My heart remembers how!

Grey recumbent tombs of the dead in desert places,
  Standing stones on the vacant wine-red moor,
Hills of sheep, and the homes of the silent vanished races,
  And winds, austere and pure:

Be it granted me to behold you again in dying,
  Hills of home! And to hear again the call;
Hear about the graves of the martyrs the peewees crying,
  And hear no more at all.

JOHN DAVIDSON (1857–1909)

from A Ballad in Blank Verse of the Making of a Poet

Greenock

His father's house looked out across a firth
Broad-bosomed like a mere, beside a town
Far in the North, where Time could take ease,
And Change hold holiday; where Old and New
Weltered upon the border of the world.

'Oh now,' he thought – a youth whose sultry eyes,
Bold brow and wanton mouth were not all lust,
But haunted from within and from without
By memories, visions, hopes, divine desires –

'Now may my life beat out upon this shore
A prouder music than the winds and waves
Can compass in their haughtiest moods. I need

No world more spacious than the region here:
The foam-embroidered firth, a purple path
For argosies that still on pinions speed,
Or fiery-hearted cleave with iron limbs
And bows precipitous the pliant sea;
The sloping shores that fringe the velvet tides
With heavy bullion and with golden lace
Of restless pebble woven and finely spun sand;
The villages that sleep the winter through,
And, wakening with the spring, keep festival
All summer and all autumn: this grey town
That pipes the morning up before the lark
With shrieking steam, and from a hundred stalks

Lacquers the sooty sky; where hammers clang
On iron hulls, and cranes in harbours creak,
Rattle and swing, whole cargoes on their necks;
Where men sweat gold that others hoard or spend,
And lurk like vermin in their narrow streets:
This old grey town, this firth, the further strand
Spangled with hamlets, and the wooded steeps,
Whose rocky tops behind each other press,
Fantastically carved like antique helms
High-hung in heaven's cloudy armoury,
Is world enough for me. Here daily dawn
Burns through the smoky east; with fire-shod feet
The sun treads heaven, and steps from hill to hill
Downward before the night that still pursues
His crimson wake; here winter plies his craft,
Soldering the years with ice; here spring appears,
Caught in a leafless brake, her garland torn,
Breathless with wonder, and the tears half-dried
Upon her rosy cheek; here summer comes
And wastes his passion like a prodigal
Right royally; and here her golden gains
Free-handed as a harlot's autumn spends;
And here are men to know, women to love...'

FRANCIS LAUDERDALE ADAMS (1862–1893)

William Wallace
(for the Ballarat statue of him)

This is Scotch William Wallace. It was he
Who in dark hours first raised his face to see:
Who watched the English tyrant nobles spurn,
Steel-clad, with iron hoofs the Scottish free:

Who armed and drilled the simple footman kern,
Yea, bade in blood and rout the proud knight learn
His feudalism was dead, and Scotland stand
Dauntless to wait the day of Bannockburn.

O Wallace, peerless lover of thy land
We need thee still, thy moulding brain and hand.
For us, thy poor, again proud tyrants spurn,
The robber rich, a yet more hateful band.

NEIL MUNRO (1864–1930)

'Hey, Jock, are ye glad ye 'listed?'

Hey, Jock, are ye glad ye 'listed?
   O Jock, but ye're far frae hame!
What d'ye think o' the fields o' Flanders?
   Jockey lad, are ye glad ye came?
Wet rigs we wrought in the land o' Lennox,
   When Hielan' hills were smeared wi' snaw;
Deer we chased through the seepin' heather,
   But the glaur o' Flanders dings them a'!

This is no' Fair o' Balloch,
   Sunday claes and a penny reel;
It's no' for dancin' at a bridal
   Willie Lawrie's bagpipes squeal.
Men are to kill in the morn's mornin';
   Here we're back to your daddy's trade;
Naething for't but to cock the bonnet,
   Buckle on graith and kiss the maid.

The Cornal's yonder deid in tartan,
   Sinclair's sheuched in Neuve Eglise;
Slipped awa wi' the sodger's fever,
   Kinder than ony auld man's disease.
Scotland! Scotland! little we're due ye',
Poor employ and skim-milk board.
But youth's a cream that maun be paid for,
   We got it reamin', so here's the sword!

Come awa, Jock, and cock your bonnet,
   Swing your kilt as best ye can;
Auld Dumbarton's Drums are dirlin',
   Come awa, Jock, and kill your man!
Far's the cry to Leven Water
   Where your fore-folks went to war,
They would swap wi' us to-morrow,
   Even in the Flanders glaur!

CHARLES MURRAY (1864–1941)

Hamewith

Hot youth ever is a ranger,
   New scenes ever its desire;
Cauld Eild, doubtfu' o' the stranger,
   Thinks but o' haudin' in the fire.

Midway, the wanderer is weary,
   Fain he'd be turnin' in his prime
Hamewith – the road that's never dreary,
   Back where his heart is a' the time.

bho Alba Saor

Cha nàimdheas do Shasann
A dhùisg mi gu ealaidh
No tnù ri cuid beairteas,
 A mòrachd 's a cliù,
Ach bhith sealltainn air Alba
'S i sìor dhol an ceannas
Gus an caill i mu dheireadh
 A toil gu bhith saor –
O èiribh, mo dhaoine,
Gu còmhstri 's chan aithreach,
A' chòmhstri nach fuilteach,
 Is sibhse mar aon
Gus am buidhinn an t-saorsa
Tha brath dol à sealladh
'Nur suain anns a' chadal
 Ás am mithich gun dùisg.

★ ★ ★ ★ ★

O Alba, mo dhùthaich
A dh 'àraich na gallain
Tha ainmeil an eachdraidh,
 Bha meanmnach gu spàirn,
A dh' fhàg dhuinn mar dhìleab
An t-saorsa ro bheannaicht' –
An dèan sinn an iomlaid
 Gu daors' chur na h-àit?
Ma chuirear gu dìochuimhn'
Leinn Brus agus Uallus
'S na fiùrain nach maireann
 A bhuidhinn ar gràdh,
Gun thoill sinn san uair sin
Ar sgiùrsadh 's ar feannadh,
'S gun iomradh oirnn tuille
 Uaith' seo gu là bhràth.

★ ★ ★ ★ ★

...Gidheadh, tha e soilleir
'S na bliadhnan dol tharainn
Alb' bhith ga cuingleachadh

Seach mar a bhà,
'S am Pàrlamaid Bhreatainn
Gur tearc is gur annamh
Na laghan a dhealbhar
    G'a feabhas 's gach ceàrn.

Gur mithich dhuinn èirigh
'S ar cùisean chur dìreach –
'S Alba an deis-làimh
    'S a daoine ga dìth,
Luchd ciùird 's tuath-cheatharn'
Ga fàgail 'nam mìltean,
A' Ghaidhealtachd gu sònraicht'
    Na fàsach 's na frìth;
Ar druim air a chromadh
Mheud 's a tha chìs oirnn
'S nach fhios leinn cuin idir
    A leagar iad sìos:
Mura comas an dìoladh
Do dhruideadh am prìosan
Aig maor agus siorram
    Gad fhòirneart gun sgìths.
Tha còmhlan nar dùthaich
Ag iarraidh le dùrachd
Gun tig Alba as ùr gu
    A Pàrlamaid fhèin,
'S an deagh ghean ri Sasann,
Gach rìoghachd gu aonaicht'
San Ìmpireachd allail...

★ ★ ★ ★ ★

from Scotland Free

No malice for England
Has aroused me to song
Nor any greed for her wealth,
    Her grandeur and fame,
But just by looking at Scotland
Bit by bit taken over
Till she loses at last
    Her desire to be free –

O rise up, my people,
To fight unrepentant,
Without shedding of blood,
   Together as one
Till you gain independence
That drops out of sight
While you stay in that sleep
   From which it's time to awake.

★ ★ ★ ★ ★

O Scotland, my country
Which nurtured the heroes
Who're famous in history,
   Courageous in combat,
Who bequeathed as their legacy
Freedom most blessed –
Will we make the exchange
   And put chains in its place?
If we let Bruce and Wallace
Slip out of our minds
With other past warriors
   Who've earned our affection,
We deserve when that happens
To be whipped, to be flayed,
And never remembered
   From here to eternity.

★ ★ ★ ★ ★

...However, it's clear
As the years roll on by
That Scotland's being strangled
   More than ever before,
It being rare and unusual
In the Parliament of Britain
For laws to be framed
   Entirely to her benefit.

It's time we arose
And put right our affairs –
Scotland's neglected
   And losing her people,
Craftsmen and labourers
Forsaking her in thousands,

The Highlands especially
    A desert and hunting-ground;
Our backs are so bent
With the burden of taxes
That we haven't a clue
    When they're going to be lowered:
If unable to pay them
You're thrown into prison
With bailiff and judge
    Harassing you tirelessly.

There's a group in our land
Who's earnestly seeking
For Scotland to have her own
    Parliament again,
Every country united
With goodwill to England
In the excellent Empire…

★ ★ ★ ★ ★

WILL H. OGILVIE (1869–1963)

The Scotch Fir

This is the tallest tree within my woods,
Lean, rugged-stemmed, and of all branches bare
Full thirty feet, with green plumes in the air
And roots among the bracken. All his moods
Are rough but kingly; whether, grand, he broods
Above his full-leaved comrades in the glare
Of summer, or in winter, still more fair,
Nods princely time to the wind's interludes.

Beauty may claim the beeches, elm and oak
Stir sentiment in England; but the fir
Stands here for Scotland and the bleak bare North.
Too tall to stoop to any servile yoke,
Too strong of heart to more than lightly stir
When the worst storm-winds of the world break forth.

RACHEL ANNAND TAYLOR (1876–1960)

The Princess of Scotland

'Who are you that so strangely woke,
      And raised a fine hand?'
Poverty wears a scarlet cloke
            In my land.

'Duchies of dreamland, emerald, rose
      Lie at your command?'
Poverty like a princess goes
            In my land.

'Wherefore the mask of silken lace
      Tied with a golden band?'
Poverty walks with wanton grace
            In my land.

'Why do you softly, richly speak
      Rhythm so sweetly-scanned?'
Poverty hath the Gaelic and Greek
            In my land.

'There's a far-off scent about you seems
      Born in Samarkand.'
Poverty hath luxurious dreams
            In my land.

'You have wounds that like passion-flowers you hide
      I cannot understand.'
Poverty hath one name with Pride
            In my land.

'Oh! Will you draw your last sad breath
      'Mid bitter bent and sand?'
Poverty begs from none but Death
            In my land.

JOHN MACDOUGALL HAY (1881–1919)

Celtic Melancholy

It is not in the sorrow of the deep,
For sunset's magic turns to pearls her tears;
Nor in old forests stiff with frost that sleep
Bowed with the legend of her ghostly years;
Nor in the sombre grandeur of the hills,
Whose snows have cold communion with the skies;
Not in the mourning of the moor with rain,
Or solemn mist that spills
Its weariness of silence: or the cries
Of great winds wandering through the glens in pain.

Thou hadst no knowledge of the market-place
And cities white and glad with statuary;
The hiving ports of a far-travelled race,
Idols in gold and jewelled sacristy;
Men hot with story from the ends o' earth,
Plaudits in theatres; an eager fleet
Taking the tide, bound for the goodly wars.
Such stuff of song and mirth
Was never thine amidst the sleet
And noise of black whales spouting to the stars.

Thine is the heritage of wandering men
Whose deeds are fragments passing like the stream;
They build the tower; they forge the shield; and then
Their labours vanish like a fragrant dream.
Wistful and dim with sad magnificence
Ye are the men destined to doom and death.
A purpose ye could never realise;
And stable recompense
Of victory was fleeting as a breath.
Only the face of death is kind and wise.

Ye are the men of perished hopes, of things
Most dear that now are ever lost – home, name,
And country – song of triumph never brings
Like requiem the meaning that's in fame.
Slogan ne'er stirred the heart to dare and die
As coronach loud wailing in the glen.

Ah! aye for you the best's beneath the sod;
Over the sea to Skye;
All's over; falls the night on broken men,
Culloden's sword with blood writes Ichabod.

ALEXANDER GRAY (1882–1968)

Scotland

Here in the uplands
The soil is ungrateful;
The fields, red with sorrel,
Are stony and bare.
A few trees, wind-twisted –
Or are they but bushes? –
Stand stubbornly guarding
A home here and there.

Scooped out like a saucer,
The land lies before me,
The waters, once scattered,
Flow orderly now
Through fields where the ghosts
Of the marsh and the moorland
Still ride the old marches,
Despising the plough.

The marsh and the moorland
Are not to be banished;
The bracken and the heather,
The glory of broom,
Usurp all the balks
And the field's broken fringes,
And claim from the sower
Their portion of the room.

This is my country,
The land that begat me.
These windy spaces are surely my own.
And those who here toil
In the sweat of their faces
Are the flesh of my flesh
And bone of my bone.

EDWIN MUIR (1887–1959)

Scotland 1941

We were a tribe, a family, a people.
Wallace and Bruce guard now a painted field,
And all may read the folio of our fable,
Pause the sword, the sceptre and the shield.
A simple sky roofed in that rustic day,
The busy corn-fields and the haunted holms,
The green road winding up the ferny brae.
But Knox and Melville clapped their preaching palms
And bundled all the harvesters away,
Hoodicrow Peden in the blighted corn
Hacked with his rusty beak the starving haulms.
Out of that desolation we were born.

Courage beyond the point and obdurate pride
Made us a nation, robbed us of a nation.
Defiance absolute and myriad-eyed
That could not pluck the palm plucked our damnation.
We with such courage and the bitter wit
To fell the ancient oak of loyalty,
And strip the peopled hill and the altar bare,
And crush the poet with an iron text,
How could we read our souls and learn to be?
Here a dull drove of faces harsh and vexed,
We watch our cities burning in their pit,
To salve our souls grinding dull lucre out,
We, fanatics of the frustrate and the half,
Who once set Purgatory Hill in doubt.
Now smoke and dearth and money everywhere,
Mean heirlooms of each fainter generation,
And mummied housegods in their musty niches,
Burns and Scott, sham bards of a sham nation,
And spiritual defeat wrapped warm in riches,
No pride but pride of pelf. Long since the young
Fought in great bloody battles to carve out
This towering pulpit of the Golden Calf,
Montrose, Mackail, Argyle, perverse and brave,
Twisted the stream, unhooped the ancestral hill.
Never had Dee or Don or Yarrow or Till
Huddled such thriftless honour in a grave.

Such wasted bravery idle as a song,
Such hard-won ill might prove Time's verdict wrong,
And melt to pity the annalist's iron tongue.

Scotland's Winter

Now the ice lays its smooth claws on the sill,
The sun looks from the hill
Helmed in his winter casket,
And sweeps his arctic sword across the sky.
The water at the mill
Sounds more hoarse and dull.
The miller's daughter walking by
With frozen fingers soldered to her basket
Seems to be knocking
Upon a hundred leagues of floor
With her light heels, and mocking
Percy and Douglas dead,
And Bruce on his burial bed,
Where he lies white as may
With wars and leprosy,
And all the kings before
This land was kingless,
And all the singers before
This land was songless,
This land that with its dead and living waits the Judgment Day.
But they, the powerless dead,
Listening can hear no more
Than a hard tapping on the sounding floor
A little overhead
Of common heels that do not know
Whence they come or where they go
And are content
With their poor frozen life and shallow banishment.

HUGH MACDIARMID (1892–1978)

from A Drunk Man Looks at the Thistle

'O wha's the bride?'

O lass, wha see'est me
As I daur hardly see,
I marvel that your bonny een
Are as they hadna seen.

Through a' my self-respect
They see the truth abject
    – Gin you could pierce their blindin' licht
    You'd see a fouler sicht!...

O wha's the bride that cairries the bunch
O' thistles blinterin' white?
Her cuckold bridegroom little dreids
What he sall ken this nicht.

For closer than gudeman can come
And close to'r than hersel',
Wha didna need her maidenheid
Has wrocht his purpose fell.

O wha's been here afore me, lass,
And hoo did he get in?
    – A man that deed or I was born
    This evil thing has din.

And left, as it were on a corpse,
Your maidenheid to me?
    – Nae lass, gudeman, sin' Time began
    'S hed ony mair to gi'e.

But I can gi'e ye kindness, lad,
And a pair o' willin hands,
And you sall ha'e my breists like stars,
My limbs like willow wands,

And on my lips ye'll heed nae mair,
And in my hair forget,
The seed o' a' the men that in
My virgin womb ha'e met...

The Little White Rose

To John Gawsworth

The rose of all the world is not for me.
I want for my part
Only the little white rose of Scotland
That smells sharp and sweet – and breaks the heart.

Scotland's Pride

Let us have no more talk of the service they gave,
Tell us no more as you have told us so long
That these were noble or clever or brave,
And deserve their place your great sons among;
Take a hundred years and let the facts decide.
Put all the conventional tributes aside,
And who's done aught for you, Scotland? Who's tried?

Have we fewer starving, fewer in want
In Scotland during the period in review?
Have we fewer slums despite all the cant,
Or thousands of homes yet that would make swine spew?
Is there less land under cultivation or more?
Aren't we worse off on every score?
Then what the Hell are they famous for?

All your nobility can be stroked off first,
Titles they may have – but none to respect.
No country in the world has ever been cursed
With such a gang of hyaenas as have somehow annexed
All your dukedoms and earldoms and historic estates,
No man of them heeds save in as much as he gets
Wealth to waste in London who would else starve on his wits.

Your divines come next. They may have served God,
But they have certainly rendered no service to man;
The prestige you give them is undoubtedly odd,
Since great though they be not even you can
Once they are dead say who the Devil they were,
But in ninety-nine cases in a hundred prefer
To forget them completely and in that do not err.

As for your politicians, not a man of them's been
Other than a servant of your deadliest foe.
Look round the whole country to-day and it's seen
Not one of them has aught to his credit to show.
Notable statesmen no doubt – but for whose good but their own?
Come, let any use they've accomplished be shown,
Your affairs all to rack and to ruin have gone.

You've had your usual supply of so-called great sons
In the period in question, but their filial regard
Wouldn't do credit, it seems, to a skunk's ones,
And if you still think that this verdict's too hard,
To problems a damned sight harder you're tied,
And the only men who have really tried
To solve them are a few on the rebel side,
Despised, rejected, hounded down and decried
By the fools on whom like a fool you've relied.

Scotland

It requires great love of it deeply to read
The configuration of a land,
Gradually grow conscious of fine shadings,
Of great meanings in slight symbols,
Hear at last the great voice that speaks softly,
See the swell and fall upon the flank
Of a statue carved out in a whole country's marble,
Be like Spring, like a hand in a window
Moving New and Old things carefully to and fro,
Moving a fraction of flower here,
Placing an inch of air there,
And without breaking anything.

So I have gathered unto myself
All the loose ends of Scotland,
And by naming them and accepting them,
Loving them and identifying myself with them,
Attempt to express the whole.

Scotland Small?

Scotland small? Our multiform, our infinite Scotland *small*?
Only as a patch of hillside may be a cliché corner
To a fool who cries 'Nothing but heather!' where in September another
Sitting there and resting and gazing round
Sees not only the heather but blaeberries
With bright green leaves and leaves already turned scarlet,
Hiding ripe blue berries; and amongst the sage-green leaves
Of the bog-myrtle the golden flowers of the tormentil shining;
And on the small bare places, where the little blackface sheep
Found grazing, milkworts blue as summer skies;
And down in neglected peat-hags, not worked
Within living memory, sphagnum moss in pastel shades
Of yellow, green, and pink; sundew and butterwort
Waiting with wide-open sticky leaves for their tiny winged prey;
And nodding harebells vying in their colour
With the blue butterflies that poise themselves delicately upon them,
And stunted rowans with harsh dry leaves of glorious colour.
'Nothing but heather!' – How marvellously descriptive! And incomplete!

A Vision of Scotland

I see my Scotland now, a puzzle
Passing the normal of her sex, going erect
Unscathed through fire, keeping her virtue
Where temptation works with violence, walking bravely,
Offering loyalty and demanding respect.

Every now and again in a girl like you,
Even in the streets of Glasgow or Dundee,
She throws her headsquare off and a mass
Of authentic flaxen hair is revealed,
Fine spun as newly-retted fibres
On a sunlit Irish bleaching field.

JOE CORRIE (1894–1968)

Scottish Pride

It's fine when ye stand in a queue
at the door o' the 'Dole'
on a snawy day,
To ken that ye leive in the bonniest
land in the world,
The bravest, tae.

It's fine when you're in a pickle
Whether or no'
you'll get your 'dough',
To sing a wee bit sang
o' the heather hills,
And the glens below.

It's fine when the clerk says,
'Nae "dole" here for you!'
To proodly turn,
and think o' the bluidy slashin'
the English got
at Bannockburn.

NAOMI MITCHISON (1897–1999)

The Scottish Renaissance in Glasgow: 1935

This city, builded on more hills than Rome was,
With a river bigger than Tiber, tidal and foamless,
I came to in the cold winter of a bad trade year,
I, Scottish too, with the same hunger for knowledge laden.
Somewhere in all this bareness, these squared, grey houses
Of harsh, unweathering stone, only ill-thoughts rousing,
Somewhere up grim stairs, steep streets of fog-greased cobbles,
In harsh, empty closes with only a dog or a child sobbing,
Somewhere among unrythmic, shattering noises of tram-ways
Or by crane and dock-yards, steel clanging and slamming,
Somewhere without colour, without beauty, without sunlight,
Amongst cautious people, some unhappy and some hungry,

There is a thing being born as it was born once in Florence:
So that a man, fearful, may find his mind fixed on tomorrow.
And tomorrow is strange for him, aye, full of tearings and breakings,
And to the very middle he feels his whole spirit shaken.
But he goes on.

WILLIAM SOUTAR (1898–1943)

Birthday

There were three men o' Scotland
Wha rade intill the nicht
Wi' nae müne lifted owre their crouns
Nor onie stern for licht:

Nane but the herryin' houlet,
The broun mouse, and the taed,
Kent whan their horses clapper'd by
And whatna road they rade.

Nae man spak to his brither,
Nor ruggit at the rein;
But drave straucht on owre burn and brae
Or half the nicht was gaen.

Nae man spak to his brither,
Nor lat his hand draw in;
But drave straucht on owre ford and fell
Or nicht was nearly düne.

There cam a flaucht o' levin
That brocht nae thunner ca'
But left ahint a lanely lowe
That wudna gang awa.

And richt afore the horsemen,
Whaur grumly nicht had been,
Stüde a' the Grampian Mountains
Wi' the dark howes atween.

Up craigie cleuch and corrie
They rade wi' stany soun',
And saftly thru the lichted mirk
The switherin' snaw cam doun.

They gaed by birk and rowan,
They gaed by pine and fir;
Aye on they gaed or nocht but snaw
And the roch whin was there.

Nae man brac'd back the bridle
Yet ilka fit stüde still
As thru the flickerin' floichan-drift
A beast cam doun the hill.

It steppit like a stallion,
Wha's heid hauds up a horn,
And weel the men o' Scotland kent
It was the unicorn.

It steppit like a stallion,
Snaw-white and siller-bricht,
And on its back there was a bairn
Wha low'd in his ain licht.

And baith gaed by richt glegly
As day was at the daw;
And glisterin' owre hicht and howe
They saftly smool'd awa.

Nae man but socht his brither
And look't him in the e'en,
And sware that he wud gang a' gates
To cry what he had seen.

There were three men o' Scotland
A' frazit and forforn;
But on the Grampian Mountains
They saw the unicorn.

Scotland

Atween the world o licht
And the world that is to be
A man wi unco sicht
Sees whaur he canna see:

Gangs whaur he canna walk:
Recks whaur he canna read:
Hauds what he canna tak:
Melts wi the unborn deid.

Atween the world o licht
And the world that is to be
A man wi unco sicht
Monie a saul maun see:

Sauls that are sterk an nesh:
Sauls that wud dree the day:
Sauls that are fain for flesh
But canna win the wey.

Hae ye the unco sicht
That sees atween an atween
This world that lowes in licht:
Yon world that hasna been?

It is owre late for fear,
Owre early for disclaim;
Whan ye come hameless here
And ken ye are at hame.

ADAM DRINAN (1903–1984)

Successful Scot

Gold pins and pearls of Columbia,
   how gross they grow by your drive,
studding an English summer
   with the back-end of your life,
     beknighted and pompous Scot!

By adding figure to figure
   you have developed never,
you have just grown bigger and bigger
   like this wee wort from the heather;
     and size is all you have got.

Your mind set towards London,
   your belly pushing you to success,
from the very day that you won
   the Bursary of the West,
     have flagged and faltered not.

Not much has your face altered!
   The man has the mouth of the child.
The Position you planted and watered
   expands from the lad's desires
     as if bound in a pot.

And would you return (for the fishing)
   to your island of humbler hours,
there in your tailored wishes
   you would trample your youth in this flower
     that you have forgotten:

Or spending a stay-at-home summer,
   you will never know what they suffer,
these bloated flowers of Columbia;
   you will own the youth of others,
     and never know what.

The Scots Greys Ride

The Scots Greys ride
Sabres by their side

Cut the mannie's ear aff!
Na jist cut it near aff!

Lea a wee bit o his lug
An next time we'll ken the dog

KATHLEEN RAINE (1908–2003)

The Ancient Speech

from Eileann Chanaidh, Isle of Canna, Inner Hebrides

A Gaelic bard they praise who in fourteen adjectives
Named the one indivisible soul of his glen;
For what are the bens and the glens but manifold qualities,
Immeasurable complexities of soul?
What are these isles but a song sung by island voices?
The herdsman sings ancestral memories
And the song makes the singer wise,
But only while he sings
Songs that were old when the old themselves were young,
Songs of these hills only, and of no isles but these.
For other hills and isles this language has no words.

The mountains are like manna, for one day given,
To each his own:
Strangers have crossed the sound, but not the sound of the dark oarsmen
Or the golden-haired sons of kings,
Strangers whose thought is not formed to the cadence of waves,
Rhythm of the sickle, oar and milking pail,
Whose words make loved things strange and small,
Emptied of all that made them heart-felt or bright.
Our words keep no faith with the soul of the world.

GEORGE BRUCE (1909–2002)

A Song for Scotland

A skull shoots sea-green grass from its sockets.
I saw it as the wave lengthened and flattened.
Moon whitened the cranium, plied its beams upon
The shooting sea green hair.

> You tell me not to stare
> So in upon myself
> Nor throw the arc-light
> Of the mind.

> But here my songs begin
> Here their first thin irregular,
> (Like the waver of the wind)
> Yet sometimes taut, music.

The oar rots on the beach.
The skua breeds on the cliff.

> A song for Scotland this,
> For the people
> Of the clearances,
> For the dead tenements,
> For the dead herring
> On the living water.
> A song for Scotland this.

ROBERT GARIOCH (1909–1981)

Scottish Scene

They're a gey antithetical folk are the Scots,
jurmummelt thegither like unctioneer's lots
or a slap-happy family of bickeran brats;
the scrauch of their squabbles wad gie ye the bats.
Twa cock-blackies wad blush fir shame
to be that ill neibors as onie of thaim –
of *thaim*: the glib third-person tells

on me anaa; whit I mean is *ourals*.
Wha's like us? Here's the answer pat:
no monie, and muckle braw thanks fir that.
And wha's gaen about like me or like you?
Ye ken the solution yirsel: gey few!
And if I'm in the richt, as I ken I sall be,
the lave are aa wrang, I think ye'll agree;
supposing ye dinnae, I'll curse and I'll ban,
and I'll cry on Jehovah to lend me a haun
to learn ye and yir upstairt gang
that I'm in the richt and ye're in the wrang.
Jehovah and I are gey faur ben
sen I chose to be yin of his chosen men.
And I dinnae fecht fir masel, forbye;
we fecht fir Scotland, Jehovah and I,
fir we ken faur better whit Scotland needs
nor onie of Scotland's lesser breeds,
owre thrawn, owre thick in the heid, or the pelt,
to listen to me and dae as they're tellt,
owre donnart, even, and owre obtuse
to curl up under my clever abuse.
Duty is duty, but it's nae joke
to sort thae curst antithetical folk.

NORMAN MACCAIG (1910–1996)

Celtic Cross

The implicated generations made
This symbol of their lives, a stone made light
By what is carved on it.
                              The plaiting masks,
But not with involutions of a shade,
What a stone says and what a stone cross asks.
Something that is not mirrored by nor trapped
In webs of water or bag-nets of cloud;
The tangled mesh of weed
                              lets it go by.
Only men's minds could ever have unmapped
Into abstraction such a territory.
No green bay going yellow over sand

Is written on by winds to tell a tale
Of death-dishevelled gull
                                    or heron, stiff
As a cruel clerk with gaunt writs in his hand
– Or even of light, that makes its depths a cliff.
Singing responses order otherwise.
The tangled generations ravelled out
In links of song whose sweet
                                    strong choruses
Are those stone involutions to the eyes
Given to the ear in abstract vocables.
The stone remains, and the cross, to let us know
Their unjust, hard demands, as symbols do.
But on them twine and grow
                                    beneath the dove
Serpents of wisdom whose cool statements show
Such understanding that it seems like love.

Patriot

My only country
is six feet high
and whether I love it or not
I'll die
for its independence.

from A Man in Assynt

Glaciers, grinding West, gouged out
these valleys, rasping the brown sandstone,
and left, on the hard rock below – the
ruffled foreland –
this frieze of mountains filed
on the blue air – Stac Polly,
Cul Beag, Cul Mor, Suilven,
Canisp – a frieze and
a litany.

Who owns this landscape?
Has owning anything to do with love?
For it and I have a love-affair, so nearly human
we even have quarrels. –
When I intrude too confidently
it rebuffs me with a wind like a hand
or puts in my way
a quaking bog or a loch
where no loch should be. Or I turn stonily
away, refusing to notice
the rouged rocks, the mascara
under a dripping ledge, even
the tossed, the stony limbs waiting.

I can't pretend
it gets sick for me in my absence,
though I get
sick for it. Yet I love it
with special gratitude, since
it sends no letters, is never
jealous and, expecting nothing
from me, gets nothing but
cigarette packets and footprints.

Who owns this landscape? –
The millionaire who bought it or
the poacher staggering downhill in the early morning
with a deer on his back?

Who possesses this landscape? –
The man who bought it or
I who am possessed by it?

False question, for
this landscape is
masterless
and intractable in any terms
that are human...

Characteristics

My American friends,
who claim Scottish ancestry,
have been touring Scotland.
In ten days they visited
eleven castles. I smiled –
How American.

They said they preferred
the ruined ones. I smiled again.
How Scottish.

SOMHAIRLE MACGILL-EAIN / SORLEY MACLEAN
(1911–1996)

Am Boilseabhach

'S mi 'm Bhoilseabhach nach tug suim
riamh do bhànrainn no do righ,
nan robh againn Alba shaor,
Alba co-shìnte ri ar gaol,
Alba gheal bheadarrach fhaoil,
Alba gheal shona laoch;
gun bhùirdeasachd bhig chrìon bhaoith,
gun sgreamhalachd luchd na maoin',
's gun chealgaireachd oillteil chlaoin,
Alba aigeannach nan saor,
Alba 'r fala, Alba 'r gaoil,
bhristinn lagh dligheach nan righ,
bhristinn lagh cinnteach shaoi,
dh' èighinn 'nad bhànrainn Albann thu
neo-ar-thaing na Poblachd ùir.

The Bolshevik

A Bolshevik who never gave heed
to queen or to king,
if we had Scotland free,
Scotland equal to our love,

a white spirited generous Scotland,
a beautiful happy heroic Scotland,
without petty paltry foolish bourgeoisie,
without the loathsomeness of capitalists,
without hateful crass graft;
the mettlesome Scotland of the free,
the Scotland of our blood, the Scotland of our love,
I would break the legitimate law of kings,
I would break the sure law of the wise,
I would proclaim you queen of Scotland
in spite of the new republic.

Hallaig

'Tha tìm, am fiadh, an coille Hallaig'

Tha bùird is tàirnean air an uinneig
troimh 'm faca mi an Àird an Iar
's tha mo ghaol aig Allt Hallaig
na craoibh bheithe, 's bha i riamh

eadar an t-Inbhir 's Poll a' Bhainne,
thall 's a bhos mu Bhaile-Chùirn:
tha i na beithe, na calltuinn,
na caorann dhìreach sheang ùir.

Ann an Screapadal mo chinnidh,
far robh Tarmad 's Eachann Mòr,
tha 'n nigheanan 's am mic nan coille
a' gabhail suas ri taobh an lòin.

Uaibhreach a-nochd na coilich ghiuthais
a' gairm air mullach Cnoc an Rà,
dìreach an druim ris a' ghealaich –
chan iadsan coille mo ghràidh.

Fuirichidh mi ris a' bheithe
gus an tig i mach an Càrn,
gus am bi am bearradh uile
o Bheinn na Lice fa sgàil.

Mura tig 's ann theàrnas mi a Hallaig
a dh' ionnsaigh sàbaid nam marbh,
far a bheil an sluagh a' tathaich,
gach aon ghinealach a dh' fhalbh.

Tha iad fhathast ann a Hallaig,
Clann Ghill-Eain's Clann MhicLeòid,
na bh' ann ri linn Mhic Ghille-Chaluim:
chunnacas na mairbh beò.

Na fir nan laighe air an lianaig
aig ceann gach taighe a bh' ann,
na h-igheanan nan coille bheithe,
dìreach an druim, crom an ceann.

Eadar an Leac is na Feàrnaibh
tha 'n rathad mòr fo chòinnich chiùin,
's na h-igheanan nam badan sàmhach
a' dol a Chlachan mar o thùs.

Agus a' tilleadh às a' Chlachan,
à Suidhisnis 's à tìr nam beò;
a chuile tè òg uallach
gun bhristeadh cridhe an sgeòil.

O Allt na Feàrnaibh gus an fhaoilinn
tha soilleir an dìomhaireachd nam beann
chan eil ach coimhthional nan nighean
a' cumail na coiseachd gun cheann.

A' tilleadh a Hallaig anns an fheasgar,
anns a' chamhanaich bhalbh bheò,
a' lìonadh nan leathadan casa,
an gàireachdaich nam chluais na ceò,

's am bòidhche na sgleò air mo chridhe
mun tig an ciaradh air na caoil,
's nuair theàrnas grian air cùl Dhùn Cana
thig peileir dian à gunna Ghaoil;

's buailear am fiadh a tha na thuaineal
a' snòtach nan làraichean feòir;
thig reothadh air a shùil sa choille:
chan flaighear lorg air fhuil ri m' bheò.

Hallaig

'Time, the deer, is in the wood of Hallaig'

The window is nailed and boarded
through which I saw the West
and my love is at the Burn of Hallaig,
a birch tree, and she has always been

between Inver and Milk Hollow,
here and there about Baile-chuirn:
she is a birch, a hazel,
a straight, slender young rowan.

In Screapadal of my people
where Norman and Big Hector were,
their daughters and their sons are a wood
going up beside the stream.

Proud tonight the pine cocks
crowing on the top of Cnoc an Ra,
straight their backs in the moonlight –
they are not the wood I love.

I will wait for the birch wood
until it comes up by the cairn,
until the whole ridge from Beinn na Lice
will be under its shade.

If it does not, I will go down to Hallaig,
to the Sabbath of the dead,
where the people are frequenting,
every single generation gone.

They are still in Hallaig,
MacLeans and MacLeods,
all who were there in the time of Mac Gille Chaluim
the dead have been seen alive.

The men lying on the green
at the end of every house that was,
the girls a wood of birches,
straight their backs, bent their heads.

Between the Leac and Fearns
the road is under mild moss
and the girls in silent bands
go to Clachan as in the beginning,

and return from Clachan
from Suisnish and the land of the living;
each one young and light-stepping,
without the heartbreak of the tale.

From the Burn of Fearns to the raised beach
that is clear in the mystery of the hills,
there is only the congregation of the girls
keeping up the endless walk,

coming back to Hallaig in the evening,
in the dumb living twilight,
filling the steep slopes,
their laughter a mist in my ears,

and their beauty a film on my heart
before the dimness comes on the kyles,
and when the sun goes down behind Dun Cana
a vehement bullet will come from the gun of Love;

and will strike the deer that goes dizzily,
sniffing at the grass-grown ruined homes;
his eye will freeze in the wood,
his blood will not be traced while I live.

SIR ALEC CAIRNCROSS (1911–1996)

Covenanting Country

In this wide moorland fringed with dirty haze
Voices fall quivering on the windless air;
The lazy seagulls trace a circling maze,
And pompous crows glean what the reapers spare.
Here the hot sky is empty of all rancour;
The quiet rivers wash away pretence.
Is this deep-rooted land a natural anchor

To peaceful living and secure good sense?
This is the home of ancient persecution,
Ungovernable wills, the spirit of denial,
Fanaticism. Men went to execution
'As to a marriage', mocking at their trial.
And we, who purpose with a calmer mind –
Can we be as implacable, less blind?

RUTHVEN TODD (1914–1978)

About Scotland, & C.

I was my own ghost that walked among the hills,
Strolled easily among the ruined stones of history;
The student of geography, concerned with fells
And screes rather than with the subtle mystery
Of action's causes – the quickly overbalanced rock
Upon the passing victim, the stab in the back.

Why did this burn run that way to the sea,
Digging a cutting through stone, moss and peat,
And so become an ingredient of whisky?
Why was this glen the cause of a defeat,
The silver bullet in the young man's lung,
The devil's puppet and hero of a song?

That queen herself was lorded by the weather,
And Knox drew sustenance from poverty,
The sharp east wind, the sickle in the heather.
The reiver was cornered in the sudden sortie
Of armoured men lying hidden in the bracken,
And a royal line was by sea-storm broken.

This way the landscape formed the people,
Controlled their deeds with cairn and gully;
And no pretender or well-favoured noble
Had power like dammed loch or empty valley.
Their history's origins lie in rock and haze
And the hero seems shorter than his winter days.

This my ghost saw from the deserted keep
And the left paper-mill forgotten in the slums,
This he saw south among the soft-fleshed sheep
And north-west where the Atlantic drums.
Then, since he'd made no claim to be an apostle,
He left, his trophy a neglected fossil.

G.S. FRASER (1915–1980)

Meditation of a Patriot

The posters show my country blonde and green,
Like some sweet siren, but the travellers know
How dull the shale sky is, the airs how keen,
And how our boorish manners freeze like snow.
Romantic Scotland was an emigrant,
Half-blooded, and escaped from sullen weather.
Here, we toss off a dram to drown a cough
And whisky has the trade-mark of the heather.
My heart yearns southwards as the shadows slant,
I wish I were an exile and I rave:
      With Byron and with Lermontov –
      Romantic Scotland's in the grave.

In Glasgow, that damned sprawling evil town,
I interview a vulgar editor,
Who, brawny, self-made, looks me up and down
And seems to wonder what my sort is for.
Do I write verse? Ah, man, but that is bad...
And, too polite, I fawn upon this tough,
But when I leave him, O my heart is sad.
He sings alone who in this province sings.
I kick a lamp-post, and in drink I rave:
      With Byron and with Lermontov
      Romantic Scotland's in the grave.

In the far islands to the north and west
Mackenzie and MacDiarmid have their peace.
St Andrews soothes that critic at her breast
Whose polished verse ne'er gave his soul release.
I have no islands and no ancient stone,
Only the sugary granite glittering crisp
Pleases the eye, but turns affection off,
Hard rhetoric, that never learned to lisp.
This town has beauty, but I walk alone
And to the flat and sallow sands I rave:
      With Byron and with Lermontov
      Romantic Scotland's in the grave.

DEÒRSA MAC IAIN DEÒRSA / GEORGE CAMPBELL HAY
(1915–1984)

Fhearaibh 's a Mhnài na h-Albann

Fhearaibh 's a mhnài na h-Albann,
stoc gailbheach mo ghràidh,
sluagh nach gabh saltairt
is nach saltair air muin chàich;
a chridheachan nach marbha,
guma fairge sibh nach tràigh
am bailtean 's glinn na h-Albann,
air a garbh chnuic 's a blàir.
      Fearann mo shinnsre Alba,
      clann Albann mo dhàimh,
      m'fheòil is sùgh mo chridhe sibh,
      mo mhisneach 's mo dheas làmh.

Seann dùthaich ghorm nam bidein,
is i thug bith dhuinn 's a thug brìgh;
is garbh, is geanail, coibhneal i,
's i toinnte 's gach aon dhinn;
air a' mhachair, air na monaidhean
dheoghail sinn a cìoch;
mas Goill, a ghaoil, mas Gaidheil sinn,
dh'àraich ise sinn.
      Fearann mo shinnsre Alba,
      clann Albann nach strìochd,
      mo bhiadh, mo dheoch is m'anail sibh –
      chan fhaic mi sibhse sìos.

Men and Women of Scotland

*Men and women of Scotland, / tempestuous race that I love, / people who are
not to be trampled on, / and who will not trample on the necks of others; / oh,
hearts that are not dull and dead, / may you be a sea that will never ebb / in the
towns and glens of Scotland, / on her rough knowes and her plains. /
Land of my forebears, Scotland, / children of Scotland, my kin, / you are my
flesh and the sap of my heart, / my courage and my right hand. //
The old blue land of the mountain pinnacles, / it is she that has given us being
and pith; / she is rough, she is cheerful and kindly, / she is interwoven in every
one of us; / on plain and on upland / we have suckled at her breast; be we
Lowland, my dear, or Gaels, / it was she that nurtured us. /
Land of my forebears, Scotland, / children of Scotland that will not yield, / my
food, my drink and my breath are you − / I will not see you brought low.*

Scotland

The white licht wellan up frae springs
            yont Asia, pales the gowd o the starns
tae a wae siller, syne consumed
            i the kendlet crucible o the East,
an ilk limestane lirk o bare Hymettus
            purples, crimsons then gowden burns,
as the new sun, kythan, glisters alang
            green waters ablow a rocky coast.

They starns that dwine frae East tae West,
            an swarf in the surgean Aegean glory,
wane abune flindert craigs − a waste
            o cairns an soopit stanes, mair weary,
mair yeld than Knoydart's heidlang coast,
            or Rannoch, lang an braid an oorie.

Sae whan the sun wasters ayont
            Aegina, an, doongaun, drains the flush
frae heich upland, heidland, island
            an the nicht owre aa things cups her hands,
ye that whan young ran on bare rocks
            an leuch tae watch green watter flash
alang a heidlang Scottish shore −
            coont ye this ane o the fremmit lands?

Bonny an kent afore elsewhere;
  new an acquent, steep, prood, sea-graven,
bare, hard, bonny, tautfeatured land,
  clear, sherp, hertsome – a land for livan.

Bare, hard, bonny – its wunds blaw clean
  across clear ridges aff the sea;
nae shoggan an flaffan o fullyerie,
  o reeshlan reeds an hedges here,
nae watter-reek o laich loanins
  tae dull the thrust o thocht an ee, .
nae braid pleuch acres o seichin brairds,
  nae plains unendan rowed in haar.

Bricht an hard – a maze sea-fretted;
  kyle an skerry, stack an strand.
Bricht an hard – a maze steep-snedded;
  scree an scaurnoch, strath an glen.
Bricht an hard – wi rocky heidlands
  derk atween lines o bleezin sand,
wi naethin boss in't, mauchy nor mauchless
  heavy nor dozent – a land for men.
A wee land, bricht an hard, whase fowk
  soared tae man's heichmaist aince, lang syne.
Still snawhite, kythan far frae land,
  their temples vaunt it as they crine.

Oor ain land wi its bitter blufferts,
  its flauchts o licht, its frosty starns,
flashes an rairs its strengthenan challence.
  What triumphs will answer frae its bairns?

Scotland

*The white light, welling up from springs beyond Asia, pales the gold of the stars
/ to a wan silver, soon consumed in the kindled crucible of the East, / and every
limestone ridge of bare Hymettus purples, crimsons, and then burns /
golden, as
the new sun, emerging, glitters along green water below a rocky coast. //
These stars that fade from east to west, and disappear in the surging Aegean
glory, / fade above splintered crags, a waste of cairns and swept stones, more
weary, / more barren than Knoydart's headlong coast, or Rannoch, long and
broad and gloomy. //*

*So when the sun goes west beyond Aegina, and, going down, drains the flush /
from high upland, headland, island, and the night cups her hands / over every-
thing, you, who when young, ran on bare rocks and laughed to watch green water
flash / along a headlong Scottish shore – do you count this one of the distant
lands? //*

*Bonny, and known before elsewhere, new and familiar, steep, proud, sea-graven,
/ bare, hard, bonny, taut-featured land, clear, sharp, heartsome – a land for
living. //*

*Bare, hard, bonny – its winds blow clean across clear ridges from the sea, / no
shaking and fluttering of foliage, of rustling reeds and hedges here, / no bog-reek
of low pastures to dull the thrust of thought and eye, / no broad ploughed acres of
sighing grain, no unending plains swathed in mist. //*

*Bright and hard – a maze sea-fretted, kyle and skerry, stack and strand. /
Bright and hard – a maze steeply cut, scree and rockfall, strath and glen. /
Bright and hard – with rocky headlands / dark between lines of blazing sand, /
with nothing waste, dirty or feeble in it, / heavy or dull, a land for men. / A
wee land, bright and hard, whose folk / soared to man's highest point once long
ago; / still snow-white, showing far from land, their temples boast of it as they
decline. //*

*Our own land with its bitter blasts, / its show of lights, its frosty stars, flashes
and roars its strengthening challenge – / what triumphs will answer from its
children?*

SYDNEY GOODSIR SMITH (1915–1975)

Epistle to John Guthrie

We've come intil a gey queer time
Whan scrievin Scots is near a crime,
'There's no one speaks like that,' they fleer,
– But wha the deil spoke like King Lear?

And onyways doon Canongate
I'll tak ye slorpin pints till late,
Ye'll hear Scots there as raff and slee –
It's no the point, sae that'll dae.

Ye'll fin the leid, praps no the fowth,
The words 're there, praps no the ferlie;
For he wha'ld rant wi Rabbie's mouth
Maun leave his play-pen unco erlie.

Nane cud talk lik Gawen Douglas writes,
He hanna the vocablerie,
Nor cud he flyte as Dunbar flytes –
Yir argy-bargy's tapsalteerie!

Did Johnnie Keats when he was drouth
Ask 'A beaker full o the warm South'?
Fegs no, he leaned across the bar
An called for 'A point o bitter, Ma!'

But the Suddron's noo a sick man's leid,
Along the flattest plains it stots;
Tae reach the hills his fantice needs
This bard maun tak the wings o Scots.

And so, dear John, ye just maun dree
My Scots; for English, man, 's near deid,
See the weeshy-washy London bree
An tell me then whaes bluid is reid!

But mind, nae poet eer writes 'common speech',
Ye'll fin eneuch o yon in prose;
His realm is heich abune its reach –
Jeez! wha'ld use ale for Athol Brose?

W.S. GRAHAM (1918–1986)

A Page About My Country

1

Quhen Alexander the king was deid
That Scotland haid to steyr and leid,
The land vj zer, and mayr perfay,
Lay desolat eftyr hys day.

And that is John Barbour making
The Bruce. Dunbar came later, A'
Enermit else as the language
Changed itself from beast to beast.

2

Where am I going to speak tonight
And in what accents? Apprentice me
To Scotland I said under the hammer
Headed crane of Harland and Wolfe
Who were very good to my father keeping
Him on. We did not need to go
Down for the Lyndoch Street soup
I mean no harm. Our bellies were common.
Dad, are we going to the Big Dam?

Curlew. The curlew cries flying
Crookedly over lonely Loch Thom.

3

Quhen I came headlong out to see
The light at the top of the land
At One Hope Street spitting the hairs
Of my mother out, to tell you the truth
I didn't know what to do. The time
Was five o'clock the bright nineteenth
Of November nineteen-eighteen.
The time is any time to tell
Whoever you are the truth. I still
Don't know what to do. Scotland?

4

A word meaning an area and
I like to see it flat pressed
By Mercator on my writing table.

Look I am looking at my sweet
Country enough to break my heart.

5

MacDiarmid's deid under a mound
O literature making no sound.

And Mars is braw in crammasy.

In Scotland Now

The last sour petrol-puff of dust has settled,
whitening the moorland road; a westering sun
silvers beneath green leaves; the yellow-petalled
iris sends lustre signals; rabbits run
with a soft flurry of sand, and prick their ears
in feigned stone-stillness, hearing the faint sound
of menace tracking through their timid years;
and a lone curlew whushers from the ground,
wheeling aloft as if it had been spun.

It startles old ghosts up from history –
Fingal advancing with his cloudy host
over the moors, his mountain mystery
towering the years since Ossian's blind toast
rang through the halls of Selma: Tearlach's ranks
broken like bracken, dead crushed down on dead,
the wounded herded in deserted fanks
to wait cold English steel; the Cause unsaid,
the Gaels' last gallant battle greatly lost!

Familiar things that keep old soldiers talking –
Hidallan's lust against young Fingal's bride:
how the old Fingal set his warriors stalking
Diarmid warm with Graunia at his side:
the talk of loot, the talk of strategy
that animated those whom Wallace led;
old women's voices hushed in tragedy,
conning the dire anatomy of dread,
uncertain when to flee or where to hide.

Knox with his rant of words forever hacking
the ancient roots of Scottish liberty;
those bleak, psalm-laden men whose souls in racking
cracked our quick joy and spilled our charity;
those gracious, gallant cellar-lords who sold
the birthright of our freedom for a bribe;
the men of smoke and steam whose lust for gold
reared slums to hide their damned, deluded tribe,
tamed by the cancerous ache of poverty.

Cold, emptied passions; scraps of stranded chatter,
worn flotsam of once ardent human pride –
what can it mean to us, or even matter
now that Time's restless and resistless tide
has rubbed away those creeds by which they stood,
altered mind's climate, tempered the heart's mood,
till most that once seemed honourably good
now lies dissected and discredited
with scarce a single gesture undenied?

So, sensing these heraldic figures tracing,
retracing their old steps, like folk turned blind,
I wonder if we met them suddenly, facing us
as man to man, could we together find
thoughts we'd all understand? Some common sign
to prove our kindred blood, each in his day
one living segment of an endless line?
Or should we learn that there no longer lay
a common frontier to a racial mind?

If words were all that mattered, we'd be staring
mutely across cold agonies of space;
for word was never made that could be tearing
those mists that blur each vague, receding face.
And there's no ultimate tongue to strip the deed
of its accomplishment, reveal that ripped despair,
those running threads of doubt, which there was need
to bind up into action, then and there,
so long ago, in each relentless place.

But they'd all recognize the spring of heather,
the curlew chantering up his changeless fears,
those wet sea-winds that modulate our weather,
sheep nibbling through contented, grassy years.
So sight and sound and touch still intersect
to keep our grim half-legendary land
a place of warm belonging and protect
our brittle senses with a friendly hand
from plunging dreams of dusty, sterile spheres.

Speaking of Scotland

What do you mean when you speak of Scotland?
The grey defeats that are dead and gone
behind the legends each generation
savours fresh, yet can't live on?

Lowland farms with their broad acres
peopling crops? The colder earth
of the North East? Or Highland mountains
shouldering up their rocky dearth?

Inheritance of guilt that our country
has never stood where we feel she should?
A nagging threat of unfinished struggle
somehow forever lost in the blood?

Scotland's a sense of change, an endless
becoming for which there was never a kind
of wholeness or ultimate category.
Scotland's an attitude of mind.

HAMISH HENDERSON (1919–2002)

The Freedom Come-All-Ye

Roch the wind in the clear day's dawin
    Blaws the cloods heelster-gowdie ow'r the bay,
But there's mair nor a roch wind blawin
    Through the great glen o' the warld the day.
It's a thocht that will gar oor rottans
    – A' they rogues that gang gallus, fresh and gay –
Tak the road, and seek ither loanins
    For their ill ploys, tae sport and play.

Nae mair will the bonnie callants
 Mairch tae war when oor braggarts crousely craw,
Nor wee weans frae pit-heid and clachan
 Mourn the ships sailin' doon the broomielaw.
Broken faimlies in lands we've herriet,
 Will curse Scotland the Brave nae mair, nae mair;
Black and white, ane til ithir mairriet,
 Mak the vile barracks o' their maisters bare.

So come all ye at hame wi' Freedom,
 Never heed whit the hoodies croak for doom.
In your hoose a' the bairns o' Adam
 Can find breid, barley-bree and painted room.
When MacLean meets wi's freens in Springburn
 A' the roses and geans will turn tae bloom,
And a black boy frae yont Nyanga
 Dings the fell gallows o' the burghers doon.

EDWIN MORGAN (1920–)

Canedolia
An Off-concrete Scotch Fantasia

Oa! hoy! awe! ba! mey!

who saw?
rhu saw rum. garve saw smoo. nigg saw tain. lairg saw lagg.
rigg saw eigg. largs saw haggs. tongue saw luss. mull saw yell.
stoer saw strone. drem saw muck. gask saw noss. unst saw cults.
echt saw banff. weem saw wick. trool saw twatt.

how far?
from largo to lunga from joppa to skibo from ratho to shona
from ulva to minto from tinto to tolsta from soutra to marsco
from braco to barra from alva to stobo from fogo to fada from
gigha to gogo from kelso to stroma from hirta to spango.

what is it like there?
och it's freuchie, it's faifley, it's wamphray, it's frandy, it's
sliddery.

what do you do?
we foindle and fungle, we bonkle and meigle and maxpoffle. we
scotstarvit, armit, wormit, and even whifflet. we play at
crossstobs, leuchars, gorbals, and finfan. we scavaig, and there's
aye a bit of tilquhilly. if it's wet, treshnish and mishnish.

what is the best of the country?
blinkbonny! airgold! thundergay!

and the worst?
scrishven, shiskine, scrabster, and snizort.

listen! what's that?
catacol and wauchope, never heed them.

tell us about last night
well, we had a wee ferintosh and we lay on the quiraing. It was
pure strontian!

but who was there?
petermoidart and craigenkenneth and cambusputtock and
ecclemuchty and corriehulish and balladolly and altnacanny and
clauchanvrechan and stronachlochan and auchenlachar and
tighnacrankie and tilliebruaich and killieharra and invervannach
and achnatudlem and machrishellach and inchtamurchan and
auchterfechan and kinlochculter and ardnawhallie and
invershuggle

and what was the toast?
schiehallion! schiehallion! schiehallion!

The Flowers of Scotland

Yes, it is too cold in Scotland for flower people, in any case
    who would be handed a thistle?
What are our flowers? Locked swings and private rivers –
and the island of Staffa for sale in the open market, which no
    one questions or thinks strange –
and lads o' pairts that run to London and Buffalo without a
    backward look while their elders say Who'd blame them –
and bonny fechters kneedeep in dead ducks with all the
    thrawn intentness of the incorrigible professional Scot –

and a Kirk Assembly that excels itself in the bad old
　　rhetoric and tries to stamp out every glow of charity and
　　change, most wrong when it thinks most loudly it is
　　most right –
and a Scottish National Party that refuses to discuss
　　Vietnam and is even applauded for doing so, do they
　　think no lesson is to be learned from what is going on
　　there? –
and the unholy power of Grouse-moor and Broad-acres to
　　prevent the smoke of useful industry from sullying
　　Invergordon or setting up linear cities among the
　　whaups –
and the banning of Beardsley and Joyce but not of course
　　of 'Monster on the Campus' or 'Curse of the Undead' –
　　those who think the former are the more degrading,
　　what are their values? –
and the steady creep of the preservationist societies,
　　wearing their pens out for slums with good leaded
　　lights – if they could buy all the amber in the Baltic and
　　melt it over Edinburgh would they be happy then? – the
　　skeleton is well-proportioned –
and by contrast the massive indifference to the slow death
　　of the Clyde estuary, decline of resorts, loss of steamers,
　　anaemia of yachting, cancer of monstrous installations of
　　a foreign power and an acquiescent government – what
　　is the smell of death on a child's spade, any more than
　　rats to leaded lights? –
and dissidence crying in the wilderness to a moor of
　　boulders and two ospreys –
these are the flowers of Scotland.

from Sonnets from Scotland

The Coin

We brushed the dirt off, held it to the light.
The obverse showed us *Scotland,* and the head
of a red deer; the antler-glint had fled
but the fine cut could still be felt. All right:
we turned it over, read easily *One Pound,*
but then the shock of Latin, like a gloss,
Respublica Scotorum, sent across

such ages as we guessed but never found
at the worn edge where once the date had been
and where as many fingers had gripped hard
as hopes their silent race had lost or gained.
The marshy scurf crept up to our machine,
sucked at our boots. Yet nothing seemed ill-starred.
And least of all the realm the coin contained.

ALEXANDER SCOTT (1920–1989)

from Scotched

Scotch God
Kent His
Faither.

Scotch Religion
Damm
Aa.

Scotch Education
I tellt ye
I tellt ye.

Scotch Equality
Kaa the feet frae
Thon big bastard.

Scotch Fraternity
Our mob uses
The same razor.

Scotch Optimism
Through a gless,
Darkly.

Scotch Initiative
Eftir
You.

Scotch Generosity
Eftir
Me.

Scotch Passion
Forgot
Mysel.

Scotch Lovebirds
Cheap
Cheap.

Scotch Astrology
Omen
In the gloamin.

Scotch Soccer
Robbery
Wi violence.

Scotch Exiles
Love ye
Further.

Scotch Unionism
Wallace bled but
Here's their transfusion.

Scotch Poets
Wha's the
T'ither?

GEORGE MACKAY BROWN (1921–1996)

Culloden: The Last Battle

The black cloud crumbled.
    My plaid that Morag wove
In Drumnakeil, three months before the eagle
Fell in the west, curled like the gray sea hag
Around my blood.
    We crouched on the long moor
And broke our last round bannock.
    Fergus Mor
Was praying to every crossed and beaded saint
That swung Iona, like the keel of Scotland,
Into the wrecking European wave.
Gow shook his flask. Alastair sang out
They would be drunker yet on German blood
Before the hawk was up. For 'Look', cried he,
'At all the hogsheads waiting to be tapped
Among the rocks'...
    Old iron-mouth spilled his brimstone,
Nodded and roared. Then all were at their thunders,
And Fergus fell, and Donald gave a cry
Like a wounded stag, and raised his steel and ran
Into the pack.
    But we were hunters too,
All smoking tongues. I picked my chosen quarry
Between the squares. Morag at her wheel
Turning the fog of wool to a thin swift line
Of August light, drew me to love no surer
Than that red man to war. And his cold stance
Seemed to expect my coming. We had hastened
Faithful as brothers from the sixth cry of God
To play this game of ghost on the long moor.
His eyes were hard as dice, his cheek was cropped
For the far tryst, his Saxon bayonet
Bright as a wolf's tooth. Our wild paths raced together,
Locked in the heather, faltered by the white stone,
Then mine went on alone.
    'Come back, come back',
Alastair cried.
    I turned.
 Three piercing shapes

Drifted about me in the drifting smoke.
We crossed like dreams.
     This was the last battle.
We had not turned up before.
     The eagle was up
And away to the Isles.
     That night we lay
Far in the west. Alastair died in the straw.
We travelled homeward, on the old lost roads,
Twilight by twilight, clachan by weeping sheepfold.

My three wounds were heavy and round as medals
Till Morag broke them with her long fingers.

Weaving, she sings of the beauty of defeat.

RUARAIDH MACTHÒMAIS / DERICK THOMSON (1921–)

Cruaidh?

Cuil-lodair, is Briseadh na h-Eaglaise,
is briseadh nan tacannan –
lamhachas-làidir dà thrian de ar comas;
's e seòltachd tha dhìth oirnn.
Nuair a theirgeas a' chruaidh air faobhar na speala
caith bhuat a' chlach-lìomhaidh;
chan eil agad ach iarann bog
mur eil de chruas nad innleachd na nì sgathadh.

Is caith bhuat briathran mìne
oir chan fhada bhios briathan agad;
tha Tuatha Dè Danann fon talamh,
tha Tìr nan Òg anns an Fhraing,
's nuair a ruigeas tu Tìr a' Gheallaidh,
mura bi thu air t' aire,
coinnichidh Sasannach riut is plìon air,
a dh' innse dhut gun tug Dia, bràthair athar, còir dha anns an fhearann.

Steel?

Culloden, the Disruption,
and the breaking up of the tack-farms –
two thirds of our power is violence;
it is cunning we need.
When the tempered steel near the edge of the scythe-blade is worn
throw away the whetstone;
you have nothing left but soft iron
unless your intellect has a steel edge that will cut clean.

And throw away soft words,
for soon you will have no words left;
the Tuatha De Danann are underground,
the Land of the Ever-young is in France,
and when you reach the Promised Land,
unless you are on your toes,
a bland Englishman will meet you,
and say to you that God, his uncle, has given him a title to the land.

Alba v. Argentina, 2/6/79

mios as dèidh Taghadh na Pàrlamaid, 3/5/79

Glaschu a' cur thairis
le gràdh dùthcha,
leòmhainn bheucach
air Sràid an Dòchais,
an Central
mùchte le breacan,
cop air Tartan bho mhoch gu dubh,
is mùn nam fineachan air a' bhlàr;
iolach-catha a' bàthadh bùrail nam busaichean –
Sco-o-t-land, Sco-o-t-land –
Alba chadalach,
mìos ro fhadalach.

Scotland v. Argentina, 2/6/79

A month after the General Election, 3/5/79

Glasgow erupting
with patriotism,

growling lions
on Hope Street,
the Central
choked with Tartan,
foaming from dawn to dusk,
and clansmen's piss on the battlefield;
the battle-cry drowning the buses' drone –
Sco-o-t-land, Sco-o-t-land –
sleepy Scotland,
a month late.

CLIFFORD HANLEY (1923–1999)

Scotland the Brave

Hark when the night is falling
Hear! hear! the pipes are calling,
Loudly and proudly calling,
Down thro' the glen.
There where the hills are sleeping,
Now feel the blood a-leaping,
High as the spirits of the old Highland men.

Chorus
Towering in gallant fame,
Scotland my mountain hame!
High may your proud standards gloriously wave!
Land of my high endeavour,
Land of the shining river,
Land of my heart for ever!
Scotland the brave!

High in the misty Highlands,
Out by the purple islands,
Brave are the hearts that beat
Beneath Scottish skies.
Wild are the winds to meet you,
Staunch are the friends that greet you,
Kind as the love that shines from fair maiden's eyes.

Chorus

Far off in sunlit places,
Sad are the Scottish faces,
Yearning to feel the kiss
Of sweet Scottish rain.
Where tropic skies are beaming,
Love sets the heart a-dreaming,
Longing and dreaming for the homeland again.

Chorus

Hot as a burning ember,
Flaming in bleak December
Burning within the hearts
Of clansmen afar!
Calling to home and fire,
Calling the sweet desire,
Shining a light that beckons from every star!

Chorus

KATHRINE SORLEY WALKER

Scottish Legacy

Tough roots, unfelt, unseen in daily life
(magnetic is the land, as are hill, bush and tree)
draw back the wandering heart to influences
deep in the past, absorbed without clear thought
but all pervasive.
So buried are these roots, so overlaid
with later, more accountable, allegiances
they rarely stir; but when they do
they have great power. Within a landscape
is strange potency. Does it derive
from the long line of generations
whose human dust, mixed with the burial earth,
scattered in ashes on the hills and glens,
speaks to me, in this land, of love of place,
kinship and ancestry?

Through the cold centuries my fathers lived
knowing this northern country.
They knew the drift-deep snow, the moors icebound,
the waves whipped high in storm. Cold dawn, cold day,
the white-cold winter night,
the moon frost-rimmed, the stars and snowflakes bright.
They tilled the armoured earth, sailed the steel sea,
and toughened flesh and spirit to resist
winter's high tyranny.
From their strong stock I sprang, thin-blooded, weak,
sapped by the heat of Indian infancy.
Bitter to me the sleet and stinging rain,
torment the chill that lay beneath my skin
deep in the ice-dipped marrow of each bone.

To Winter they bequeathed me – he, their friend,
always my enemy. Yet there were days of summer heat,
high in the hills and on the open heath,
drawing the scents from juniper and ling,
wild rose and golden gorse. And I, as they,
was with such delights.

So the long skein of genealogy is spun
that ends in me. So is the history unrolled
that chronicles quiet, far from famous, lives,
each to itself important, as mine to me.
They are my people, blood-linked by marriage nets
spread across families of diverse kinds.
Their varied backgrounds, traits, abilities,
merge in my temperament as, within this earth,
by right of legacy, winters and summers lie –
the contrasts and the complements of life.

The Scottish Soldier (The Green Hills of Tyrol)

There was a soldier,
A Scottish soldier
Who wandered far away
And soldiered far away
There was none bolder,
With good broad shoulders
He'd fought in many a fray,
And fought and won.
He'd seen the glory
And told the story
Of battles glorious
And deeds victorious
But now he's sighing,
His heart is crying
To leave these green hills of Tyrol.

Chorus
Because these green hills
Are not highland hills
Or the island hills,
They're not my land's hills
And fair as these green foreign hills may be
They are not the hills of home.

And now this soldier,
This Scottish soldier
Who wandered far away
And soldiered far away
Sees leaves are falling
And death is calling
And he will fade away,
In that far land.
He called his piper,
His trusty piper
And bade him sound a lay
A pibroch sad to play
Upon a hillside,
A Scottish hillside
Not on these green hills of Tyrol.

And so this soldier
This Scottish soldier
Will wander far no more
And soldier far no more
And on a hillside,
A Scottish hillside
You'll see a piper play
His soldier home.
He'd seen the glory,
He'd told his story
Of battles glorious
And deeds victorious
The bugles cease now,
He is at peace now
Far from those green hills of Tyrol.

Chorus

WILLIAM NEILL (1922–)

Scotland

I have sailed on the viking sea,
Sumburgh on the skies' rim
and with the inner eye
seen dragon ships, warriors drinking the wind
travelling westward, bloody for loot and land;
the smoke of burning abbeys on the isles;
the jewelled bindings wrenched,
the pages scorched and scattered,
the words our fathers heard, scattered
as the vikings scattered their seed,
the seed of our fathers.

I have sailed on the sea of Moyle,
the islands emerald on a silken cloth,
gazing on Fodla through the wind's eye,
on Calum's Derry, Suibhne's mountains and woods:
old stories, chariots racing in the mind.

High blue Donegal and green, green Antrim
whence they came to our land with their swords and saints,
blooding their blades in the flesh of our father's bodies
sowing the words of their book in our father's minds,
these men of Cuchulainn's land, the land of our fathers.

I have wandered and sought through this fair hard land:
Dunnet to Drummore and the Butt to Berwick,
scratching a saltire of wanderings on its soil;
and blood must answer the echoes that do not die,
slogans that rise from the craigs and mosses and cairns,
where the carven stone of the Pict is a family tomb.

Western wind over Barra blessed in the sun
Darkness at noon in the mountain clefts of Argyle,
the howes and the hills of Kyle, cool Carrick burns
and the mist in its brooding silence above Glentrool.

These are as much myself as my flesh and blood.

Then and Now

I can see Wallace now
A man who burned like a flame
Stand in their perjured court
His pride and glory sold to mockery:
See the cold Norman sneers
The hollow advocates
The secret envy in each Quisling heart
And one who saw his duty stark and clear,
Watching, regretful of past infamy.

This is now as it was;
Time stills no truth,
No less obliged to answer for our blood
We stand condemned.
Our limbs and sinews feel the pain he felt
But gain no honour in dismemberment.

Yon steadfast, mighty man,
Whose torture stained their loud proclaimed nobility,
Is like our Scotland; with the same mind again
They draw the living bowels from our country;
Not now our manhood, but our nationhood
Emasculate.

G.F. DUTTON (1924–)

as so often in Scotland

as so often in Scotland
the sun travelled
dyke over dyke, burning
dead grass golden and ending,
after a wallow of foothills,
on one brown summit;
that flared its moment, too,
and was gone.

ALASTAIR REID (1926–)

Scotland

It was a day peculiar to this piece of the planet,
when larks rose on long thin strings of singing
and the air shifted with the shimmer of actual angels.
Greenness entered the body. The grasses
shivered with presences, and sunlight
stayed like a halo on hair and heather and hills.
Walking into town, I saw, in a radiant raincoat,
the woman from the fish-shop. 'What a day it is!'
cried I, like a sunstruck madman.
And what did she have to say for it?
Her brow grew bleak, her ancestors raged in their graves
as she spoke with their ancient misery:
'We'll pay for it, we'll pay for it, we'll pay for it!'

To Have Found One's Country

To have found one's country
after a long journey
and it to be here
around one all the time.
It is like taking a girl
from the house next door,
after all that travel
that black dense wall.

To have fallen in love with
stone, thistle and strath,
to see the blood flow
in wandering old rivers,
this wound is not stanched
by handkerchiefs or verse.
This wound was after all
love and a deep curse.

Now I'm frightened to name it
lest some witch should spring
screaming out of the tombs
with a perverted broom.
I'm almost frightened to
name all the waters,
these seas, tall hills,
these misty bordered bibles.

Love's such a transient thing
except for that hard slogging
which, though it's love, we don't
name it by that ring
in which, tortured, we fight
with all the bones about us
in these cemeteries that hold
the feet in living grass.

from The White Air of March

This is the land God gave to Andy Stewart –
    we have our inheritance,
There shall be no ardour, there shall be indifference.
There shall not be excellence, there shall be the average.
We shall be the intrepid hunters of golf balls.

Have you not known, have you not heard, has it not been reported
that Mrs Macdonald has given an hour-long lecture on Islay
and at the conclusion was presented with a bouquet of flowers
by Marjory, aged five?
                Have you not noted
the photograph of the whist drive, skeleton hands,
rings on skeleton fingers?
                Have you not seen
the glossy weddings in the glossy pages,
champagne and a 'shared joke'.
                  Do you not see
the Music Hall's still alive here in the North? and on the stage
the yellow gorse is growing.
                    'Tragedy,' said Walpole, 'for those who feel.
For those who think, it's comic.'
                Pity then those who feel
and, as for the Scottish Soldier, off to the wars!
The Cuillins stand and will forever stand.
Their streams scream in the moonlight.

★ ★ ★ ★ ★

The exiles have departed,
                leaving old houses.
The Wind wanders like an old man who has lost his mind.
'What do you want?' asks the wind. 'Why are you crying?
Are those your tears or the rain?'
I do not know. I touch my cheek. It is wet.
I think it must be the rain.

It is bitter
to be an exile in one's own land.
It is bitter
to walk among strangers
when the strangers are in one's own land.

It is bitter
to dip a pen in continuous water
to write poems of exile
in a verse without honour or style.

★ ★ ★ ★ ★

The tall buses pass by.
        The cottages trail their roses.

Look at the witch at the waterfall.
        She does Bed and Breakfast.

'Ah, Freedom is a noble thing.'

        Around the Cuillins
the clouds drift like green dollars.

★ ★ ★ ★ ★

The Cuillins tower high in the air –
                            Excellence...

MARGARET GILLIES BROWN (1929–)

Scottish Woman

I am this century's Scot,
One whose native tongue
Was borrowed from the south
By forebears – language heard
From the moment of birth
Rich with the roll of sound,
Rivered in consonants,
Vowel-round as the hills I wake to.
I speak in idioms
Strange to the southern ear,
Unaware that I do.

I am a Scot, be in no doubt,
Have no other ancestors
Save a French fisherman
Tossed on a wild shore

Before union with England.
I live through my country's history
Breathe through its rugged land
As it breathes through me.
Know its strengths and weaknesses,
Storms, dourness, its glorious
Clearness and cleanness,
Leanness of winter sheep,
Fatness of summer cattle;
Its darkness, enveloping mists and moods,
Mourning, rejoicing.

I know its people –
The tillers of the ground,
Men who weld steel
With dangerous flashes,
The carpenters loving the wood
That they work with,
The fishermen risking their lives
Against breakers:

Women renouncing, when they conceive,
A separate existence,
Teaching the children, nursing the sick,
Cleaning, cooking, sewing
Making life smoother and rounder.

Scotland –
I know its birds and trees
Wild flowers and animals,
Red deer on the hill, roe deer in the woods,
The hare with no home.
How the land lies sweetly in summer,
Triumphant in autumn, in banners of gold,
Bleakly and whitely in winter,
Vibrant in spring.

I've been child of its urban arms,
Child of its country airs,
Know its various faces,
Been nursed in its round hollows,
Nurtured at the breast of its hills
Shaped by its angry stormings.

TOM BUCHAN (1931–1995)

Scotland the wee

Scotland the wee, crèche of the soul,
of thee I sing

land of the millionaire draper, whisky vomit
and the Hillman Imp

staked out with church halls, gaelic sangs
and the pan loaf

eventide home for teachers and christians,
nirvana of the keelie imagination

Stenhousemuir, Glenrothes, Auchterarder, Renton
– one way street to the coup of the mind.

Stones of Scotland

Stones of Scotland chipped
and rough in my hand – 2 flints
of pink quartz, a malty slice of opal
and a blue stone I cannot name
which I think may be your heart.

The Low Road

Bohannan held onto a birch branch
by yon bonny banks and looked down
through several strata of liquid
– there is someone somewhere
aiming a missile at me (he thought)
for the mountain behind him
was drilled with caves
each one crammed with nuclear hardware
and the sea-loch over the mountain
lay easy with obsolescent new submarines.

Would an underwater burst at Faslane
kill me (Walter Bohannan)
and for how many seconds/split seconds
would its bubble of steam swell and rupture
and swell and rupture again as it rose
to its final spiflification
sending fission products skimming
across the surface to Rhu and Roseneath
and Garelochhead and Greenock and Rothesay?

But no doubt they'll have arranged
for an airburst over Glen Douglas
the fireball of which will defrost Inchlonaig,
vaporize Cailness and Rowchoish, fry
the Glasgow councillors fishing for free
on Loch Katrine and kill all the spiders
and earwigs between here and Crianlarich
and me (he thought) as through the soft air
trucks, cars, buses and articulated lorries
accelerated their loads of Omo, people and bricks
towards Oban and Inveraray.

GEORGE MACBETH (1932–1992)

from My Scotland

Oatcakes

They come in a high tin, cylindrical, sealed with cellophane. Each night,
sometime after eleven, I come downstairs into the kitchen and reach up
for it. In a corrugated tube of paper, dished a little, and resting in each
other like the bowls of spoons, they confront the eye with the solidity of
porridge. When I was little, I used to know the thicker ones as
bannocks. These are neither one thing nor the other, they rest in
between, perhaps nearer the norm than the cheaper varieties I remember
before the war. Those were brittle triangles in folded paper. These are
medallions, rough shields. Targes, almost. If Bruce were to come back
now in fire along the glen, he could seize one to his arm again and win
that famous battle. Bannockburn. The apotheosis of oatmeal.

Bagpipes

Their sound is perhaps the only one I know that works in the stomach. It comes like a hard meat, stringy with gristle. For anyone who was born in the scattered landscape it summons and governs, there is no escaping its bitter, outmoded rallying-cry. More than the drab gauds of Caledonia they still flaunt in for Burns suppers and tourism, it steams and twitches in the cauldron of belonging, the long vault of Celtic exile. Every man who hears it is a king in the blood, returned out of the foreign slime to renew his dead alliance.

Scottish

If it were just a matter of words, no doubt we should all fall in the gap between *skittish* and *sottish*. We have the dry wit of the fairies, a touch fey and feline, and we cross it with the dream of blood like clear water from the rocks, potent as Strathisla. Somewhere in the space between dancing like angels on pins, and lying face down in the flooded brook of the arteries, we live, rise, and dwindle, miraculous as centaurs in the double-nature of Highland and Lowland. Elsewhere the pincers close. Here it is all division, *Scottish* into twin bits.

Scotch

As for that other word, already ennobled in a world coinage of wanting, how shall we all deny there is gold and honey, maple and pure syrup, in the pure malt? If this were what it meant to be of it, a long race would engender in the bowels of Finland, St Lucia and Paraguay, no more known to the forgotten corners of the loch-spitted anvil we call Scotland than butter-scotch, or scotched snakes.

The Idea of Scotland as a Scattered Universal

Somewhere in that man with a name like a pirate captain, Willard van Orman Quine, there extrudes an anchor, a hook through to the under-lying nexus. There in the concept of universals as everywhere, as disintegrated, as finalities, I come into the gut's truth of Scotland. Here, in the South, four hundred miles from the Cannongate, the intrinsic resonance still aims and thunders out of the fur of dogs, the meal of food, the vowels even of converts. Shatter and split it how you will, it veers and collapses, triumphing, veridical, and as prevalent as the dirt under nails. In the North it intensifies and thickens. Here it is all diffusion, adulterate with water, occasional only. And yet it teases, like tartan, like Burns. I follow it, as the will o' the wisp.

DUNCAN GLEN (1933–)

The Hert o Scotland

I hae problems.

I would scrieve o Scotland
and mak a unity o it

but
ken nae word o Gaelic
though I've had three fortnichts in the hielants
and went on a boat to Lochboisdale
wi hauf an 'oor ashore. In Inverness I was that lanely
I went to bed early. In Fort William it rained
and though I sclimed Ben Nevis in record time
it was sae misty I could haurdly see the path at my feet.

Dundee I hae forgotten frae an efternoon veesit
and Union Street Aiberdeen I've never seen to forget.
Perth I reached efter a lang bike ride
and had to turn back as soon as I got there
haein nae lichts.
Stirling Castle I hae stood on and surveyed the scene
but I mind the girl mair than the panorama.
The Borders I ken weill enterin or leavin by a sign
SCOTLAND
but I've never got aff the train.

I hae problems.

Fife noo is different.
It I ken frae pushin an auld bike to the limits
and stood on baith Lomonds and Largo Law. I hae kent it
early and late wi the extremes o youth. And mony
girls
but aw the faces and names noo forgetten
but yin that coonts
in or oot o Fife and she was born in Mallaig
whaur I'd never been.
Fife is different.
I hae my Glesca voice and Fifers notice that.
And I've never played golf at St Andrews.

I hae problems.

Still there's Edinburgh
and that gies a bit o status if no unity
for aw that awbody kens Edinburgh
(they'd hae us believe!)
I had the advantage o digs in Marchmont
and days at the Art College
– but aye a visitor wi a time limit
as still
wi sae mony ithers.

I hae problems
being frae Lanarkshire.

It's true there's the hills by Symington
and orchards in the upper Clyde valley
and Kirkfieldbank. But
I was yin that never went to see the Spring blossom
steyin pit in grey streets
in the shadow o pits and bings and steelwarks.
The ugliest stretch in aw Scotland
those that ken their Scotland hae tellt us
and I only kent aboot as faur as I could walk.

I hae problems.

There's my Scotland. A wee corner o Lanarkshire
and Glesca (I should mention!)
whaur as message boy
at fifteen I kent aw the addresses
and short cuts. There I belonged

– till I left at echteen!

ANNE STEVENSON (1933–)

American Rhetoric for Scotland

North in the mind, ragged edged, stubborn ribbed,
with your bald soils and scoured hills and cold ruined massacres,
disasters no one is expected to inhabit...
however you ignore them, you are one with your bones.
'Admire,' you implore, 'my redemptory achievements,
my swift roads, my smooth steel, my pylons and high voltages,
my slums reduced to powder, reassembled as skyscrapers,
my lochs relieved of romance, rehabilitated as electrons.'
Nobody believes you. The first mist disposes of them.
You build in your stone ghost.

It takes a man's full arrogance to sing out in your weather,
'I am the the creator. Everything is for me.'
The scraped countryside groups itself around him, without him.
It is over his lighthouse that the gulls swing, buffeted...
wailing, repeating reminiscences, grievances.
These are his sheep, soft boulders till they move,
cropping expertly, inflexibly along the rainswept ridges,
leaving among thistles and torn matted grasses
nests of round, moist, unhatchable black eggs.

Occasional crofts or byres, or parts of crofts
or half byres, knot the irregular, useless walls
with which the land seems tied. Or is it the land that ties?
Did the house give way painfully to its tightening,
the lintels sag, the roofs buckle, the beams split
as the ground took its stones back one by one,
with the people rooted to them or rooted out
or shrugged off into Queensland, Ontario, Birmingham,
or that gaunt crease or angle of yourself spreading east
out of Glasgow?
                                        Some settled for it.
Others borrowed Cleveland, Toronto, made themselves indispensible.
The new world still uses them like engines.

And what are they to say to the strangers they come back to?
If they do come back, with their easy ways and smart daughters,
to be chilled in your houses, homesick for midwestern summers,
too rich for your sun and for the kind, shrewd nephews

who keep, nevertheless, an oblique ascendancy,
who copy or accuse or make fun of what they envy,
who are in turn wistfully envied, since under their
preposterous assertions, their necessary frugality, their greed,
lies that which is forever whispering their release...
'No day is property. There is little purpose. Living is enough.'

Living. Its clumsy satisfactions. Its tea and football.
Its women and shows and kids and drams of an evening –
ambitions an honest man attends to if he's lucky,
if the drams are enough and the friends plentiful,
or even if the wife is enough and the tea plentiful –
though it may be he is evil in his seed,
that the jolt of conceiving him is evil,
that beyond the shimmering coasts and the barren islands
Great Doom is readying itself for a descent –
sea that will rise and lash inland, lapping him up,
receding over his tangled, indelible evidences,
quays upended, boats stoved in, offices gutted,
cranes caught and petrified in the wince of action,
their bony necks twisted or hurled back or
bent to the swirling water as if to drink it.

But you know better. The two-faced familiar antagonist
still asks for its share of husbands,
still plays fairly or unfairly with the slippery herring,
but clings to you, nevertheless, with its legends in tatters,
its white waters and grey waters repetitious in old age,
old tediums, memories old women live by
as they knit or make trifles for the
waves that break again and again over your moorlands,
running northwards and outwards out of Clydeside into
Morven and Sutherland and Inverness, and over
Ardnamurchan into Skye and Barra.

Will your mountains be wild enough and strong enough?
Or will you drown, devour whatever feeds you,
melt into the undifferentiated mind that wants you,
with its cameras and appetites and little boredoms,
or even its bewildered fumblings for a simple life,
the better way it half hopes it can pay you for?
You're not for sale, though you give to one or two:
blood-gold sunsets. One white seagull, perhaps,

rising in contradiction to a cataract. Perhaps in sandstone
a pattern like braided hair. Always the sound of water.

Quiet stone.

The raw grey villages subsist on little, settle uneasily
into the shifting hills. Below them some soft bays open
or dwindle. Some islands vanish. The sun, using the scarce,
indefinable, frail pigments sparingly, moves something like yellow
from one valley to another. This gentleness is moss thin.
Stones don't need nourishment. They break through. They harden.

STEWART CONN (1936–)

Cappella Nova at Greyfriars' Kirk

Rare as whorls of gold-leaf floating in air
the cadences of Carver and the Inchcolm
Antiphoner are followed by the radiance
of a present-day elegy for Colum Cille –
he should have been Scotland's patron saint.

Emerging afterwards into a grainy twilight
(itself enough to make you catch your breath)
and walking to where the Covenant was signed
past the domed tomb of 'bluidy Mackenzie',
it fully registers that the priestly composer

of another piece, all exultant counterpoint,
was Robert Johnston who fled to England,
charged with heresy, after the martyrdom
of Patrick Hamilton by Archbishop Beaton;
a torch which ignited the Reformation.

How swiftly beauty and horror intertwine,
the one so often a means of purging
the other; in this instance the singers
our intermediaries, the dark abyss bridged
by such poise... such perfect harmonies.

WILLIAM MCILVANNEY (1936–)

The Cowardly Lion

A parable: March, 1979

There was a lion dormant, with the mange.
Its roar was out of practice and its teeth
Were brown with eating scraps or something worse.
There was a smell of carrion on its breath.
Asleep it dreamed of a past that never was;
Awake, lapped spirit from a drinking bowl
The keepers had allowed it, walked its cage
In which a full length mirror was installed.
All day it watched itself and practised rage,
Whispered 'I am a lion,' bared its fangs
And sometimes snarled so fiercely that it ran
In fear of its own image to the end
Of its small cage, and hid its head and then
Peeped out, approached the mirror once again.
'I can remember being strong,' it said.
Then it lay down and licked the wounds
It didn't have and thought of all the cubs
The keepers took away and taught strange tricks.
Throughout the world those cubs had won great fame,
Performing always in the keepers' name.
And wondering where they were, where was its soul,
It would return to find it in the bowl
And gather strange, imaginary strength
And roar and fill itself with its own terror
And beat itself unconscious in the mirror.

But lions will be lions and one day
It saw behind it in the mirror keepers laughing
At its preposterous enactment of itself.
They giggled, winked and nodded and it turned
And in an instant lionhood was formed.
The roar was real. In the eyes a dark past burned.
It saw its own horizons without bars.
It saw that keepers only keep the past
And it was present and its powerful paws
Could free it from injustice of the laws.
It took its strength and ran and the bars shook.
The keepers were afraid. They mustn't lose
The cubs and revenues the lion gave.

It was a prize exhibit in their zoo.
They watched it lying down, ignore the mirror
And stare at them in hunger, leave the bowl.
They watched it gather strength from day to day
Towards when it would smash the bars away.

The keepers held a conference. A plan
Was needed or the lion would escape.
It wanted freedom. Why not give it some,
Extend its compound but still keep it trapped?
Some nodded sagely who were not asleep.
They would pretend to free it but still keep
It as their pet. And even some of those
Who loved the lion said the plan was good.
These in their cunning thought they understood
The lion would escape this half-way house.
This was a lion. It was not a mouse
To be content with just a little room.
The compound was constructed. Every stone
Was argued over fiercely. Like a tomb
It never would escape the thing was made.
Still those who loved it acquiesced. They said
In private, 'Things will work out very well.
Give it one sniff of freedom and we'll see.
The lion will be a lion and will be
True to itself again. Don't be afraid.'
Some sleepers wakened briefly and agreed.
The day of 'freedom' came. The cage-door creaked
Out on its ancient hinges and swung open.
In awe the keepers waited. What would happen?
Would the lion attack and had they been too bold
In their decisions? Would the compound hold?
The lion approached the door. Its head emerged
Noble and proud, its snout raised to the wind.
It smelt the terrible distances of freedom,
It felt the risk of not being confined,
It knew the pain of hunger unassauged,
It sensed the emptiness where self is found,
It heard the bitterness where life is waged.

Slowly the keepers relaxed into a smile
And giggled and nodded again, were winking while
Those who loved the lion had nothing to say.
For the lion had turned to its cage and slunk away
And lives still among stinking straw today.

Scotia Deserta

All those kyles, lochs and sounds...

★ ★ ★ ★ ★

And the gulls at Largs pier:
sitting in that café
at the big window full of wind and light
reading and watching

★ ★ ★ ★ ★

Thinking back to the ice
watching it move
from the high middle spine
out into the Atlantic

feeling it gouge out lochs
and sculpt craggy pinnacles
and smoothe long beaches

the land emerges
bruised and dazed
in the arctic light

gannets gather on the islands
eagles on the piney hills
cotton grass tosses in the wind

men come
gazing around them
what name shall it be given?
Alba

★ ★ ★ ★ ★

White beach meditations
mountain contemplations
imprinted on the mind

★ ★ ★ ★ ★

One left traces of his presence
out there in Bute and the Garvellach Isles
and in Kilbrannan Sound –
the holy voyager, Brandan

Brandan was maybe a believer
but that's neither here nor there
first and foremost
he was a navigator
a figure moving mile by mile
along the headlands
among the islands
tracing a way
between foam and cloud
with an eye to outlines:

Sound of Islay
the Firth of Lorn
Tiree passage
the Sound of Mull
Skerryvore and Barra Head
Loch Alsh, Kyle Rhea
Sound of Raasay

★ ★ ★ ★ ★

Ah, the clear-sounding words
and a world
opening, opening!

★ ★ ★ ★ ★

Other figures cross the scene
like this one:
Kentigern they cried him

in the church I attended
around the age of nine
was that stained glass window
showing a man
with a book in his hand
standing on a seashore
preaching to the gulls

I'd be gazing at the window
and forgetting the sermon
(all about good and evil
with a lot of mangled metaphor
and heavy comparison)
eager to get back out
on to the naked shore
there to walk for hours on end
with a book sometimes in my hand
but never a thought of preaching in my mind

trying to grasp at something
that wanted no godly name
something that took the form
of blue waves and grey rock
and that tasted of salt

★ ★ ★ ★ ★

A rocky walk
and the smell of kelp
between Fairlie and Largs

Drifting smoke
the glint of autumn leaves
on Loch Lomondside

Ghostly gulls in the greyness
keeya, keeya, keeya, keeya
September at Applecross

Tiree
on a March morning
the kingdom of the wind

Seven islands
in the August sunlight
Islay, Jura, Scarba, Lunga, Luing, Shuna, Seil

★ ★ ★ ★ ★

Walking the coast
all those kyles, lochs and sounds

sensing the openness
feeling out the lines

order and anarchy
chaos and cosmology

a mental geography

★ ★ ★ ★ ★

Have you heard Corrievreckan
at the Spring flood
and a westerly blowing?

the roaring's so great
you can hear it twenty miles
along the mainland coast

admiralty charts
show a 9–knot race

to the senses
that do no calculations

but take it all in
it's a rushing white flurry

birthplace
of a wave-and-wind philosophy

★ ★ ★ ★ ★

Let the images
go bright and fast

and the concepts be extravagant
(wild host to erratic guest)

that's the only way
to say the coast

all the irregular reality
of the rocky sea-washed West

★ ★ ★ ★ ★

Pelagian discourse
atlantic poetics

from first to last.

ROY WILLIAMSON (1937–1990)

Flower of Scotland

O, Flower of Scotland
When will we see
Your like again
That fought and died for
Your wee bit hill and glen
And stood against him
Proud Edward's army
And sent him homeward
Tae think again.

The hills are bare now
And autumn leaves
Lie thick and still
O'er land that is lost now
Which those so dearly held
That stood against him
Proud Edward's army
And sent him homewards
Tae think again.

Those days are past now
And in the past
They must remain
But we can still rise now
And be the nation again
That stood against him
Proud Edward's army
And sent him homeward
Tae think again.

ALAN JACKSON (1938–)

A Scotch Poet Speaks

Och, I wish you hadn't come right now;
You've put me off my balance.

I was just translating my last wee poem
Into the dear auld Lallans.

LES A. MURRAY (1938–)

Elegy for Angus Macdonald of Cnoclinn

The oldest tree in Europe's lost
a knotty branch it could ill spare
to make a hump in Sydney ground,
not for the first time. No. But the last.
A genus of honey bees has died out,
a strain that came to us from the lost world.

Anger at that coarse canting fool
who tried to bury you meanings and all
under his turnip-cairn of texts
– you with the knowledge, he with the talk –
kept us from tears, the day you rode
down ropes in your chest of polished wood.

You were as strange in our waters as
the Atlantis-reef Rocabarraidh. Students,
we came for ancestral language, but you,
no teacher of grammar, gave us lore,
a sight down usages to the Bronze Age
and ideal from then, older than Heaven,
the 'harmony of the men of peace'.

The highest folk culture in the West
and terms from a lost, non-Greek Agora
mingled in you, our giver of words:
feallsanachd, oine, foidhirlisg.
Late on and far from heirs, you wrote
your oral learning down in a book,
a dense heaped Cadbury Hill of a book,

the history of your island, songs
and steadings of Heisgir under the sea,
black crimes from the Age of Forays, wise
folk government in the Lordship of the Isles,
astronomy and logic of the men
who taught in that curious late druidical
university of the White Mountain;

you were oath-bound to transmit these things
and you did transmit them. The book remains,
cranky, magnificent, pregnant with rethinkings
as the Watts Towers or Fort's museum,
a Celtic history indeed, a line –
for this is the meaning of the drowned lands –
by which to haul from the conqueror's sea
of myth, our alternative antiquity.

Teacher of my heart, you'll not approve
my making this in the conqueror's language
(though Calgacus used their Latin finely:
'You have made a desert and called it peace').
Even the claim I make at times
to writing Gaelic in English words
would make you sniff (but also smile),

but my fathers were Highlanders long ago
then Borderers, before this landfall
– 'savages' once, now we are 'settlers'
in the mouth of the deathless enemy –
but I am seized of this future now.
I am not European. Nor is my English.

And perhaps you too were better served here
than in Uist of the Sheldrakes and the tides
watching the old life fade, the *toradh*,
the good, go out of the island world.
Exile's a rampart, sometimes, to the past,
a distiller of spirit from bruised grains;
this is a meaning of the New World.

The good does not go out of the past.
Angles of the moving moon and sun
elicit fresh lights from it continually;
now, in the new lands, everyone's Ethnic
and we too, the Scots Australians, who've been
henchmen of much in our self-loss
may recover ourselves, and put off oppression.

This, then, for the good you put on us,
round-tower of Gaelic, grand wrongheaded one,
now you have gone to the dark crofts:
the oldest tree in Europe's shed
a seed to us – and the Otherworld
becomes ancestral, a code of history,
a style of fingering, an echo of vowels,
honey that comes to us from the lost world.

DONALD CAMPBELL (1940–)

Anthem o the Unco Guid

'We are the People, we're the braw boys
Beluvit o Gode, His ain guid choice
Sing it wi virr, gie it aa yer voice!
            We are the People!
            Rejoice! Rejoice!

We are the People, whitever ye say
Wi Gode on oor side, we ken the richt way
Wi Gode on our side – whitever we dae
            We are the People!
            Hurray! Hurray!

We are the People, we hae nae sin
We staun unitit, we're kith an kin
Let oor enemies come, we'll gar them rin
        We are the people!
        We'll win! We'll win!

We are the People an fine we ken
That ane o us 's warth mair than ten
o *ony* communion o *ither* men
        We are the People!
        Amen. Amen.'

JOHN PURSER (1942–)

Northern Latitudes

They, whose solstice bears
the urgency of fear
far from the sun,
have they not passed beyond
the civilised assertions
and made their compromise
with all their origins
on tougher rock?
Living on the extremities,
their attentive eyes
focus on distant objects,
universal skies.

Only in stories
or the weather's phrase
remembering kings
and currents of the sea
do they evoke the heroes
summoning tragedy
they tighten their religion,
clean the wells,
and dig fertility
into the ground,
knowing the ice may yet return
and germination die
within the seed.

DOUGLAS DUNN (1942–)

Here and There

'Everybody's got to be somewhere.'
Woody Allen

You say it's mad to love this east-coast weather –
I'll praise it, though, and claim its subtle light's
Perfect for places that abut on water
Where swans on tidal aviaries preen their whites.
You whisper in the south that even the rain
Wins my affection, and I won't deny it,
Watching it drench my intimate domain:
I love the rain and winds that magnify it.
The evening's paper-boy goes round the doors
At his hour of November when the day's
Closing in goose-cries and the sycamores
Darken to silhouettes by darker hedges –

I love that too. 'Provincial', you describe
Devotion's minutes as the seasons shift
On the planet: I suppose your diatribe
Last week was meant to undercut the uplift
Boundaries give me, witnessed from the brae
Recording weather-signs and what birds pass
Across the year. More like a world, I'd say,
Infinite, curious, sky, sea and grass
In natural minutiae that bind
Body to lifetimes that we all inhabit.
So spin your globe: Tayport is Trebizond
As easily as a regenerate

Country in which to reconstruct a self
From local water, timber, light and earth,
Drawing the line (this might please you) at golf
or watersports on a sub-Arctic Firth.
It matters where you cast your only shadow,
And that's my answer to, 'Why did you choose
Grey northland as your smalltown El Dorado?
You've literature and a career to lose...'
It isn't always grey. And what is grey?
A colour like the others, snubbed by smart

Depressives who can't stroll an estuary
without its scope of sky bleaching their hearts.

'... *You'll twist your art on the parochial lie.*'
I love the barbed hush in the holly tree.
'*An inner émigré, you'll versify,*
Not write. You'll turn your back on history.'
Old friend, you're good for me, but what I want's
Not what your southern bigotry suspects.
Here on imagination's waterfronts
It's even simpler: fidelity directs
Love to its place, the eye to what it sees
And who we live with, and the *whys* and *whens*
That follow *ifs* and *buts*, as, on our knees,
We hope for spirit and intelligence.

Turbulence reaches here: the RAF
Loosens the earwax – so, not paradise
Unless you're awkward, Tory, daft or deaf
Or dealing in destruction's merchandise.
I hold my infant son at the window.
Look, there's the blue; I show him sky and the leaf
On the puddle. What does a baby know
Of the hazardous world? An acrid *if*
Diseases happiness, the damned *perhaps*
Perfected by the uniforms of State.
Our sunlit roofs look nothing on their maps

Other than pulverable stone and slate.
A ferry town, a place to cross from... Verse
Enjoys connections: fugitive Macduff
Escaped Macbeth by it. Lacking his purse,
He paid in bread – The Ferry of the Loaf...
'*Ferries? Fairies! That's medieval farce!*'
The wizard, Michael Scot, was born near here...
'*I might have guessed you'd more like that, and worse...*'
... Alchemist, polymath, astrologer
To the Holy Roman Empire; Tayport's son
Mastered all knowledge, too controversial
For Dante who invented his damnation
In the *Inferno*: 'Tayport Man in Hell,'

They'd say in the *Fife Herald* – 'Sorcerer
From Tayport Slandered by Tuscan Poet.'
'Worse than parochial! Literature
Ought to be everywhere...' Friend, I know that;
It's why I'm here. My accent feels at home
In the grocer's and in Tentsmuir Forest.
Without a Scottish voice, its monostome
Dictionary, I'm a contortionist –
Tongue, teeth and larynx swallowing an R's
Frog-croak and spittle, social agility,
Its range of fraudulence and repertoires
Disguising place and nationality.

'What's this about Tayport's centenary?
I never thought you'd prime a parish pump.'
Not me. Who's said I have? *'It's scenery*
You're there for.' No, it isn't. *'Mugwump!'*
You're wrong again, old friend. Your Englishness
Misleads you into Albionic pride,
Westminstered mockery and prejudice –
You're the provincial, an undignified
Anachronism. The Pax Britannica's
Dismissed, a second-rate Byzantium,
Self-plundered inner empire's Age of Brass.
No houseroom's left in the imperial slum.

And as for scenery, what's wrong with love's
Preferred country, the light, water and sky
Around a town, centennial removes
From time? – The universe within the eye,
Cosmogyny, not parish-governed stars
Cultured above the Tay, but seen from here
When late-night amateur philosophers
Puzzle the substance of their hemisphere.
Time, space and yours truly: all men deserve
Somewhere, if only that, fruition's place,
Quotidian but extra, on a curve
That's capable of upwards into grace,

Eccentric elegance, the personal life
Sharing its ordinariness of days
With speculative spirit which is midwife
To nation, intellect and poetry's

Occurrence. *'You're looking for a chance to wear*
A three-piece suit in tweeds with heavy brogues,
Rehearsing presbyterian despair
On a shoreline, in Reithean monologues.'
So what, if I talk to myself in the woods?
'Perverse retreat into the safe and small
Suggests fake self-denial.' These latitudes
Enlarge me, comfort me, and make me whole.

'No, you're evasive, knowing it might be wrong
To hedge ambition into quietude
That serves a lowered will with local song,
Beachcombing an iambic neighbourhood.'
It serves my loyalty. It serves increase.
I'll keep no secrets from you: it serves love;
It serves responsibility and caprice.
Damn all careers; I'd rather *be* than *have.*
'You mean, it serves you right?' I hope so, friend.
Pay me a visit and we'll drink to life
One evening when the light and water blend
On the conjectural points of coastal Fife.

Come by the backroads with a sense of time.
Come like Edward Thomas on a holiday
In search of passages of wild-flowered rhyme
No Scot or Irishman would dare betray.
Now, though, I'm going out to the black twigs,
Shy waterbuds reflecting as they drop
To the neighbourly, where the good ground swigs
Any libation from its earthen cup.
Scottishness, if you say so; but I see
Plurals and distances in voiceless wet
Enough to harbour all my history
Inside a house protected from regret.

mise, alba

mise, alba, cluaran sporach
dèan tighinn faisg orm le meatag stàilinn,
ach èist –

mar a ruith an ceòl thar nan stùc
ann a neòil de chainntearachd
gach lid a glaothaich mise *beatha*

mar a ruith a ghaoth ris a chòrsa fada
linn thar linn
a giùlain a luchd de dh'eòin beag gearanach

a dìon, nam b'urrainn dhaibh, am fearann
mise? alba? cluaran sporach?
nach tig thu staigh, gabh dràm leam

i, scotland

i, scotland, prickly thistle
if you must approach wear gloves of steel,
but listen –

how the music races over peaks
in clouds of cainntearachd
each syllable crying i am a life

how the wind races on the long coasts
century on century
carrying its cargo of small complaining birds

protecting, if they could, their territory
i? scotland? prickly thistle?
why don't you come in, let's have a dram

from Situations Theoretical and Contemporary

Scotland has become an independent socialist republic.
At last.

Eh?
You pinch yourself.
Jesus Christ. You've slept in again!

The Voyeur

what's your favourite word dearie
is it wee
I hope it's wee
wee's such a nice wee word
like a wee hairy dog
with two wee eyes
such a nice wee word to play with dearie
you can say it quickly
with a wee smile
and a wee glance to the side
or you can say it slowly dearie
with your mouth a wee bit open
and a wee sigh dearie
a wee sigh
put your wee head on my shoulder dearie
oh my
a great wee word
and Scottish
it makes you proud

Simile Please / Say Cheese

as the sea comes ogling ogling up the sand
and drops down its hankie of seaweed for the land to
    hand over
but the land doesn't bother for the land still fancies the
    sky
and the sea goes away in the huff but it always comes
    back

like a small man standing at the bottom of Big Ben
    holding a long thread tied to the top
which slowly bends over as the man creeps furtively
    away

only the clock tower has been secretly made of rubber
    which straightens up to hurl the man away up to Scotland
only the man has been secretly made of Scottish rubber
    so that he bounces to his feet amang his ain folk

darling...

THOMAS A. CLARK (1944–)

The Homecoming

the true south and the upland grass
the bright glade and the fallen lintel
the driving rain and the sudden calm
the fiddle tune and the rowan berries
the ruined chapel and the black water

the hard road and the steady light
the heat haze and the peat smoke
the pebble bed and the yellow flag
the grey song and the fault line
the dog rose and the meeting place

the keen air and the pine needles
the furze blossom and the brown trout
the far hills and the broken boat
the bleached bones and the summer dwelling
the slack tide and the raised beach

the blue sky and the summit cairn
the hanged crow and the sheep dip
the bracken fronds and the healing pool
the lobster pots and the teasel patch
the old fort and the malt whisky

the scree slope and the circling buzzard
the lonely glen and the heather fire
the sphagnum moss and the golden lichen
the bladder wrack and the shell mound
the west wind and the last harebell

the lark notes and the ripe brambles
the tweed jacket and the grouse moor
the barbed wire and the holy island
the standing stone and the loud burn
the wild goats and the bog myrtle

MAOILIOS M. CAIMBEUL / MYLES M. CAMPBELL (1944–)

An Referendum airson Pàrlamaid ann an Alba 1/3/79

Air latha an Referendum

Tha sneachda ga do chòmhdach
mar òigh a' dol gu a banais,
's ged a dhiùltas do ghilead na tràillean
bidh tu ann an ceangal a' phòsaidh
mus bi an oidhche seachad,
Alba bhòidheach dhan tug mi gràdh.
Tha thu air tighinn gu inbhe,
fàgaidh tu taigh t' athar
agus seasaidh tu ann an comann saor
ris a' chòrr den t-saoghal.
Bidh tu fhèin agus saorsa

nan càraid a' fàs gu suairce
agus air an latha seo èiridh tu suas
agus canaidh tu, cha dhealaich sinn gu bràth.
Agus cuimhnichidh tu air do latha bòidheach,
air an latha a sheas thu nad chulaidh ghil,
agus bidh tu moiteil agus glan agus saor.

ach air an latha an dèidh an Referendum

A thruaghain!
'S tu nad òigh fhathast
gun saorsa, gun solas, gun ola.
Nach bochd nach tàirngeadh cuideigin thu!
Ach tha eagal orm gum fàs thu
nad sheann mhaighdeann, gearanach, crosta,
ag èisteachd ris a' ghaoith anns an t-simileir
agus anns na craobhan fàsail,
a' feitheamh ris a' phosta a' tighinn,
a' faicinn do thiormachd anns an sgàthan,
a' tarraing do shàilean an taigh t' athar –
thu na thaice gu h-iomlan –
a' smaoineachadh air na seòid
nach tig gu bràth gad iarraidh.
Theich do bhòidhchead.
Cha bhi eòlas agad air gràdh.
Agus càite bheil na mnathan a nì gaoir
no a bhuaileas basan aig do thuireadh?

The Referendum for a Scottish Assembly 1/3/79

On the day of the Referendum

Snow covers you
like a virgin going to her wedding,
and though your whiteness repels slaves
you'll be in the bonds of marriage
before the night is out,
beautiful Scotland whom I have loved.
You have come of age,
you will leave your father's house
and stand in free communion
with the rest of the world.

You and freedom
will be a couple growing civilly
and on this day you will rise up
and you will say, we will never part.
And you will remember your beautiful day,
the day that you stood in your white dress,
and you will be proud and pure and free.

but on the day after the Referendum

You wretch!
A virgin yet
without freedom, or happiness, or oil.
How sad that no-one could nail you!
But I'm afraid you will grow
to be an old maid, complaining, bad-tempered,
listening to the wind in the chimney
and in the desolate trees,
waiting for the postman to come,
seeing your barrenness in the mirror,
dragging your heels in your father's house –
completely dependent on him for support –
thinking of the suitors
who will never come back to seek you.
Your beauty has fled.
You'll have no knowledge of love.
And where are the women who will keen
or strike palms at your funeral?

ROBIN MUNRO (1946–)

Patriotism

If you mean the gean
and the blackthorn blossom,
I am your reluctant patriot,

the universal countryman.
And if I live above no betterland
than this reluctant soil,
then it must serve me.

I notice trees feel blind into the earth
like calves snouting for the udder.

I love this roaring winter,
for want of another, and this rock,
which is the shape of kingdoms.

LIZ LOCHHEAD (1947–)

Inter-City

Hammered like a bolt
diagonally through Scotland (my
small dark country) this
train's a
swaying caveful of half-
seas over oil-men (fuck
this fuck that fuck
everything) bound for Aberdeen and
North Sea Crude.
Empty beercans of
spun aluminium roll like ballbearings
underfoot and
sloshing amber's a
storm in whisky glass or two.
Outside's all
black absolutely
but for fizzing starbursts
of weirdblue or orange streetlights
and lit-up grids of windows.
Only bits of my own blurred
back-to-front face and
my mind elsewhere.
The artsyfartsy magazine I'm
not even pretending to read
wide open
at a photograph called Portrait of Absence.

Scotch Mist (The Scotsport Song)

Lazy Sunday Afternoon in Central Scotland.
You scoosh 'Yes please'
Behind your knees
And ask him what he's got planned?
All over Central Scotland, men are pulling down the blinds.
The men of Central Scotland got something
Sort of Sunday Afternoonish on their minds.

Match of the day, action replay it's on Scotsport.
Chuck us a can, a man's not a man without Scotsport.
You can cook good, you can look good
You can play hard to get.
To turn him on's impossible –
He's turning on the set.
He'll never tell you he loves you
Unless he's pissed.
Love in a Cold Climate,
Scotch Mist!

Pissed off with life
Your average wife
Is quite entitled to feel
He's a waste of a bottle of Bad–E–Das
And a damned good Meal.
He'll say, after Scotsport
You're next on the list.
Love in a Cold Climate,
Scotch mist!

from Mary Queen of Scots Got Her Head Chopped Off

'Scotland, Whit Like?'

Alone, FIDDLER *charges up the space with eldritch tune, wild and sad, then goes. Enter into the ring, whip in hand, our 'chorus',* LA CORBIE. *An interesting, ragged ambiguous creature in her cold spotlight.*

LA CORBIE: Country: Scotland. Whit like is it?
It's a peatbog, it's a daurk forest.
It's a cauldron o' lye, a saltpan or a coal mine.
If you're gey lucky it's a bricht bere meadow, or a park o' kye.
Or mibbe... it's a field o' stanes.
It's a tenement or a merchant's ha'.
It's a hure hoose or a humble cot. Princes Street or Paddy's Merkit.
It's a fistfu' o' fish or a pickle o' oatmeal.
It's a queen's banquet o' roast meats and junketts.
It depends. It depends... Ah dinna ken whit like your *Scotland* is.

Here's mines.

National flower: the thistle.
National pastime: nostalgia.
National weather: smirr, haar, drizzle, snow.
National bird: the crow, the corbie, le corbeau, moi!
How me? Eh? Eh? Eh? Voice like a choked laugh. Ragbag o' a
burd in ma black duds, a' angles and elbows and broken oxter
feathers, black beady een in ma executioner's hood. No braw,
but Ah think Ah ha'e a sort of black glamour.
Do I no put ye in mind of a skating minister, or, on the other
fit, the parish priest, the dirty beast?
My nest's a rickle o' sticks.
I live on lamb's eyes and road accidents.
Oh, see, after the battle, after the battle man, it's a pure feast – ma eyes
are owre big even for my belly, in lean years o' peace, my belly thinks
my throat's been cut.
(Laughing, LA CORBIE *cracks whip for* THE ENTRANCE OF THE ANIMALS.
In a strange circus our characters, gorgeous or pathetic, parade: MARY,
ELIZABETH, HEPBURN, DANCER/RICCIO, KNOX, DARNLEY *all dirty and
down on his luck. They circle, snarling, smiling, posing. And halt. Drumbeat
ceases.)*
(With both Queens by the hand, parading them) Once upon a time
there were twa queens on the wan green island, and the wan green
island was split inty twa kingdoms...

Advertisement for a Scottish Servant

Would you like a very Scottish servant all your own
who'll do for, spiritually speaking, you alone?
A lad o' pairts: a prophet, a historian and more,
a therapist/composer who understands the score?
Guaranteed – your past and future contrapuntally combined
into a pre-determined present so defined
you'll never need to think or feel again!

Your gardener for life, his motto: prune first then restrain
the slightest sign of growth. He'll cut you down to size
(for your own good) then train your roots to do
their darkest: dig deep, grasp, immobilise;
if needs be, split your soul into two.
He'll anticipate your every beck and call –
he *kent your faither*, after all!

As a Scottish-school economist he takes great pains
where pain was never due. Never credit-giving Keynes,
he soon has Adam Smith's close-fistedness outclassed
insisting every childhood trauma last
your lifetime. All you'll need to know is what he'll tell you,
even when you're sleeping he'll compel you
treat his dreams as if they were your own.

Say 'yes' – he's yours! Your very own: flesh, blood and bone
passed on as Scottish fathers pass him on
to Scottish sons (with references supplied
unto the seventh generation). A tendency to patricide
but nothing serious – just words – so never heed him.
This very Scottish servant –
who needs him?

RAYMOND VETTESE (1950–)

Scotland '79

This is the place o the deid,
tho resurrection promised
canna happen here;
sae lourd the stane o the past is,
e'en miracle cuidna shift it.

Gin as the angels o Heiven
and God Himsel cam doon,
they wadna gar oor dry banes jink;
we're a tribe no juist lost
but abandoned, e'en by oorsels.

Scottish Names

I love the names o Scotland:
Ecclefechan, Auchenblae,
Fordoun, Gourdon, Forfar, Kirkcudbright,
Dunnichen, Echt, Panadram, Drumtochty,
and wha could ignore Auchtermuchty?

I love the names o Scotland:
hoo they dirl thro me, the stounds
o consonants, nieves o sounds
that dunt on the map; ilka ane redounds
wi stickit pride: these are my boonds!

I love the names o Scotland:
Friockheim, Fettes, Pittenweem, Pitcaithly,
Dunnotar, Dunfermline, Aberdower, Invertay,
Catterline, Corstorphine, Craigmillar, Cruden Bay,
and wha could ignore Clachnaharry?

I love the names o Scotland:
hoo e'en the prosaic is owreset
intil a ferlie ye canna forget,
tho it's aiblins but a place whaur burns aince met
or wee wuid fort wis, and is yet,

but only in the name. Oor past's
chairted for us, oor history's here,
in Balmaha, Birnam, Dunblane, Ardersier:
the names clash oot, tirl on the ear,
and wha could ignore braw Durisdeer?

I love the names o Scotland,
the names that are oors, and tho Wounded Knee
is fine and fair and sad, it's no Fyvie,
and gin Montrose, whaun I dee, winna hae me:
bury my hairt in the cricket-pitch o Freuchie!

GERALD MANGAN (1951–)

Scotland the Ghost

It's no deid, the auld land, it's no deid in spirit:
All it wants is a stirrup-cup, and a coronach to stir it.
Drinking up at closing-time, it's girning in its chains:
O when, O floo'er o Scotland, will we see your like again?

It's no deid in spirit, no, it's never done with haunting;
But it never makes its mind up, to tell us what it's wanting.
The spirit's weak without the flesh, but still it lifts the hackles –
With its head below its arm-pit, and its ankle still in shackles.

It drags the sword off Wallace, it's lugging Bruce's helmet;
But spiders make their webs in it, and a draught would overwhelm it.
The heart inside the armour's like the queen inside her cell:
The breath of Knox has chilled it, and blasted it to hell.

The crown fell off with Jamie, when he took the English tiller;
The head fell off with Saltoun, who sold the tongue for siller.
When Bonnie Charlie dreamed his dream, to stick it back together,
He met a butcher's cleaver, and it ended up in slivers.

The heart grew black as Glasgow, then, and rumbled underground;
The disembodied head was known as Edinburgh town.
When Burns sprang up to sing of flesh, and earth, and barley-grain,
He sang too low, too late to touch the Socratean brain.

Sheriff Walter found the body stripped to bare essentials,
And shivering in the heather; but he saw its true potential.
He dressed it up in tartan plaid and kilt, for exhibition,
Installed it in his stately home, and charged them all admission.

Victoria had it dance a fling, and played it for a puppet –
A gillie on a string, without a *sgian dubh* to cut it.
Mass-produced in clockwork, it made the perfect vassal
To paint the atlas red for her, or dandle in her castle.

Burke and Hare worked double-time, supplying all the clients
Who analysed the body in the interests of science.
Doctor Jekyll knew the head was severed from the heart,
And drank a heady potion to explore the private parts.

GERRIE FELLOWS (1954–)

At the Aliens' Gate

I

The one saying
> You have no street
> You have no town
> Your voice is nothing we know

is the one who pushed the burning rags
through the letterbox

The one saying
> You have no voice
> Your voice is nothing

is the uniformed man at the Aliens' Gate
willing himself to believe
that the person
with the careful suitcase
is out to put one over on him
has uprooted himself from his own language
in order to do this

The man at the Aliens' Gate
carrying in his suitcase the floods of the rainy season
is darker than he is   braver

II

Scotland   my touchpaper
red rag to an enraged girl

I become a stranger again
listener   to foreign tongues
strange utterances
from those who consider their speech
to be commonplace and true
repeated, made perfect   each consonant
a wheel turning a whole revolution
in the mouth

> You have no street
> You have no town
> You have no voice

My voice no longer fits me

Another woman
is a wee wifey asking me to tea
> There is a gale above Glen Shiel
> I am broken in two
> Help me to be made whole

But I become a stranger
close up   a bog asphodel
whispering
> I will not   be broken

BASHABI FRASER (1954–)

Between My Two Worlds

When I left London
I wrote of English summers
Of bluebells and blackbirds
And dreamt of the snow.

I came back to Scotland
And longed for the Monsoons,
The flocks flying homewards
In the deep sunset glow.

My mother's concern, my father's care
My daughter's soft body that wasn't there;
So I switched my priorities and went back to stay
Carrying deep longings when I went away

To be enfolded in India
In its rich living spree
Yet turning to Britain
In my memory;

Till the unexpected happened
And my worlds switched again
To experience long daylight
And pine for the rain

Of a country burning
With the sun and my pain
Of living between two worlds
That I cannot maintain.

While my mother falters
And my father grows old
I hold *this* my country
As my daughter holds.

Originally

We came from our own country in a red room
which fell through the fields, our mother singing
our father's name to the turn of the wheels.
My brothers cried, one of them bawling *Home,*
Home, as the miles rushed back to the city,
the street, the house, the vacant rooms
where we didn't live any more. I stared
at the eyes of a blind toy, holding its paw.

All childhood is an emigration. Some are slow,
leaving you standing, resigned, up an avenue
where no one you know stays. Others are sudden.
Your accent wrong. Corners, which seem familiar,
leading to unimagined, pebble-dashed estates, big boys
eating worms and shouting words you don't understand.
My parents' anxiety stirred like a loose tooth
in my head. *I want our own country*, I said.

But then you forget, or don't recall, or change,
and, seeing your brother swallow a slug, feel only
a skelf of shame. I remember my tongue
shedding its skin like a snake, my voice
in the classroom sounding just like the rest. Do I only think
I lost a river, culture, speech, sense of first space
and the right place? Now. *Where do you come from?*
strangers ask. *Originally?* And I hesitate.

Anglophobia

Sometimes, after ten pints of Pale in Mather's,
my pals and I discuss, with reasoned calm,
the origins of Anglophobia.

The philosophy was mother's milk to me.
Our cat was called Moggy the Bruce.
In 1966 my uncle Billy died on his knees
before the telly screaming 'It didnae
cross the line ye blind bastard!'
I remember my Grandad, seventy five
and ridged with nicotine, sitting, grimly watching
a schoolgirls' hockey match. Hands like shovels,
he'd never even seen a game with sticks
but he was bawling 'Bully up, Fiji,
get intae these English!'

An expression of lost identity, they say.
Some identity.
We were the most manic crew of cut-throats
out, never happy unless we were fighting,
preferably each other; any venue,
Turkestan to Guadeloupe.
It was only after the Pax Britannica
that any of us had a free minute between rounds
to contribute to the culture of the world.

By some strange alchemy we had however found
the untapped source of arrogance and up
to our arses in mud we could thumb our noses
at the Florentines and all the other poofs
of the Renaissance and take some solace
from thumpings by our betters by claiming
moral victory; a piece of turf from Solway
Moss and the crossbar from Culloden.

But despite all that, and sober, the limp
red lions stir the blood and in a crowd of
fellow ba-heids I'll conjure up the pantheon
of Scotland's past and jewel it with lies.
Unswerving stubborness.
I suppose that in the graveyard of nations
Scotland's epitaph will not be a volume
like the French but a single line:
'Ye'll be hearing from us.'

PETER MCCAREY (1956–)

Referendum Day 3

Irrefutable, and unconvincing,
said David Hume of Bishop Berkeley's argument
that a tree unseen by anyone in a wood
is undemonstrable and does not exist.
Hume wouldn't let in God for the trees to root in His attention,
nor would he let the leprechaun of reason from his grip,
but the thought that those elaborate dendrological arrangements
were a class that snapped to attention when the teacher turned from
the board,
must have driven him crackers (I can see him in the staffroom).
Don't fret: the raptor that patrols Ben Vorlich
brings great clefts of pine to be as it seeks out other things;
the cushioned thump at the back of the woodpecker's skull,
the stuck of sap when it wags itself like a dog that grips a stick,
the ramp and tilt of slaters in the gullies of its bark
suggest that, yes, the tree is there. Says Berkeley, 'show it to me!'
I can't. And when I fly away from Scotland,
packing it carefully down in cotton wool for another year,
when I think of it, near as old as any tree,
am I using a Roman stone for a step? Is this the last
light from a done star reeling into my eye like a measuring tape?

Referendum Day 2

Was it Kelvin or Clerk-Maxwell, Satie or Tobias Hume
orchestrated this foregathering on the darker side of
Metis (one of Jupiter's wee satellites),
up to our ears in aspic, re-rehearsing Brigadoon?

It would seem (though I can't say what Dunce or Watt or Michael Scot
concocted the theology) that we're staying here
in Corkerhill West – 'a Tibetan assembly' –
until our heirs decide, like, if we are or if we're not.

I mean, severally and jointly are we a nation or a neep?
(Neep! Neep!) This thing's not working! Yogi Bear and his
cheap laser link to the front page of the *Herald*...
Tea break's over: back on your heids.

Referendum Day 1

St Columba voted no
from the orbit of Io
which is where the skilful go
        skating in the autumn.

Scots wha peddled kingdom come
Knox and Marx and opium,
cattle prods and, eh, the Drum,
        birl there in tandem.

Early exit polls from Hell
(...*reel and set, cross and...*) tell
'Don't Think Twice' is doing well
        out of pandemonium.

Did I say Columba neg?
What I meant was good St Meg.
Sub-sub editor, I beg
        take a corrigendum.

Reader, think on them and me,
disenfranchised over sea and time:
we're waiting breathlessly
on YOUR decision.

ELIZABETH BURNS (1957–)

Scotland

    – a broken thistle
    on a bare hillside
    the purple of its flowers
    bent to earth
    spikey leaves withered
    wisps of thistledown
    blown off across
    fields of exile

ALAN RIACH (1957–)

The Dogs of Scotland

You only cross this border once –

The rain pulls back its curtains once again, and light
falls like sheaves from the clouds, harvests across
the horizon, stooked in the earth, leaning into sky.
The rain twists off like helter-skelter figures of eight
on roller-skateboard fluency and turning all the time,
never to be predicted, and the light says hello to the call
of all the dogs of Scotland, opening their throats to the air.

You can hear them bark in sunshine in the city parks, while foxes nose
through bins in alleys, brazen it out on the edge of their domain,
on borderlands, like David, three years old, running in the snowfall,
                                                          all hands up,
a million unending of tiny wet kisses, now, for the first time only,
                                                          blessings
in the country and the city, in an air too filthy and too clean
to want any more or less of, yet, so doggedly –
except this particular piece of the planet forever.

WILLIAM HERSHAW (1957–)

June: Songs of the Scottish Examination Board English Marker

1

The High Schools, Academics, Colleges, Saints,
I shuffle between my hands.

Morgan, Madras, Kelvinside, Wester Hailes,
I red ink their mistakes.

Dalbeattie, Lochgelly, Our Lady's, Balfron,
I envelope, number and grade.

Selkirk, Dalziel, Balwearie, Nairn,
I process their thoughts, dreams and lives.

Without passion, reproach or approval
I Standard Grade and Higher.

So many lives pass before my eyes
on the way to the rest of theirs
while mine stops here with this slow and painful business.

Through the small glass square in my attic roof
the sound of children's laughter in the street
upsets my penning rhythm.

I lift up my head in the summer heat then,
Hazelhead, Sandwick, St Columba's, Arbroath,
Royal High, Bannockburn, Dalkeith.

2

No future 'A' pass Higher here:
she wrote of her father and feelings,
how he lay on a waterbed
whey-faced and skeletal from fighting the cancer
the last time her mother had taken her
to the hospice for the dying.

I wrote on it:
gives a clear account of personal experience;
communicates a sense of involvement;
sentences accurate but not varied;
does not demonstrate skill with language
or overall distinction of Credit English;
General, Grade 3.

O God,
when my final examination comes,
do not measure me
by the same pitiless criteria.

JAMES ROBERTSON (1958–)

Very Scottish Weather

You watch the weather arrive in droves:
Bitter, fierce, grim and unrelenting.
A batch of Scottish stereotypes perhaps?
When this thought strikes you, idly you begin
To toy with it – November's squalls as images
of Scottish poetry.
Those angry blasts battering the window
And, in between, the sudden calming lulls
Are such a meeting of extremes they might be
MacDiarmid in full flow.
That rise and fall in the wind –
Is that not the very sound of Sorley intoning,
Breaking off to tell you that the English version
Is no good at all, at all?
This gust snatching and ditching down the street's
A bit of Morgan surely, throwing up all kinds of wonders
In the mind – beer-cans and newspapers
The percussion and confetti of a great parade.
And on the glass, close to your face,
Raindrops track like the little poems
Of MacCaig
Trickling drily
Down the page.

You could go on, but then someone comes in with the tea,
Like your mother, saying,
'You wouldn't want to go out in that.'

Cream of Scottish Youth

rolled

trousers to knees and
danced a weird waltz.

Chucked bangers at club-feet,
snow at girls' faces,
crisp bags full of frogspawn slop.

Sat among ropes, wore Harlequin socks,
rabbit ear collars and baratheas, spat
on the heads of waggy yap dogs
allowed to run free by owners.
Rolled

jumper sleeves to elbows
and pretended to be Thalidomide.
Smoked
singles
bought from ice-cream vans,
scuffed mushy leaves with best shoes, kicked
puddle-twigs at the dumb sun as the wind
swiped through big branches, scurried
among big shadows.
Tumbled,

yelling, from dizzy swish roundabouts,
pelted the swans in the dam with cans,
tore the pages from the brainyboy's books
then tipped his schoolbag upside down,
lit fires just for the hell of it, splashed
scruffy steam gold against the oaks

that had seen it all before.

Ate banana and marmite rolls
as gloom curdled in the cloakroom.
Looked at photos of whopper breasts,
studied photos of open legs,

fell over each other to sniff
the future.
Fumbled
in panties at puberty parties,
swallowed Pale Ale, Newcastle Brown,
Breaker Malt Liquor and Eldorado.
Gathered at night to sit on walls
or topple sun-dials onto grass.
Made scratchy marks on sheds and lamp-posts,
squirted stinking, chemist perfumes
onto clothes of teeth-brace boys,
spluttered over thick Panatellas,
chewed on borrowed plastic pipes.
Dropped lit matches into postboxes,
said the words 'fanny', 'gobble' and 'spunk',
spooned in shagalley toothpaste dark,
fell over each other to reach

the sex.
Grew
hair long, got it chopped off,
did everything wrong, everything
right.
Threw slushballs at respectable windows,
stones at clocks, rocks at stars
and cruised cobbled wynds with springs
in heels,
skated, laughing into the void, fell over
each other to ask

the time.
Rolled

Trousers to knees and
danced a daft can-can.
Rolled back to ankles, hobbled
for home, the whipped

cream of Scotland's dream.

DAVID KINLOCH (1959–)

Braveheart

O Mel! Mel of the hair extenders! Braveheart!
O Mad Mac Mel! It is I,
Walt, Walt Whitman, who salutes you.
When I heard at the close of the day
That your heroic film of the Wallace
would premiere in Stirling, I floated

From Mount Florida, high above Glasgow, floated
From the residence of my comrade Kinloch, a brave heart
Like you, I crossed the hummock-land of Shotts as Wallace
Did on leaving Elderslie, I
Sped through that dun-coloured upland (beside the great M8) that day
To celebrate your epic but most of all to be with you

O Mel! But also to petition you,
Dark singer of Democracy, you who floated
Like a Moses through Scottish bogs, waiting for the day
To release your noble, simple people, their brave brave heart
Clasped in an English vice. O Mel, I
Confuse you, mix you in my mind with Wallace.

And who could blame me? For you and Wallace
Commingle in my scented breast, you
Two and I, comrades all, shooting the film of liberty I
Crave above all else, I crave and lost as my successors floated
Back up stream to a land of villanelles and sonnets. Bravehearts!
Brave Walt! a bearded Ariel imprisoned in a bad sestina who would this day

Be free again by your example, free today
To live today, to sing the love of comrades as Wallace
Did. He could not rhyme, his only beat the braveheart
Quad-pumping the eclectic plaid above his knees (What knees!). You
Saw him Mel, as clearly as I see you who floated
From Australia via Hollywood to this premiere. I

Name the perfumed guests as they arrive, I
Shake the manly hand of Jodie Foster, day
Dream as Christian Slater – he of the slow doe-eyes – floats
In. We sit transfixed as the credits of your Wallace
Roll but I have eyes alone for you,
Peach of a biceps – your musk white thighs – muncher of
power-breakfasts, Braveheart!

Mel Wallace, Will Gibson, this day
Your barbaric yawp injects its braveheart
Into me. You and I floating and free.

ROBERT CRAWFORD (1959–)

Scotland

Semiconductor country, land crammed with intimate expanses,
Your cities are superlattices, heterojunctive
Graphed from the air, your cropmarked farmlands
Are epitaxies of tweed.

All night motorways carry your signal, swept
To East Kilbride or Dunfermline. A brightness of low headlands
Beams-in the dawn to Fife's interstices,
Optoelectronics of hay.

Micro-nation. So small you cannot be forgotten,
Bible inscribed on a ricegrain, hi-tech's key
Locked into the earth, your televised Glasgows
Are broadcast in Rio. Among circuitboard crowsteps

To be minaturised is not small-minded.
To love you needs more details than the Book of Kells –
Your harbours, your photography, your democratic intellect
Still boundless, chip of a nation.

Alba 1997

Cumaidh sinn an gàrradh
Fhathast is an dìg fhèin, seadh,
A tha mar gum b' ann mar chrìoch
Eadar dùthaich na h-Albann 's an còrr,
Eadar sinn fhèin is coimhearsnaich
Bun na h-ursainn
Ach, bho seo a-mach,
An àite bhith 'n còmhnaidh ri sadail
'S ri sadail ar cuid sgudail
Thairis air uile gu lèir,
Saoil nach glèidh sin againn fhìn
A' chuid-mhòr dheth mar eallach,
Dìreach air ghaol na rèite
Eadrainn mar Chlann Mhic-an-Duine

'S cò aig' a tha fios dè dh' fhàsas
As an lagais a dh' èireas às?

Scotland 1997

We'll keep the dividing wall
A wee whilie yet, and the dyke
Which is like a border
Between Scotland and the rest,
Between ourselves
And the folk next door
But, from now on,
Instead of forever flinging
All our rubbish over it,
Suppose we keep most of it ourselves,
For the sake of reconciliation, you understand,
Between us as Jock's wee bairns

And who knows what'll emerge
From the resultant midden?

JACKIE KAY (1961–)

In my country

walking by the waters
down where an honest river
shakes hands with the sea,
a woman passed round me
in a slow watchful circle,
as if I were a superstition;

or the worst dregs of her imagination,
so when she finally spoke
her words spliced into bars
of an old wheel. A segment of air.
Where do you come from?
'Here,' I said, 'Here. These parts.'

The Broons' Bairn's Black

a skipping rhyme

Scotland is having a heart attack
Scotland is having a heart attack
Scotland is having a heart attack
The Broons' Bairn's Black.

W.N. HERBERT (1961–)

The Postcards of Scotland

My country is being delivered repeatedly
onto the 'WELCOME' mat of my mind
with the light patter of postcards falling
like flattened raindrops; postcards from
its very moniply, its each extremity:
the drunk dog's profile of Fife,
the dangling penis of Kintyre,
the appendix of the Mull of Galloway,
the uvula of Ulva and the septum and

spat-out dentures of the Western Isles,
the whale's maw of the Moray Firth
and the steam-snort cockade
of the Orkneys.
                              Every village sends me
its image like a sweetheart's *Vergissemienicht*,
to be carried in the wallet on a dangerous journey,
for I am voyaging so far within
all thoughts of 'home',
it is as though I were stationary, and
it is they who fly away in every direction;
Scotland exploding like a hand-grenade until
its clachans catch up with the stars,
its cities collide with galaxies, scattering
the contents of their galleries, unspooling
their cinemas, bargain-basketing
their shopping precincts.

Only their postcards survive,
like the familiarity of light
still travelling from extinguished stars.

But what postcards can endure transmission
across such addressless gulfs, insertion
in such a black hole as
the letterbox of my discrimination?

Certainly the tartan-fringed idylls
of small dogs and pretty girls
hypnotised by the contents of a flapping kilt
despite the rubicund obesity of its owner
and the fact that he wears his gingery beard
sans moustache:
                              nothing shall destroy
these, not even the incendiary glance
of the Angel of Death,
for which reason Auld Clootie sends him them
weekly, along with their sib,
the fisherman catching Nessie,
because Auld Nick kens weel this degraduation
of Thor's mythic encounter with
the Midgard Serpent
is a pain in the angelic butt.

But these I throw aside negligently
in the search for my true home.

Not the misty-lensed monstrosities
of quality pap-merchants, with
their dug-up zombie shots, their same old
purpling panoramas of hills and lochs
giving the glad eye in weathers that never were.
Nor the shampooing of sheep and the oiling
of Highland cattles' horns; nor
the photographic humping of Belties
and the image-maker's posing hand
fist-fucking the cute black bun. Nor
the fascinating 'Doors of Many Post Offices' shot,
presenting such a quaint contrast
to the works of Bernhard und Hilla Becher
with series of urban water towers,
or the disused mines' pit-heads of Sanquhar,
and the lowland belt across to Fife.
Nor the orange and viridian 'Closes of Glasgow' series,
each tile personally signed
by Rennie Mackintosh, miraculously free
of asbestosis-tinged alcoholics' vomit.
Give me the postcards of muncipal Scotland;
each caravan park lovingly identified
by a zen-succinct description printed
on a white border along the postcard's base:
each children's playpark accurately defined
down to the lack of smiles on the weans' faces;
each council flowerbed pointlessly recorded.
Here are the proud wastes of our city centres
accurately seen for the first time,
begotten from the copulation
of councillors with cement-mixers,
the tight wads of backhanders jammed
up their quivering rectums.

Here is the genuine face of eternity,
where 'swimming pool' means
a kidney-shaped pond eighteen inches deep,
the colour of chopped jobbies
full of pale bodies and pink flotation aids;
where 'beach' is a silver fingernail,

clipped and spinning from the camera like
a boomerang covered in lice.
Observe the two old men leaning towards
the water, out of focus; they
are transfixed by a monster more fecund
than any Nessie: that brown weasel shape
is a wet spaniel bitch,
you have only to scratch
the postcard to release the perfume
of soggy dog. Observe
that child on the sliver of toe-cheese
called the 'beach' at Portpatrick:
she has one foot in a plastic bucket
forever. Paradise smells
of tarry seaweed, it tastes of sand
in lettuce and tomato sandwiches.
I couldn't think of never dying
anywhere else.

Here is my only home,
my Heaven; observe
these photographs of Mercat crosses
and town centres packed with Anglias,
the ghosts of Hillman Minxes.
Surely those figures eating fried egg rolls
behind the glass of Italian cafes
are the philosophers of the Enlightenment.
Surely that is Susan Ferrier gossiping
outside the crappy dress shop
with Margaret Oliphant. Surely
Robert Burns is buying a haggis supper
from that chipper in Annan,
William Dunbar is stotting from
The Cement-Mixer's Arms.

Only in these images do I recognise
the beautiful nincompoop face
of my nation; the sullen brows
of the stultified young farmer
speeding out of shot;
the *Sweetheart Stout* expression
of the girl with a knife in her handbag.
Only in these postcards
can I ever be at rest.

The Queen of Sheba

Scotland, you have invoked her name
just once too often
in your Presbyterian living rooms.
She's heard, yea
even unto heathenish Arabia
your vixen's bark of poverty, come down
the family like a lang neb, a thrawn streak,
a wally dug you never liked
but can't get shot of.

She's had enough. She's come.
Whit, tae this dump? Yes!
She rides first camel
of a swaying caravan
from her desert sands
to the peat and bracken
of the Pentland hills
across the fit-ba pitch
to the thin mirage
of the swings and chute; scattered with glass.
Breathe that streamy musk
on the Curriehill Road, not mutton-shanks
boiled for broth, nor the chlorine stink
of the swimming pool where skinny girls
accuse each other of verrucas.
In her bathhouses women bear
warm pot-bellied terracotta pitchers
on their laughing hips.
All that she desires, whatever she asks
She will make the bottled dreams
of your wee lasses
look like *sweeties*.

Spangles scarcely cover
her gorgeous breasts, hanging gardens
jewels, frankincense; more voluptuous
even than Vi-next-door, whose
high-heeled slippers
keeked from dressing gowns

like little hooves, wee tails
of pink fur stuffed in the cleavage of her toes;
more audacious even than Currie Liz
who led the gala floats
through the Wimpey scheme
in a ruby-red Lotus Elan
before the Boys' Brigade band
and the Brownies' borrowed coal-truck;
hair piled like candy-floss;
who lifted her hands from the neat wheel
to tinkle her fingers
at her tricks
      among the masons and the elders and the police.

The cool black skin
of the Bible couldn't hold her,
nor the atlas green
on the kitchen table,
you stuck with thumbs
and split to fruity hemispheres –
yellow Yemen, Red Sea, *Ethiopia*. Stick in
with the homework and you'll be
cliver like yer faither.
but no too cliver,
no *above yersel*.

See her lead those great soft camels
widdershins round the kirk-yaird,
smiling
as she eats
avocados with apostle spoons
she'll teach us how. But first

she wants to strip the willow
she desires the keys
to the National Library
she is beckoning
      the lasses
      in the awestruck crowd...

Yes, we'd like to
     clap the camels,
to smell the spice,

admire her hairy legs and
bonny wicked smile, we want to take
PhDs in Persian, be vice
to her president: we want
to help her
      ask some Difficult Questions

she's shouting for our wisest man
to test her mettle:

      Scour Scotland for a Solomon!

Sure enough: from the back of the crowd
someone growls:
      whae do you think y'ur?

and a thousand laughing girls and she
      draw our hot breath
      and shout:

THE QUEEN OF SHEBA!

On the Design Chosen for the New Scottish Parliament Building by Architect Enric Miralles

An upturned boat
    – a watershed.

RICHARD PRICE (1965–)

Hinges

On the airstrip: fog.
Nothing taking off.
Five in the afternoon
more or less.

I'd have called it a 'flitting'
but it was a year before I was born –
to my father it was 'moving house'.

He was Ma's envoy in Scotland:
he'd just chosen a field
that would grow into a bungalow
and he'd pay for it
whenever the bathroom,
opening on the hall
with a frosted glass door,
trapped her, towelnaked,
before the postman
and something to be signed for.

Through the same melted glass
I saw my first memory:
my eldest brother, nine or ten,
was stretching and not touching anything,
petrolburns on his face and hands,
a human X at the front door
(on a building site a friend
had clicked him alight;
we still don't know the bet).

On the airstrip: fog, night.
Eleven o'clock.
My father is being practical
on the hotel phone:
'I am speaking
back in my room.'

In the morning in England,
like a new couple
two police officers stood back
as Ma opened the door.
They had to be reassured:
she gave them tea in the fine bone.
(Just beyond the wicker of radar
the first plane out, just past midnight,
had dropped like a figurine.)

In the afternoon
my mother met my father in Arrivals.
Before they held held held each other
he says they just shook hands.

HAMID SHAMI (1969–)

Lost

To quote my distant friend Imran MacLeod,
'A man with no culture has no identity.'

The last I heard from him was, he was off
To the Himalayas.

He had a very confused childhood.

Father was Scottish,
Mother Pakistani.

They'd always be arguing over many things
Concerning him.

One was religion.

Father wanted him brought up
A Catholic; mother wanted a Muslim.

Was the only boy on our street who went
To mosque on Fridays and chapel on Sundays.

But in the mountains

God's sure to find him.

KEVIN MACNEIL (1972–)

Young Chinese and Scottish

These bastards I feed.
I serve them sourfaced
from this lair's fiery kitchen,
dish up noodles of rich-crispy-chicken
in an atmosphere thick
with soy, sweat and steam.

Ape-drunk, certain, they'll swagger in,
pie-eyed and slobbering on my thin
silken blouse: '(Hur hur) Hello rare
mah wee China doll, er...
Ah'll havvuh speshl (hur hur) sixty-nine
(hur hur) uhna bedduh speshl flied lice.'

My folks tell tales of dragons, but I have tasted haggis!
See, Buddha-sure, I just hunger for dancing, drinks
and a Scot I adore. How I love to not
taste homesweethome in his plain Scottish food.
I'll serve no more. Take away
the Chinese till I'm half understood.

IRFAN MERCHANT (1973–)

I'm a Racist

'If this is a paki, a darkie and a chinky, you're a racist.'
Slogan on a poster produced by the City of Edinburgh Council, with three
appropriate head-and-shoulder photos.

I saw a paki
on the side of a bus.

I'm a paki.

I thought to myself:

How nice. A paki
on the side of a bus.

Growing up Black in Scotland

Growing up black in Scotland and I wonder if we exist
We look in school history books but we don't exist
We buy plasters that are pink cause we don't exist
Use tinted cream that is white cause we don't exist
We look for black make up but it don't exist
We search TV screens, papers but we don't exist

On weddings and birthdays we look at smiling
white faces on cards cause we don't exist
On the birth of our children we see rosebud mothers
And pink chubby babies smiling up from rows of cards

We don't exist now
Our children don't exist
Growing up black in Britain
I wonder if we exist at all

Envoi and Prelude

ANNE FRATER (1967–)

Dealachadh

Cheannaich e thu mar thràille,
a' creidsinn
air sgàth 's gur ann le òr a phàigh e
gum biodh tu modhail.

Thug e air èiginn thu
uair an dèidh uair;
thug e ort a dhol a shabaid dhà
fhad 's a bha e fhèin na shuidh'
ri taobh an teine;
chuir e air falbh do chlann
mus fhàsadh iad neartmhor
agus lìon e a bhroinn le do bhiadh
fhad 's a bha thu a' gal leis an acras.

Ghoid e gach nì a bh' agad:
ghoid e na fàdan a-mach às do theine;
ghèarr e do ghruag agus reic e i;
thug e 'n fhuil fhèin
a-mach às do chuislean,
agus rinn e siùrsach dhìot,
ga do reic ri 'chuid fhèin.

Alba àlainn
cuimhnich
air a' bhean uasal a bh' unnad,
agus bris am pòsadh seo
mus bi na trì ceud bliadhna suas.

Divorce

He bought you like a slave
thinking
that because he paid with gold
you would be submissive.

Time and again
he raped you;

he forced you to fight his wars
while he sat
beside the fire;
he sent your children away
in case they grew strong,
and he filled his belly with food
while you cried with hunger.

He stole everything that you had:
he stole the peats from your fire;
he cut your hair and sold it;
he took the very blood
from your veins
and turned you into a whore,
selling you to his own kind.

Beautiful Alba
remember
the noble woman that you were
and end this marriage
before the three hundred years have passed.

IAIN CRICHTON SMITH (1928–1998)

The Beginning of a New Song

Let our three-voiced country
Sing in a new world
Joining the other rivers without dogma,
But with friendliness to all around her.
Let her new river shine on a day
That is fresh and glittering and contemporary;
Let it be true to itself and to its origins
Inventive, original, philosophical,
Its institutions mirror its beauty;
Then without shame we can esteem ourselves.

INDEX OF POETS

INDEX OF TITLES AND FIRST LINES

INDEX OF TITLES AND FIRST LINES   257

ACKNOWLEDGEMENTS

Thanks to Gerard Carruthers for drawing our attention to Allan Ramsay's hitherto uncollected 'A Poem' and the 'Epistle' by Alexander Geddes and for comments on the manuscript; to John Purser for providing the text of 'Deirdre's Farewell' and to Thomas Clancy and to Michel Byrne for their continuing help and advice; to Stewart Conn for providing a previously unpublished poem for the anthology; to the staff of the Scottish Poetry Library for exceptional professionalism and helpfulness; and to Calum Colvin for permission to use his work as our cover illustration. Special thanks are due to Robyn Marsack and Julie Johnstone of the Scottish Poetry Library, Edinburgh, and to our editorial assistant Susan Neil.

Acknowledgements are due to the following copyright holders and translators:

Kenneth Hurlston Jackson, translator, 'Deirdre's Farewell to Scotland', from *A Celtic Miscellany* (Harmondsworth: Penguin Books, 1971).

Thomas Owen Clancy, editor, *The Triumph Tree* (Edinburgh: Canongate, 1998), for his translations from the Gaelic originals: Mugron, Abbot of Iona, 'In Praise of Colum Cille'; Anonymous, 'On Oengus, son of Fergus'; Anonymous, 'On the Death of Cinnead son of Ailpin'; Anonymous, 'A Verse on David Son of Mael Coluim'; Anonymous, 'On the Battle of Stirling Bridge'. Thanks also to Gilbert Markus for his translations from the same volume of Latin originals: Anonymous (partly 14th century), from the *Inchcolm Antiphoner*; Anonymous, 'Advice to Malcolm from MacDuff'; Anonymous, 'On the Death of Alexander II, King of the Scots'; Anonymous, 'Song for the Wedding of Margaret of Scotland and Eirik, King of Norway'; Anonymous, 'On the Death of Edward I'; Anonymous, 'William Wallace's Uncle's Proverb'; Anonymous, 'King Robert's Testament'; Anonymous, 'Scotland's Strategy of Guerrilla Warfare'; Anonymous, 'The Epitaph of Robert Bruce'.

Derick Thomson translated the anonymous 1513 poem, 'To fight the Saxons'; Robert Crawford translated George Buchanan, 'To Henry Darnley, King of Scots'; of the poems by Iain Lom/John MacDonald, 'Song Against the Union' was translated by William Neill and 'A Lament for the State of the Country' was translated by Meg Bateman. The extract from 'Alba Saor' / 'Scotland Free' by Aonghas Moireasdan/Angus Morrison was translated by Ronald Black.

Douglas Gifford provided the English versions of Andrew of Wyntoun, 'Macbeth'; Anonymous, 'Scotland After Alexander'; Anonymous, 'Jok Upalland'; Sir David Lyndsay, 'Of the Realme of Scotland' and 'The

Collected Poems (Edinburgh University Press, 1971), reprinted by permission of the George Bruce Estate; Robert Garioch: 'Scottish Scene' from *Complete Poetical Works*, edited by Robin Fulton (Loanhead, Midlothian: Macdonald Publishers, 1983), reprinted by permission of the Saltire Society; Norman MacCaig: 'Celtic Cross', 'Patriot', from 'A Man in Assynt' and 'Characteristics' from *Collected Poems* (London: Chatto & Windus, 1990), reprinted by permission of The Random House Group Limited; Sorley Maclean: 'The Bolshevik' and 'Hallaig' from *From Wood to Ridge: Collected Poems* (Manchester: Carcanet Press, 1989), reprinted by permission of the publisher; Sir Alec Cairncross: 'Covenanting Country' from *Snatches* (Gerrards Cross: Colin Smythe, 1980), reprinted by permission of Frances Cairncross; Ruthven Todd: 'About Scotland, & C.' from *Garland for the Winter Solstice: Selected Poems* (London: J.M. Dent & Sons Ltd., 1961), reprinted by permission of David Higham Associates; G.S. Fraser: 'Meditation of a Patriot' from *Poems*, edited by Ian Fletcher and John Lucas (Leicester University Press, 1981), reprinted by permission of the Estate of G.S. Fraser; George Campbell Hay: 'Scotland' and 'Men and Women of Scotland' from *Collected Poems and Songs*, edited by Michel Byrne (Edinburgh University Press, 2000), reprinted by permission of the publisher (the poem 'Scotland' carries this title in its first journal publication, in *Poetry Scotland 4* (Glasgow: MacLellan, 1949), but in the *Collected Poems and Songs* it is entitled 'The White Licht...'; the English version of 'Scotland' is by Douglas Gifford and 'Men and Women of Scotland' is translated by the author); Sydney Goodsir Smith: 'Epistle to John Guthrie' from *Collected Poems: 1941–1975* (London: Calder Publications, 1975), reprinted by permission of the publisher; W.S. Graham: 'A Page About My Country' from *New Collected Poems* (London: Faber & Faber, 2004), reprinted by permission of the Estate of W.S. Graham; Maurice Lindsay: 'Speaking of Scotland' from *Scotland: An Anthology* (London: Robert Hale, 1974) and 'In Scotland Now', reprinted by permission of the author; Hamish Henderson: 'The Freedom Come-All-Ye' from *Collected Poems and Songs* (Edinburgh: Curly Snake Publishing, 2000), reprinted by permission of the Estate of Hamish Henderson; Edwin Morgan: 'Canedolia', 'The Flowers of Scotland' and 'The Coin' (from *Sonnets from Scotland*, 1984) from *Collected Poems* (Manchester: Carcanet Press, 1990), reprinted by permission of the publisher; Alexander Scott: from 'Scotched' from *The Collected Poems of Alexander Scott*, edited by David S. Robb (Edinburgh: Mercat Press, 1975), reprinted by permission of Mrs Scott; George Mackay Brown: 'Culloden: The Last Battle' from *Selected Poems 1954–92* (London: John Murray, 1996), reprinted by permission of John Murray Publishers; Derick Thomson/Ruaraidh MacThòmais: 'Steel?' and 'Scotland v. Argentina, 2/6/79' from *Creachadh na Clàrsaich: Cruinneachadh de Bhardachd / Plundering the Harp: Collected Poems 1940–1980* (Edinburgh: Macdonald

Publishers, 1982), reprinted by permission of the author; Clifford Hanley: 'Scotland the Brave', reprinted by permission of Kerr's Music Corporation Limited; Kathrine Sorley Walker: 'Scottish Legacy' from *Modern Scottish Women Poets*, edited by Dorothy McMillan and Michel Byrne (Edinburgh: Canongate Books, 2003); William Neill: 'Scotland' and 'Then and Now' from *Four Points of a Saltire* (Edinburgh: Reprographia, 1970) reprinted by permission of the author; G.F. Dutton: 'as so often in Scotland' from *The Bare Abundance: Selected Poems 1975–2001* (Tarset: Bloodaxe Books, 2002), reprinted by permission of the publisher; Alastair Reid: 'Scotland' from *Oases: Poems and Prose* (Edinburgh: Canongate Books, 1997), reprinted by permission of the author; Iain Crichton Smith: 'To Have Found One's Country' from 'The White Air of March' from *Selected Poems* (Manchester: Carcanet Press, 1985), reprinted by permission of the publisher; Margaret Gillies Brown: 'Scottish Woman' from *Looking Towards Light* (Dundee: Blind Serpent Press, 1988), reprinted by permission of the author; Tom Buchan: 'Scotland the wee' and 'The Low Road' from *Dolphins at Cochin* (London: The Cresset Press, 1969) and 'Stones of Scotland' from *Poems 1969–72* (Edinburgh: The Poni Press, 1972); George MacBeth: 'Oatcakes', 'Bagpipes', 'Scottish', 'Scotch' and 'The Idea of Scotland as a Scattered Universal' from *My Scotland: Fragments of a State of Mind* (London: Pan Macmillan, 1973), reprinted by permission of the publisher; Duncan Glen: 'The Hert o Scotland' from *Selected Poems, 1965–90* (Edinburgh: Akros, 1991), reprinted by permission of the author; Anne Stevenson: 'American Rhetoric for Scotland' from *Scottish Poetry* 7, edited by Maurice Lindsay, Alexander Scott and Roderick Watson (University of Glasgow Press, 1974), reprinted by permission of the author; Stewart Conn: 'Cappella Nova at Greyfriars' Kirk', reprinted by permission of the author; William McIlvanney: 'The Cowardly Lion' from *In Through the Head* (Edinburgh: Mainstream, 1988), reprinted by permission of the author; Kenneth White: 'Scotia Deserta' from *Open World: Collected Poems 1960–2000* (Edinburgh: Polygon, 2003), reprinted by permission of the publisher; Roy Williamson: 'The Flower of Scotland', reprinted by permission of The Corries (Music) Limited; Alan Jackson: 'A Scotch Poet Speaks' from *Salutations: Collected Poems 1960–1989* (Edinburgh: Polygon, 1990), reprinted by permission of the publisher; Les A. Murray: 'Elegy for Angus Macdonald of Cnoclinn' from *New Collected Poems* (Manchester: Carcanet Press, 2003), reprinted by permission of the publisher; Donald Campbell: 'Anthem o the Unco Guid' from *Rhymes n' Reasons* (Edinburgh: Reprographia, 1972), reprinted by permission of the author; John Purser: 'Northern Latitudes' from *The Counting Stick* (Breakish: Aquil, 1976), reprinted by permission of the author; Douglas Dunn: 'Here and There' from *New Selected Poems 1964–2000* (London: Faber & Faber, 2003), reprinted by permission of the publisher; Aonghas MacNeacail: 'mise alba

/ i, scotland' from *Present Poets* (Edinburgh: National Museums of Scotland, 1998), reprinted by permission of the author; Tom Leonard: 'simile please / say cheese' and 'The Voyeur' from *Intimate Voices: Selected Work 1965–1983* (London: Vintage, 1995), reprinted by permission of the author, and 'Scotland has become an Independent Socialist Republic' from *Reports from the Present: Selected Work 1982–94* (London: Jonathan Cape, 1995), reprinted by permission of The Random House Group Limited; Thomas A. Clark: 'The Homecoming' from *Tormentil and Bleached Bones* (Edinburgh: Polygon, 1993), reprinted by permission of the publisher; Myles Campbell: 'The Referendum for a Scottish Assembly 1/3/79' from *An Tuil: Dunaire Gaidhlig an 20mh Ceud / Anthology of 20th Century Gaelic Verse*, edited by Ronald I.M. Black (Edinburgh: Polygon, 1999), reprinted by permission of the author; Robin Munro: 'Patriotism' from *Shetland, like the world* (Aberdeen: Triangle Press, 1973), reprinted by permission of the author; Liz Lochhead: 'Inter-City' from 'In Alberta' from *Dreaming Frankenstein and collected poems* (Edinburgh: Polygon, 1984), 'Scotch Mist (The Scotsport Song)' from *True Confessions and New Cliches* (Edinburgh: Polygon, 1985), reprinted by permission of the publisher, and 'Scotland, Whit Like?' from *Mary Queen of Scots Got Her Head Chopped Off and Dracula* (London: Penguin Books, 1989), reprinted by permission of the publisher; Ron Butlin: 'Advertisement for a Scottish Servant' from *Histories of Desire* (Newcastle: Bloodaxe Books, 1995), reprinted by permission of the author; Raymond Vettese: 'Scotland '79' and 'Scottish Names' from *The Richt Voice and Ither Poems* (Edinburgh: Macdonald Publishers, 1988), reprinted by permission of the Saltire Society; Gerald Mangan: 'Scotland the Ghost' from *Waiting for the Storm* (Newcastle: Bloodaxe Books, 1990), reprinted by permission of the author; Gerrie Fellows: 'At the Aliens' Gate' from *Wish I Was Here: An Anthology* (Edinburgh: pocketbooks, 2000), reprinted by permission of the author; Bashabi Fraser: 'Between My Two Worlds' from *Wish I Was Here: An Anthology* (Edinburgh: pocketbooks, 2000), reprinted by permission of the author; Carol Ann Duffy: 'Originally' from *The Other Country* (London: Anvil Poetry Press, 1990), reprinted by permission of the publisher; Hugh McMillan: 'Anglophobia' from *Aphrodite's Anorak* (Calstock: Peterloo Poets, 1996), reprinted by permission of the publisher; Peter McCarey: 'Referendum Day 3', 'Referendum Day 2' and 'Referendum Day 1' from *In the Metaforest* (London: Vennel Press, 2000), reprinted by permission of the author; Elizabeth Burns: 'Scotland' from *Poems* (Edinburgh: School of Poets, 1986), reprinted by permission of the author; Alan Riach: 'The Dogs of Scotland', reprinted by permission of the author; William Hershaw: 'June, Songs of The Scottish Examination Board English Marker' from *The Cowdenbeath Man* (Edinburgh: Scottish Cultural Press, 1997), reprinted by permission of the author; James Robertson: 'Very Scottish Weather' from *Sound Shadow*

(Edinburgh: B&W Publishing, 1995), reprinted by permission of the author; Graham Fulton: 'Cream of Scottish Youth' from *Knights of the Lower Floor* (Edinburgh: Polygon, 1994), reprinted by permission of the publisher; David Kinloch: 'Braveheart' from *Un Tour d'Ecosse* (Manchester: Carcanet Press, 2001), reprinted by permission of the publisher; Robert Crawford: 'Scotland' from *A Scottish Assembly* (London: Chatto & Windus, 1990), reprinted by permission of The Random House Group Limited; Rody Gorman: 'Scotland 1997' from *On the Underground / Air a' Charbad fo Thalamh* (Edinburgh: Polygon, 2000), reprinted by permission of the publisher; Jackie Kay: 'In my country' from *Other Lovers* (Newcastle: Bloodaxe Books, 1993) and 'The Broons' Bairn's Black' from *Off Colour* (Newcastle: Bloodaxe Books, 1998), reprinted by permission of the publisher; W.N. Herbert: 'The Postcards of Scotland' from *Cabaret McGonagall* (Newcastle: Bloodaxe Books, 1996); Kathleen Jamie: 'The Queen of Sheba' from *The Queen of Sheba* (Newcastle: Bloodaxe Books, 1994), reprinted by permission of the publisher; Kathleen Jamie: 'On the Design Chosen for the New Scottish Parliament Building by Architect Enric Miralles' from *Jizzen* (London: Picador, 1999), reprinted by permission of Pan Macmillan; Richard Price: 'Hinges' from *Frosted, Melted* (Callander: diehard, 2002), reprinted by permission of the publisher; Hamid Shami: 'Lost' from *Wish I Was Here: An Anthology* (Edinburgh: pocketbooks, 2000); Kevin MacNeil: 'Young Chinese and Scottish' from *Love and Zen in the Outer Hebrides* (Edinburgh: Canongate Books, 1998), reprinted by permission of the publisher; Irfan Merchant: 'I'm a Racist' from *Wish I Was Here: An Anthology* (Edinburgh: pocketbooks, 2000); Kokumo Rocks: 'Growing up Black in Scotland' from *Bad Ass Raindrop* (Edinburgh: Luath Press, 2002), reprinted by permission of the publisher; Anne Frater: 'Divorce' from *Fon T-Slige: Bardachd / Under the Shell: Poems* (Glasgow: Gairm Publications, 1995), reprinted by permission of the publisher; Iain Crichton Smith: 'The Beginning of a New Song' from *Variations on a New Song* (Edinburgh: Scottish Poetry Library, 2000), reprinted by permission of the Estate of Iain Crichton Smith.

Every effort has been made to trace the copyright holders of the poems published in this book. The editors and publishers apologise if any material has been included without the appropriate acknowledgement, and would be glad to correct any oversights in future editions.